GUERRILLA P.R.

OTHER BOOKS BY
MICHAEL LEVINE

The Address Book—How to Reach Anyone Who Is Anyone

The Corporate Address Book

The Music Address Book

The Environmental Address Book

The Kid's Address Book

GUERRILLA P.R.

HOW YOU CAN WAGE AN EFFECTIVE

PUBLICITY CAMPAIGN . . .

WITHOUT GOING BROKE

MICHAEL LEVINE

HarperBusiness
A Division of HarperCollins*Publishers*

HarperCollins books may be purchased for educational, business, or sales promotional use. For information please write: Special Markets Department, HarperCollins Publishers, Inc., 10 East 53rd Street, New York, NY 10022.

FIRST EDITION

Designed by George J. McKeon

Library of Congress Cataloging-in-Publication Data

Levine, Michael, 1954–
    Guerrilla P.R. : how you can wage an effective publicity campaign . . .
without going broke / Michael Levine. — 1st ed.
        p.   cm.
    ISBN 0–88730–608–X
    1. Public relations. 2. Industrial publicity. 3. Small business.
I. Title. II. Title: Guerrilla P.R.
HD59.L48   1993
659—dc20 92–53331

93 94 95 96 97 CC/RRD 10 9 8 7 6 5 4 3 2 1

To Dennis Prager, who changed my life by making the most compelling case for the belief in God I've ever heard.

The best effect of any book is that it excites the reader to self activity.

——THOMAS CARLYLE

I agree!

——MICHAEL LEVINE

CONTENTS

ACKNOWLEDGMENTS

With lovers and friends, I still can recall,
some are dead and some are living.
In my life, I've loved them all.

Saying thank you to my friends and family somehow seems so inadequate. It's what I say to people who hold the elevator door open for me.

So, to the following loyal friends and family I send my love and deepest appreciation through these words.

My brilliant literary agent and good friend, Alice Martell and her assistant Paul Plunkett.

My encouraging friends at Putnam Publishing Company (where I've been published since 1984): my dynamic editor Laura Shephard, John Duff, Rena Walner, and Christine DelRey.

My dedicated and loving father Author O. Levine, stepmother Marilyn, and sister Patty.

My special friends: Keith Atkinson, Rana Bendixon and Sorrell, Ken Bostic, Leo Buscaglia, Ron Byrd, Bill Calkins, Susan Gauthier, Karen L'Heureux, Heather Lawrence, Richard Imprescia, Bette Geller Jackson, Lori and Lisa Kleinman, Robert Kotler, Bonnie and Gordon Larson, Richard Lawson, Nancy Mager, John McKillop, Lynn Novatt, David Newman, Dennis Prager, Steven Short, Peter Smaha, Joshua Trabulus, and Earlene White.

My wonderful business partners Mitchell Schneider and Monique Moss.

My office family Amanda Cagan, Todd Brodginski, Marla Capra, Katherine Caulfield, Vivianna Ceballos, Naomi Goldman, Kim Kaiman, Matt Labov, Julie Nathanson, Robert Pietranton, Kelly Reichard, Tresa Reburn-Cody, Julie Rona, Marcee Rondan, Rhonda Saenz, Jane Singer, Kimberley Smith, Melissa Spraul, Brigid Walsh, Julie Wheeler, Allison Whyte, Staci Wolfe, and Lesley Zimmerman.

My business associates Bob and Lori Bernstein, Laura Herlovich, Barry Langberg, Matt Lichtenberg, Dan Pine, and Joy Sapieka.

My special thanks to Kathleen Conner for her incredible committment to excellence in the researching of this book.

Assembling a book like this would be impossible without the input from my professional colleagues in the various media. There are many I need to thank: Cary Darling, John Horn, Debbie Farr, Kristen Brown, Randy Taraborelli, Jane Kaplan, Martha Smilgis, Bob Serling, Randi Gelfand, Sandy and Howard Benjamin, Doug Washington, Rebecca Coudret, Jerry Porter, Peggy Klaus, Keith Atkinson, and Julian Meyers, all contributed enormously to this effort, and I'm forever grateful.

A special thank you to my Guerrilla P.R. Commandos, who embody the spirit of this book: Bob Columbe, Luke Dommer, Wayne Perryman, Angelyne, Candy Lightner, Dick Rutan, Si Frumkin, and Andy Lipkis.

To the guerrillas—Dave Schwartz, Michael Viner, Dale Faye, Richard Epcar and Ellyn Stern, Jefferey Ullman, Sandy Tang, Will Ackerman, and the thousands of others out there working hard to find their niche in the media—my heartfelt thanks.

Deepest appreciation to Lester Pine.

Endless and deep appreciation to Dan Pine whose constant support and timeless effort were invaluable.

FOREWORD

I have to admit, I smiled visibly when I first read *Guerrilla P.R.* Not because I found anything in the text unseemly or laughable. On the contrary, this book is about as true and cogent an examination of the role media play in our society as any I have ever read. No, I laughed because, on nearly every page, I saw something of myself. Turns out, in an effort to serve my clients, I've been practicing Guerrilla P.R. for years. I just didn't know it.

Michael Levine would be the first to state he did not invent Guerrilla P.R. Rather, he assembled its constituent parts, codified it, and gave this rather timeless concept a distinct shape and color. Clearly, entrepreneurs, businessmen and -women, civic leaders, and countless others from all walks of life have for years comprehended the importance of media coverage. Not all had the wherewithal to afford the luxury of press agentry to get it. Many, like myself, found it more expedient—and more effective—to try for it themselves.

In my life and career, I have naturally gravitated toward statements and actions that have resulted in an increased public profile. It wasn't my doing when the judge ordered the entire courtroom to rise and sing "Happy Birthday" to me on my eighty-fourth birthday not long ago. But having gone through it, I wasn't inclined to keep it to myself.

Likewise, it has always been incumbent upon myself to appeal to the court of public opinion when I take on certain controversial cases, like that of victims of Ferdinand Marcos' torturers in the Philippines, or the sheep farmer whose flock of rare multinippled sheep was poisoned by tainted animal feed (and if you don't like the fact that I sent a photo of a multinippled sheep to *Playboy* magazine, well, I offer my sincerest apology). One of the blessings of our legal system is that it is indeed a very public institution, and, being so, entitles me to engage the public mind in representing my clients.

What Michael Levine has written here goes far beyond other do-it-yourself publicity manuals. As he writes early on, his goal is to help the reader "think like a publicist," rather than simply plod along in a connect-the-dots fashion. I don't care how much training one receives in one's given field, real life situations almost always result in throwing a measure of the classroom theory out the window (that's certainly true in the law).

Real life *is* the best teacher. Even in this book, though it is replete with real-life examples, Michael makes it clear that the best way to learn Guerrilla P.R. is to *do* Guerrilla P.R. It is this aspect of action, of protagonism, that I find so refreshing. This is not a volume for daydreamers. It's meant for people who are prepared to rise off their duffs, roll up their sleeves, and dig in to some hard yet potentially rewarding work.

And it is work (though it need not be drudgery). I know from my own encounters with media people that they are indeed a tough bunch. Unsentimental, cynical, leery, often curt and condescending— you truly swim in a piranha tank if you skinnydip with America's press corps.

But don't let that ominous admonition stop you. The media are not impenetrable, nor are they altogether disinterested in the occasional unsolicited story. As Michael makes clear, they're interested in but one thing: reporting news. The trick is feeling comfortable creating news, making news, being news. If it weren't for my own zest for this pursuit, I would not have enjoyed the same glorious career.

I value Levine's effort to demystify and demythologize the media. I'm afraid most people have come to view them as something of a monolithic monster, unblinking and pitiless as the sun. There's a large degree of truth to that; however Guerrilla P.R. dictates that one confront the media—and all other people for that matter—on an individual basis. The human factor plays the greatest role in Michael Levine's methodology. I believe that's why it works so well.

All his life Michael Levine maintained but two vocational passions, entertainment and politics. At age twelve, while his peers were reading *Mad* magazine, he was reading *Variety*. He left college after a brief stint to enter the workplace, and he quickly excelled in public relations. In the early eighties he launched his own P.R. company and, within a short span of time, built it into one of the most dominant in Hollywood.

His warmth and creativity energize those around him, but what is most striking about Michael is his apparent inner restlessness. Though outwardly calm and collected to a fault, he is a churning caldron of ideas. His favorite word is "synergism," a term that implies both synthesis and energy. I can think of no more fitting description of Michael Levine.

Significantly, his P.R. prescription is founded on an inviolable sense of ethics. Somehow, the notion that "the worst thing a person can do is get caught" has emerged as a credo for our time. Not so, says Michael, who, though quick to teach the subtle art of persuasion, draws the line well before the ethical boundaries are reached. Call him a throwback, call him a fool, call him a cab, but his stand is undeniably admirable.

Levine is a superb teacher, in that he both instructs and inspires. Yet ultimately, as is fitting, he turns the process back over to the reader, demanding of him or her the actual effort required. Pulling together the disparate elements of a media campaign is time-consuming, and requires great forethought in addition to honed instincts. Michael likes to say there is no shortcut through the firewalk, and I'm convinced he's correct. But for those willing to traipse over the coals of the media pathway, Michael Levine and *Guerrilla P.R.* pad the soles quite well.

I join him in wishing you the reader "Good luck."

Melvin Belli

INTRODUCTION

*There are conditions of survival in a guerrilla force: they
include constant mobility and constant vigilance.*

—CHE GUEVARA

OPPORTUNITY KNOCKS

In the middle of the worst drought in California history, a sudden
downpour deluged Los Angeles back in March 1991. Though the city
was grateful for the moisture, the rain caused problems. Under a
two-block section of Ventura Boulevard in the San Fernando Valley,
a water main burst, causing the street to split apart.

Torrents of water cascaded over the sidewalk. Traffic and business came to a standstill. As workmen toiled to repair the damage
along the thoroughfare, no customers could reach any shops. One
such hapless establishment was Mel's Diner, a kitschy fifties-style
eatery located right in the middle of the affected area. The situation
looked bleak as Mel's lunch business dried up amid the floodwaters.

So what did Mel do? He gave away free hamburgers to the street
maintenance crew; and he invited local TV news outlets to witness
this noble act of charity. For the cost of a couple of dozen beef patties
and a few phone calls, Mel's Diner was all over the airwaves that
night, and ever since, business has been better than ever.

Mel showed himself a master of Guerrilla P.R.

In 1970, an ambitious young businessman named Michael Viner
sought a way to enter the music industry, though he had little money

to invest, and no recording artists lined up. With no other resources than his native creativity, Viner pressed several thousand copies of an album titled, *The Best of Marcel Marceo*. It was thirty-five minutes of silence, punctuated by applause. He sent copies not to record distributors, but to newspaper writers like Vernon Scott of UPI, who ran an amusing story on the prank record, which was picked up by every paper in America. Other stories ran in major outlets like *Newsweek*.

The record even hit *Billboard*'s Album Chart. Orders began pouring in, and Michael Viner built up a financial war chest with which he then entered the record business in earnest, releasing albums like *Candyman* by Sammy Davis, Jr.

Michael Viner is a master of Guerrilla P.R.

The examples of Mel's Diner and Michael Viner illustrate the central premise of this book: the world is overflowing with opportunities. Opportunities in work, in love, for spiritual growth and emotional fulfillment. It's your mission to remain "constantly vigilant," so that opportunities do not pass you by.

That's how I view the world. As founder of one of the nation's largest independent public relations companies, I've constantly sought new and more effective ways to heighten the profiles of my clients, and I have scoured every resource available to me in order to find them.

This approach has worked, at least according to my clients, who have included Charlton Heston, Mickey Rooney, Jon Voight, Vanna White, Michael J. Fox, Linda Evans, Fleetwood Mac, and hundreds more. They chose our firm in part because of our attitude, stemming from my ceaseless quest for opportunity.

When I read the morning paper, I don't just keep up with the headlines. I'm scanning for possibilities: letters-to-the-editor or guest editorials for my clients, trends that may end up as surveys, predictions, or other kinds of press releases. When I watch television, I'm not zonking out with a bowl of popcorn by my side. I'm looking for talk shows that might book my clients as guests. I'm looking at news programs to get a feel for the angles of the day. In everything I do, I stress an outlook different from that of most people: I'm looking for opportunity.

As I suggested, this view can be applied to any field of endeavor, work-related or otherwise. As it relates to P.R., anyone—pro and non-pro—can benefit from it. But if you wish to tackle a publicity campaign on your own, this opportunity-driven perspective is key. Adopt it and you'll have joined the ranks of the Guerrilla P.R. army.

WHAT THE PROS CAN AND CANNOT DO

The difficult we do right now; the impossible will take a little longer.

—SEABEES MOTTO

Today, most colleges and universities offer degrees in communications and public relations. Professional P.R. trade associations and think tanks abound. If a teen tells his parents, "I want to go into public relations," he or she will likely get the same approving hugs from Mom and Dad as if the kid chose medicine or law.

That's because P.R. is a true profession. The money's good, the status high, the demand for services strong. My company has seen a steady stream of clients who want what we've got, and every year the business grows exponentially.

What is it the professional publicists do for clients they cannot do for themselves? For one, we give them the hard-driving personality of that unique human subspecies, the Professional Publicist. The venerated *"Dartnell P.R. Handbook,"* considered by some the bible of the business, says: "The P.R. careerist with great potential always exhibits a lively interest in people, events, action. He has an insatiable curiosity and a high energy quotient that lead him to a number of activities not necessarily related to his school courses or working life." Sounds like a good prescription for anyone; but it's a positive I.D. on any capable publicist.

I can tell you that, in general, publicists and P.R. careerists are among the most upbeat, lively, curious, well-spoken, and enthusiastic people you'll ever meet. Their attraction to media is a direct outgrowth of an inner desire to know what's going on in the world, to make sense of the world, and to leave a mark on the world. They merely took that driving passion and channeled it into a logical career direction.

In addition to energy and curiosity, the pro has contacts. More than anything, we offer clients *entree* to the media. We know the reporters, editors, hosts, and producers of every newspaper, magazine, radio station, TV news program, and morning show in America. We also know the subtle art of pitching a client. Every day we do the journalists' work for them, coming up with ideas, devising angles, showing them why they should do stories on our clients. We tell them what's news and we get them to agree.

(I can't count the number of times I have spoken with intelligent media people who have expected me, the publicist, to concoct their *entire* story. They tell us, "We just report the news, we don't manufacture it." Personally, I don't buy that. Seventy-five percent of potential news items that reach the average news desk every day never reach the public. The veto power of news people decides what's news. Journalists are among the most creative people I know, but the natural laws of inertia come into play, and they customarily expect us to connect their dots.)

Top professional publicists are good writers too. We dash off press releases as easily as grocery lists. We conceptualize attractive press kits, photo opportunities, clever press releases, information-packed biographies, and eye-catching events to reshape media perception (and therefore public perception) of our clients. That ability to use language persuasively, whether orally or on paper, is arguably the single most important attribute of the topnotch professional publicist.

With major clients, such as governments, Fortune 500 companies, and other powerful institutions, the role of the P.R. professional takes on even greater dimensions. Clients of this nature aren't merely looking for "good press." They expect public relations counselors to foster a widespread and permanent positive perception, an inexorable bending of the public mind toward the "correct" point of view: theirs.

I can cite a classic example. The multinational oil companies have led the entire Western world to believe that life, as we know it, would cease if society were to deviate in any way from reliance on their products. Forget that fossil fuels are steadily choking the planet to death; forget that there are plenty of viable energy alternatives available. Thanks to skillful management of public relations, the oil companies—though largely perceived as avaricious—are nevertheless generally accepted as our best hope for an energy-rich future. It may or may not be true—but we believe it. And you have their hired P.R. geniuses to thank.

Essentially, the pros see things from two points of view: the media's and the client's. They tailor a client's image to meet the needs of the press. At the same time, they challenge the media to perceive the client *as we wish them to.* The pros don't always know what's best, but often they're called upon to make critical image decisions for clients, based on experience with what goes over well in print and on the air. It's a formidable assignment; when it works, it's extraordinarily gratifying.

Still, there are some things the pros cannot do. No matter how hard they try to muster a genuine sense of enthusiasm about a client, the bottom line is—the pros are just doing a job. They are paid to pitch. If the client stops paying, they stop pitching. So concern, caring, and devotion can be turned on and off with the bounce of a check. *Nobody will care about the client and his goals as much as the client himself.*

Similarly, because the pros are in business, there may be certain kinds of assignments they may be unable or unwilling to take on. Some potential clients are too narrowly focused, such as a small business in a secondary market. Others may be unable to afford the cost of professional P.R., which can be considerable (up to $5,000 a month, and more). Still others may present image problems. After a change in senior management in 1992, top Washington P.R. firm H&K severed its relationship with several controversial clients, including the scandal-ridden BCCI bank. Said H&K CEO Tom Edison at the time, "We have no business representing sleaze."

So you can see there are as many doors closed to the professional as are closed to prospective clients. Add it up and there may be countless businesspeople, civic leaders, inventors, performers, scholars, directors of charitable groups, and others who could greatly benefit from the services of a professional P.R. firm, yet are unable to connect.

To them I say there is a way out that bypasses the pros, that avoids the high costs, and proves as effective—if not more effective—in securing publicity than the efforts of most professional P.R. companies. It's a method that incorporates everything the pros have—energy, contacts, written and oral skills, and broad perspective—by teaching a new approach. I call it Guerrilla P.R.

THE JUNGLE FIGHTER

A guerrilla is a jungle fighter, a lightning-quick devotee of the sneak attack. A guerrilla knows his terrain better than his opponents, believes passionately in his cause, and is nearly impossible to defeat. A Guerrilla publicist works in such a fashion. Agile, confident, dynamic, making do with far less than his desk-bound professional counterpart, the Guerrilla is a model of compact efficiency.

Resourcefulness is next to godliness. That's the cornerstone of my technique. What a Guerrilla lacks in funds, he or she makes up in moxie. Every press campaign, even the most expensive and sophisticated, is ultimately a grass-roots crusade. The goal of any publicist, professional or Guerrilla, is to reach individuals. The pros, as paid pitchmen, can't help but take a less credible posture in representing a client. By taking a close-to-the-ground, one-on-one approach, and wearing his passion on his sleeve, the Guerrilla P.R. trooper cuts to the chase.

Today, technology permits millions to launch cottage industries at home. Everyone has access to the prime tools: phone, fax, computer, modem, and mailbox. But these tools mean nothing to the Guerrilla publicist without the attitude I've described. I'm talking about the attitude that says, "My project is the most important thing in the world, and I'll stop at nothing to tell the world about it!"

So who are the Guerrillas?

• The owners of a Utah ski resort who noticed their guests developing runny noses standing in long lines at frigid ski lifts. Management installed tissue dispensers, and made sure the local media knew about it. That year, business climbed, and it's still referred to as the "Kleenex resort."

• The Miami florist who ran a campaign in his shop dubbed, "Who Would You Most Like To Send Flowers To?" Entry blanks were available to all customers, who enjoyed filling them out. The florist issued a press release announcing the winners (Tom Cruise and Cybill Shepard). The flower shop gained a good deal of notoriety and business increased sharply.

• Candy Lightner, who formed Mothers Against Drunk Driving (M.A.D.D.) in response to the death of her daughter at the hands of a drunk driver. At her first press conference, she and her surviving daughter wept openly while describing their ordeal. An electrifying photo of the two women flashed around the country, and M.A.D.D. was off and running. Though her emotion was genuine, Candy knew touching hearts would reach minds.

• The heavy metal band Immaculate Mary, which sought to distinguish itself from the hundreds of competing bands in L.A. At every show, the lead singer threw foil-wrapped condoms into the crowd. Weird, yes, but different and eye-catching.

• The owners of the Improvisation Comedy Club, who wanted to increase the club's visibility. They launched a petition drive to demand a Best Comedy Oscar. Thousands signed the petitions, which were delivered by the boxload to the Motion Picture Academy. Press releases announcing the campaign, the tally, the delivery were sent, and they even wrote a guest editorial in the *Los Angeles Times*.

• The out-of-work accountant in Los Angeles, tired of discouraging headhunters and go-nowhere want ads, who strapped a sandwich board over his body and hit the streets of Beverly Hills. Emblazoned on his homemade billboard were the words: "Unemployee of the Month." He got a good job a few days later.

The Guerrillas are those who take responsibility for their own success or failure. They reject the smug conventions of our specialized society. They say "no" to the advisers, the naysayers, the consultants, and bring to their projects the kind of spunky cleverness that typified the old Hollywood. People say movies were better back then. They say cars were built better back then. They're right. It's because in those days individuals cared more, complained less, and took pride in the whole, the final product, no matter how little may have been the piece of the puzzle they claimed as their own.

WHO NEEDS IT?

The 1990s have been dubbed the Age of the Entrepreneur. Every year more and more people jump into the marketplace, seeking to turn products, projects, and concepts into successful and lucrative ventures. What kind of individuals need Guerrilla P.R.?

• A fledgling manager of a local rock band hoping to be spotted by major record companies.

• A director of a free clinic or shelter for the homeless seeking to increase public support.

• The designer of a bold new look in apparel ready to excite the tastemakers in the fashion world.

• An actor or actress appearing in a small production, hoping to be "discovered" by top casting agents.

• A shopkeeper in a competitive mall trying to focus attention on his store.

• The inventor of an environmentally safe automobile engine attempting to attract the interest of Detroit.

• A crusader against drug abuse needing increased community involvement and financial support.

• A restaurateur seeking loyal clientele for her newly opened cafe.

• A medical practitioner hoping to expand his practice.

• Professors from the rarefied halls of academia who lost touch with the real world of business.

• The franchisor seeking to distinguish his own store from the scores of copycats in the neighborhood.

• The author in search of the widest possible audience for his new book.

• And even the journalist or other media professional who would like a deeper understanding of the people vying for his or her attention.

You may already have in place an ongoing marketing, advertising, and merchandising campaign on behalf of your business or project. If so, great! Assuming your campaign is working, there's no need to stop. Guerrilla P.R. can simply serve as an ancillary marketing tool. But if you don't have any such campaign, and/or you cannot afford one, then listen up. This book was expressly written for you.

WHY A MANIFESTO?

This is by no means the first book on the subject of P.R. I make no claim of originality on that score. However, thumbing through previously published volumes on the subject, I noticed a major defect running through many of them. Though each explained what to do (some more lucidly than others), none that I saw showed the reader how to *think* like a publicist.

Consider the difference between learning a few phrases in a "Traveler's Guide to Spanish" and really learning the syntax of the language. Once you've mastered "Where can I get my pants pressed?" you're no better off than before. You have to learn to conjugate. You have to learn sentence structure. You have to feel the music of the language. This book teaches the grammar of directing public perception.

If you can't think like a publicist, you won't know what to do if something unexpected happens. You won't pitch the talent coordinator at your local morning show in a persuasive way. You won't know whom to call or what to write when an innovative campaign idea occurs to you. In fact, you might not even conjure up those ideas in the first place.

Guerrilla P.R. is as much manifesto as textbook. I show you not only what to do, but why to do it. Throughout, I offer my own partisan philosophy of public relations. Granted, it may not be shared by all my colleagues in the profession, but it has worked very effectively for me, especially early in my career before I had a large and well-connected company, and I know it can work for anyone who applies Guerrilla P.R. techniques.

This book is designed to change the way you see the world, insofar as the media are concerned. If you apply my principles, you will emerge a media-savvy urban guerrilla, fighting and winning the battle for public attention.

But that's not all. I truly believe many of the philosophical principles of Guerrilla P.R. offer a prescription for living, a manner of interacting with others. It's not a new idea. From Aristotle to Dale Carnegie, the premier minds of their time have pondered the intangibles of human relations. The ideology undergirding my plan for gaining media attention works just as well in getting ahead in your office, or with making friends or customers, as it does in getting your name in the paper.

Just as hard work and initiative in one area of your life have a beneficial spillover effect in other areas, so can your Guerrilla P.R. efforts make you a better—and better-liked—person. I've seen it happen many times.

HOW TO USE THIS BOOK

Guerrilla P.R. is a tool for empowerment. But it only works if you use it. In each chapter, I outline several principles, give examples, methods for practical application, and frequently offer Tips & Traps. In some sections I suggest exercises. Do them. Practice is the key to thinking like a Guerrilla.

Throughout the book, I give real-life examples of creative ideas that have kicked selected P.R. efforts into overdrive. I also cite individuals—I call them Guerrilla P.R. Commandos—who best exemplify the Guerrilla P.R. spirit. Some of them are well known, some are not. All have successfully engineered their own P.R. campaigns. You can learn from them. I have.

Most importantly, I've designed this to be an action manual. That means you should utilize the principles as you devise and instigate your campaign. Refer often to the book. Use it like a jungle fighter would use a map. Check back frequently to see if you're on-track. Don't worry, I'm right behind you.

DREAM ON

We can't all be Beethoven, but we can all make music. If you own a hamburger stand, don't be consumed with a desire to become the next McDonald's, because you probably won't. But that doesn't mean the game is over. Perhaps you can turn your place into the best burger stand in the city. For that you can strive.

I'm not telling you to avoid dreaming big. If you're not dreaming big I question why you're in business in the first place. But dreams occur while we're sleeping. I focus on the waking hours, when steel-eyed practicality goes a long way in making dreams come true.

What you can achieve is limited only by internal factors. Fear and laziness are tougher obstacles than irascible reporters and distracted talk-show producers. Basically, all it costs to make it in the Fame Factory is the price of a few stamps and a telephone. What cannot be appraised is the value of imagination.

If you see yourself benefiting from media exposure; if you feel you have enough creative energy to devote to planning and engineering an original, self-directed P.R. campaign; if you're up to acquiring new skills that will help you comprehend the world of the mass media; if you are prepared to look at media and society in a new and positive way, then you are a conscript in the Guerrilla P.R. forces.

It would be a mistake to promise you too much. In the beginning you may find the going rough. Not every newspaper or radio station is going to be interested in what you have to offer, and you may feel discouraged at times. But don't be afraid of failure. Teddy Roosevelt said, "He who has never made a mistake is one who never does anything." If you follow my system, you'll not only pull off a first-rate public relations campaign, but you'll gain a new sense of yourself. The seeds are within you right now.

Forward, march!

1

A BRIEF HISTORY OF TIME . . . AND
NEWSWEEK AND *USA TODAY*

*Three hostile newspapers are more to be feared than a
thousand bayonets.*

—NAPOLEON

THE NATURE OF MEDIA

Thirty years ago, Marshall McCluhan, the father of modern communications, wrote the immortal words, "The medium is the message."
Today I would amend that to, "The medium is the media." Our
civilization is utterly dominated by the force of media. After our own
families, no influence holds greater sway in shaping the text of our
being than do the media that cloak us like an electronic membrane.

We all think of ourselves as unique, unlike any person past or
present. Indeed, what gives human life its divine spark is the distinct
quality of every individual. Yet in many ways we are all the same.
The task of market analysts, pollsters, and demographers is to identify
those characteristics we share, and group us accordingly. If you are
in your early forties, male, Caucasian, a father of two, earn $50,000
or more, and listen to a Top 40 radio station, there are total strangers
out there who know an awful lot about you.

That's because they understand a lot about your upbringing.
They know you watched "The Mickey Mouse Club" in the fifties,
"The Man From U.N.C.L.E." in the sixties, "Saturday Night Live" in
the seventies, became environmentally conscious in the eighties, and
were probably sorry ABC canceled "Thirtysomething" in the nine-

ties. They've got your number because they understand the role the media have played in your life from the moment you Boomed as a Baby.

Today, in America, we tune in to over 9,000 commercial radio stations, 1,100 television stations, 11,000 periodicals, and over 11,-000 newspapers with a combined circulation of nearly seventy million. These are the sources of our opinions on everything from nuclear disarmament to Madonna's love life. Nobody likes to be told what to think, but all of us, every single day, are told precisely what to think about.

As Anthony Pratkanis and Elliot Aronson show in their insightful book, *Age of Propaganda*, the mass media are most effective in terms of persuading the public for two primary reasons. First, they teach new behavior and, second, they let us know that certain behaviors are legitimate and appropriate. So, if the media are encouraging certain buying patterns, fashion trends, modes of thinking, the unstated message we receive is "It's okay for me to like that, do that, feel that." In this way, our culture evolves, is accelerated, and disseminated.

Like the transcontinental railroad of the last century, the media link every city, gully, farmhouse, and mountaintop in North America. Regionalism is fading. The American accent is more uniform; our penchant for migration and blending in is like the smoothing out of a great national blanket. We are fast becoming one.

A common grammatical error occurs when people say "The media *is*" rather than "The media *are*" ("media" being the plural of "medium"). Yet I sense people who say "the media is" are on to something. They perceive the many arms of the media—TV, newspapers, radio, etc.—as part of one monstrously monolithic creature. The media are "one" too.

Consider "Baby Jessica" McClure, for whom my firm donated public relations services. Jessica was the toddler from Midland, Texas, who fell down a narrow pipe in her backyard in 1987. For thirty-six hours, America was mesmerized by press coverage of her rescue. Acting as a concerned neighbor, the media conveyed Jessica's plight to the nation. The private agony of the McClure family became the anguish of all America.

Think of it: the temporary suffering of one "insignificant" little girl stopped the world's most powerful country dead in its tracks.

(Then, to canonize the experience, the TV movie version of Jessica's story made it to the small screen within a year.)

Without those cameras there to catch it, and those TV stations to broadcast it, Baby Jessica's ordeal would have made absolutely no impact on anyone other than her family and those who saved her. Because of the media, all of America for two days became part of Jessica's family.

CONTRACTION AND EXPANSION

Journalists and talk-show hosts like to claim they're in the information business or the news business. But you know and I know they're in the money business just like everyone else. Because practically all media are privately held profit-making ventures, they behave much like any other enterprise, looking for ways to increase the bottom line.

To do that they must expand their consumer base, that is, their audience. They must give the customer what he or she wants. So if your local news station runs a few too many five-part specials on the illicit sex lives of nuns during "Sweeps Month," remember they're only trying to please the viewers.

Creating a successful product means citizens may not always get the information they need. A Harvard researcher found the average network sound byte from presidential campaigns dropped from 42.5 seconds per broadcast in 1968 to just under 10 seconds in 1988. That translates into roughly sixteen words a night with which to make up our minds on who should run the country. We absorb more information, yet understand less than ever before.

This is a logical consequence of big media. Their existence depends on keeping the audience tuned in. If TV station "A" covers candidate "B" droning on about farm subsidies, most of the audience will probably switch to station "C" running a story about the stray cat raised by an affectionate pig. Station "A" would be wise to ditch candidate "B" and send a crew out to film Porky and Tabby.

Along with this contraction of information is a parallel expansion of media. Because social scientists have us so precisely categorized, outlets targeted to specific groups flourish. *Lear's* caters to mature, high-income women. *Details* appeals to middle-income, fast-tracker men. *Essence* aims for black women.

Peter Yarrow, of Peter, Paul, and Mary, tells a great story in his stage show to illustrate how narrowly focused we've become as a society. In the 1940s and 1950s we had the all-encompassing *Life* magazine. Then, we cropped our vision down to *People* magazine in the seventies (all of Life wasn't good enough anymore). Things tightened up even more with *Us*. Now we have *Self.* Somewhere, there's just gotta be a magazine just for you. I can just imagine it: on sale now, "Fred Morganstern Monthly."

Not only do we see more media outlets, but the flow of information has likewise increased dramatically the past few years. Fax machines, cellular phones, modems, fiber-optic cables, Low Power TV, satellite down-links, all have reshaped the way we get our information, when we get it, and what we do with it.

During China's "Goddess of Democracy" protests in 1989, the students kept in touch with the outside world via fax. Instantly, China seemed to leap forward from feudal empire to modern nation. Vietnam was the first "we'll be right back after these messages" war. As napalm rained down on the jungle, we saw it live as it happened. We had no time to process information or analyze events as we were barraged by them. Because of improved communications, the Gulf War had the same effect, only with infinitely more drama.

The media may have accelerated the process of dissemination, but as we found out in the days of the first supersonic jets, breaking the sound barrier did not, as some scientists feared, cause planes to disintegrate. Likewise, instant news did not cause us to psychologically disintegrate.

There's no way to assess what this means to society. To be carpet-bombed by information must have far-reaching consequences to our civilization, but that's for future observers to sort out. Today, we face an intimidating media-driven culture. Anyone looking to succeed in business must first master the fundamentals of navigating the media. To reach customers, donors, or investors—to reach the public—one must rely on the media as the prime intermediary. The methodology to achieve this is known as Public Relations.

THE NATURE OF PUBLIC RELATIONS

*Half the world is composed of people who have something
to say and can't, and the other half who have nothing to say
and keep on saying it.*

—ROBERT FROST

I'm often asked whether public relations is a science or an art. That's
a valid question. In science, two plus two equals four. It will always
equal four whether added by a Republican from Iowa, a shaman from
New Guinea, or an alien from Planet X. However, in public relations,
two plus two may equal four. It may equal five. It may equal zero
today and fifty tomorrow.

Public relations is an art.

Like any art, there are rules of form, proven techniques, and
standards of excellence. But, overall, it's a mercurial enterprise, where
instinct is as legitimate as convention.

Public relations was once defined as the ability to provide the
answers before the public knows enough to ask the questions. Another P.R. pundit once stated, "We don't persuade people. We simply
offer them reasons to persuade themselves." I define what I do as
gift-wrapping. If you package a bracelet in a Tiffany box, it will have
a higher perceived value than if presented in a K Mart box. Same
bracelet, different perception.

PERCEPTION IS REALITY

Don Burr, former CEO of People Express Airlines, once said, "In the
airline industry, if passengers see coffee stains on the food tray, they
assume the engine maintenance isn't done right." That may seem
irrational, but in this game, perception, not the objective truth, matters most.

How one comprehends given information is all-important in
public relations. For decades, baby harp seals were bludgeoned to
death by fur hunters, but until the public saw the cute little critters
up close and personal and perceived the hunt as unacceptable, the
problem didn't exist. Before that, it was a matter of trappers preserving their hardy way of life. The seals ultimately hired the better
publicist.

This also works in negative ways. The congressional check-bouncing scandal was a case in which individual congressmen's visibility skyrocketed, while their credibility plummeted. The Tobacco Institute, a Washington-based lobbying and P.R. outfit, spends its time and money claiming cigarettes are okay. Nothing they do or say will ever make that true, but they may go a long way in changing public perception of their product. A few years ago they sponsored a national tour of the original Bill of Rights document, implying subliminally that no-smoking regulations infringe on our basic liberties. How's that for a P.R. stretch?

Ultimately, the goal of any public relations campaign is to either reorient, or solidify, perception of a product, client, policy, or event. From there, nature takes its course. If the public perceives the product as good, the movie star as sexy, the pet rock as indispensable, then the public will fork over its money. As the brilliant business author Dr. Judith Bardwick explained, "To be perceived as visible increasingly means one is perceived as successful."

Some may charge that stressing perception as reality is tantamount to sanctioning falsehood. I disagree. As the great historian Max Dimont argued, it didn't matter if Moses really did have a chat with the Lord up on Mount Sinai or not. What matters is that the Jewish people believed it and carved their unique place in world civilization because of it. Perception became reality.

Likewise, on a more mundane scale, one will succeed in a P.R. campaign only if the perception fostered truly resonates with the public. I do not believe people are easily duped. You may try everything in your bag of tricks to get the public to see things your way. You'll pull it off only if the perception you seek to convey fits the reality of the public, the reality of the times. As Pratkanis and Aronson argue, credibility today is manufactured, and not earned.

P.R. OR PUBLICITY?

Often, the terms "public relations" and "publicity" are used interchangeably. They shouldn't be. Publicity is only one manifestation of P.R.—specifically, achieving notoriety through accumulated press exposure. A publicist knows newspapers, magazines, and TV talk shows. Public Relations is much more than that. The Public Relations expert is as well versed in human nature as in editorial deadlines and sound bytes.

P.R. can be as macro as a campaign to persuade foreign governments to buy U.S. soybeans, or as micro as a warm handshake. The notion that P.R. is simply a matter of mailing press releases is nuttier than a squirrel's breakfast. As producer, manager, and publicist Jay Bernstein says, "P.R. is getting a front table at the right restaurant, getting you invited to the right party, and getting into first class with a tourist ticket."

A man who has greatly affected my thinking, the esteemed business author and lecturer Tom Peters, tells the story of a visit to a neighborhood convenience store. "American Express was being a little user-unfriendly," Tom recalls, "and it took a good three minutes for my AMEX card to clear. When it finally did, the cashier bagged my purchase, and as I turned to go, he reached into a jar of two-cent foil-wrapped mints. He pulled one out, dropped it in my bag, and said, 'The delay you experienced was inexcusable. I apologize and hope it doesn't happen again. Come back soon.' For two cents, he bought my loyalty for life."

This story is about one small business owner and only one customer, but it's a perfect example of good P.R. But what about bad P.R.? I doubt there's anyone on the scene who has mastered that dubious craft better than sometime-billionaire Donald Trump. This is a man who has lost control of his own gilded ship. His lurid infidelities, his profligate spending, his precipitous fall from fortune, and, worst of all, his attempt to exploit the Mike Tyson rape tragedy to promote a prize fight, collectively paint a portrait of a thoroughly vulgar mind.

The Donald doesn't care what you say about him, as long as you spell his name right. True, whenever he opens his mouth or makes a move, the press is all over him. But his massive celebrity has made him only a famous fool. You are not likely to achieve the degree of fame that Mr. Trump has, but, given his shameful image, I would congratulate you on that.

P.R. VS. MARKETING

With Guerrilla P.R. (and P.R. in general), you do not tell the public that your new digital fish cleaner is the greatest invention since the dawn of time. You could easily do that in an ad. Your goal is to lead people to draw that same conclusion for themselves. Otherwise, you're engaging in good old-fashioned—or is it new-fashioned?—marketing strategy.

Companies often relegate public relations to their marketing departments. That might make sense from a corporate point of view, but there's a distinct difference between P.R. and marketing. Going back to the "science vs. art" analogy, whereas P.R. is the art, marketing is the science.

Bob Serling, president of the Stratford Marketing Group, an L.A.–based marketing firm, has written, "Marketing is *everything* you do to make sure your customers find out about, and buy, your products and services." That's a tall order, and to go about filling it, marketing executives lug around a hefty bag of tricks.

To a large degree, they rely on surveys, demographic analyses, and established sales and advertising procedures to accomplish their goals. But in Public Relations, intangibles play a far greater role. How do you measure a feeling? It's not easy, but in P.R. we trade in the realm of feelings every day. We may use the media as the vehicle, but the landscape we traverse is contoured by human emotion.

Marketing often goes hand-in-hand with advertising. The undeniable advantage with advertising is that the advertiser retains full control. He knows exactly what his message will say and precisely when it will be seen. But remember this little fact of life: most top ad agencies consider a 1–2 percent response rate a triumph. That's all it takes to make them happy. And, like it or not, most people don't take ads as seriously as advertisers would like. Everybody knows they're bought and paid for.

I prefer the odds with major media exposure. True, you do lose a large measure of control, and you never know for sure when or how your message will be conveyed. But the public is far likelier to accept what it gleans from the news media over what it sees in commercials. If Dan Rather says a new sports shoe is a daring innovation, people will give that more credence than if company spokesman Bo Jackson says it. The news, indeed the truth, is what Dan Rather says it is.

So who tells Dan Rather what's news? The media like to boast they rely on ace newsgathering staffs; but in fact they depend a great deal on public relations people. That doesn't mean the journalists of America are saps. They're just looking for good stories. A hungry reporter and a smart publicist is a match made in heaven, and it's been that way since the dawn of the Communication Age.

FROM THE GUERRILLA P.R. FILE
In Amarillo, Texas, you'll find the Big Texan Steak Ranch, where the owner issues the following challenge: if you can eat a seventy-two-ounce steak in an hour, you get it free. News of the deal traveled far and wide, even to the skies, where I first read about it in an airline magazine.

GLORY DAYS: THE FOUNDING OF THE P.R. INDUSTRY

The public relations industry flourished with the growth of twentieth-century mass media, although sensitivity to public opinion on the part of public figures is nothing new. Even Abraham Lincoln got into the act, declaring once, "What kills a skunk is the publicity it gives itself." The fathers of modern P.R. knew the value of simple images to convey powerful messages.

Edward Bernays, founder of modern P.R., defined his mission as the engineering of consent. He was a nephew of Sigmund Freud, and he strikes me as having been just as perceptive about human nature as his esteemed uncle. Bernays displayed a genius for concocting indelible images, something good P.R. campaigns require. In one early triumph, he arranged for young debutantes to smoke Lucky Strikes while strolling in New York's 1929 Easter Parade. What Bernays sold to the press as a bold political statement on women's rights was no more than a gimmick to sell cigarettes.

Pioneers like publicist/film producer A. C. Lyles set the pace for generations of publicists to follow. Another innovator, Ivy Hill, is often credited with inventing the press release. Hill believed telling the "truth" in journalistic fashion would help shape public opinion. He sensed editors would not dismiss press releases as ads, but rather would perceive their real news value. He was right.

The publicist's ability to appeal to newspapers proved invaluable to captains of industry seeking to shore up their images. Back in the 1920s, Hill masterminded industrialist John D. Rockefeller's much-ridiculed habit of handing out dimes to every child he met. Ridiculous but effective in its time. (Imagine T. Boone Pickens trying that today.)

Occasionally, clients got less than they bargained for. In the late 1950s, the Ford Motor Company hired P.R. trail-blazer Ben Sonnenberg to help overcome the negative fallout from the Edsel fiasco. He charged Ford $50,000 for a foolproof P.R. plan, and after three days submitted it in person. Sonnenberg looked the breathless executives in the eye and intoned, "Do nothing." With that, the dapper publicist pocketed his check and walked out, much to the slack-jawed shock of the Ford brain trust.

Even nations sometimes need help. During the 1970s, Argentina developed a little P.R. problem when its government kidnapped and murdered thousands of its own citizens. Buenos Aires hired the high-powered U.S. firm of Burson-Marsteller to tidy things up. For a cool $1,000,000, the firm launched an extensive campaign involving opinion-makers from around the world: a stream of press releases stressed, among other things, the Argentine regime's record in fighting terrorism. Sometimes the truth can be stretched until it tears itself in half.

I don't wish to give the impression that P.R. is strictly a polite version of lying. That's not the case. As I said, P.R. is gift-wrapping. Whether delivered in fancy or plain paper, truth is truth, and the public ultimately comprehends it. The trick is packaging the truth on your own terms.

How often have you read about a big movie star storming off the set of a film because of "creative differences" with the director? We all know the two egomaniacs probably hated each other's guts. But if the papers printed that, we'd perceive the situation very differently. By our soft-pedaling the row with words like "creative differences," the movie star's reputation remains intact, even though intuition tells us he's "difficult."

MORE THAN ONE PUBLIC

Thus far, when referring to the public, I've generalized to mean the population at large: We the People. The sophisticated modern art of P.R. encompasses many more "publics" than that. In fact, selective targeting is a primary tactic in sound P.R. strategies. As you will see, bigger is not always better.

Depending on the goals, a publicist could target any one of various business, consumer, or governmental communities. An inventor seeking financial backing aims for the financial press and relevant trade publications. A rock musician zeroes in on the local music rags. A lobbyist might need nothing more than a friendly article in the *Washington Post*, a retailer only the residents in his immediate neighborhood.

Though I've found a few clients easily dazzled by quantity, in P.R. quality is what really counts. A seven-inch stack of press clippings means nothing unless the objectives of the campaign have been met. The scrapbook makes a great Mother's Day gift, but I'd rather see my clients' careers advanced in the right direction.

Figuring out which public to reach is one of the most critical decisions a publicist makes. My orientation—and, I hope, yours—is geared toward the most significant audience vis-à-vis your objectives, which is not necessarily the widest. You may want to target the people you buy from, the people you sell to, the people you hope to buy from, the people you hope to sell to, the people you work for, the people that work for you, and so on. It's a big world full of little worlds when you look closely.

In most cases I spell out precisely who and what I'm going after, and then proceed aggressively. Don't go for the moon all at once. Set a goal, achieve it, then build on that base. Any good planner knows the advantages of thinking three steps ahead while proceeding one step at a time.

FROM THE GUERRILLA P.R. FILE

The history-making August 1991 revolution in the former Soviet Union began when then-president Mikhail Gorbachev left Moscow for a vacation on the Crimean Sea. Because the whole affair had a happy ending, everybody laughed when, only a few days later, the president of an outdoor billboard company in Detroit ran a series of large ads all over town reading: "Welcome Back, Gorby! Next Time Vacation in Michigan."

2

BASIC TRAINING

I don't care what they call me, as long as they spell my name right.

—GEORGE M. COHAN/AMERICAN ENTERTAINER

IDEAS AND INNOVATION

The challenge before me was formidable. I realized my client, Oscar-winning actor Charlton Heston, couldn't possibly be made any more famous than he'd already been for the last four decades. But as his public relations counselor, I was responsible for enhancing his distinguished image and career.

Because of his legendary status, due in no small part to the epic nature of the characters he's portrayed on screen, one area in which I felt Mr. Heston could benefit was showing the public that he was a regular human being, just like the rest of us. I also know him to be among the wittiest gentlemen I'd ever met. Suddenly, one of those light bulbs went off: why not have Mr. Heston guest-host "Saturday Night Live"?

It was perfect. Though selling the concept to both the show and my client took some doing, in the end Mr. Heston did host the show. He was a big hit, and many critics at the time called his appearance a "P.R. masterpiece." It all began with a simple brainstorm.

There's a theme running through the examples used in this book. All are based on ideas, not skills. The tricks of the trade are simple to acquire, and easily adapted to a tight budget. The mechanics are not what count. What must be emphasized above all else is the idea itself. From there, all things are possible. As author H. G. Wells said, "Human history is in essence a history of ideas."

So often I've heard people lament that they don't know how to come up with ideas. As my friend, psychologist Dr. Joyce Brothers, explained to me, "Our most creative thoughts do not come when we try to force them. They come as a by-product, while lying in the bathtub or when we're busy with the kids." She's right. Robert Louis Stevenson based *Dr. Jekyll and Mr. Hyde* on a dream. Igor Stravinsky composed in his mind the entire ballet *The Rite of Spring* while asleep. Our best ideas derive from the unconscious, and that's a realm to which we have no practical access.

Yet the challenge to you is to base your Guerrilla P.R. campaign on ideas. But perhaps you're unsure of your ability to generate them. Take it from me, you possess all you need to conjure up clever and effective ideas. Over the years, I've found the best of them are based on four fundamental principles.

Utility. Juxtaposition. Humor. Image.

Not all four are interchangeable, and not all four work equally well for any given project. But if you look closely, within one of these principles lies the pathway to your own sensational ideas—ideas that will fuel your campaign.

Utility means usefulness. Most ideas, inventions, and innovations are based on this simple principle. The question to ask yourself is, "What do people need or want that they haven't thought of before?" One large bank offered customers $10 for every bank error they discovered in their checking accounts. Not only did this help the bank cut down on internal audit procedures, it also brought in 15,000 new accounts and $65,000,000 in deposits within two months.

What better form of utility can anyone in business imagine than in fostering good customer relations? Successful Dallas obstetrician Walter Evans sends his new mothers and their babies home from the hospital in a chauffeured limousine. Estee Lauder, the international cosmetics and beauty products giant, originated the idea of giving away a free gift with every purchase. Today, of course, the company is worth billions, and everybody else in that industry similarly gives away gifts.

Los Angeles radio station KTWV, known as "The Wave," scored points by dotting southern California beaches with "Wave" trash cans, encouraging beachgoers to put their litter in the proper place. It was useful, it was effective, and it made the Wave a much better-known radio station than before.

Don't worry if the usefulness of your ideas isn't immediately apparent to others. Federal Express founder Fred Smith first cooked up his idea for overnight courier service while still a student at Yale. In fact, a paper he wrote about the idea was returned with a "C" grade and a scoffing note from his professor. It took six more years before Smith launched Fed-Ex. Today, I imagine his ex-professor is coaching high school badminton, or should be.

The utility principle works not only in business, but in shaping a P.R. campaign as well. When a mother and daughter country music duo first began to get their career off the ground ten years ago, instead of performing in circuslike mob showcases at well-known clubs, they performed short sets in intimate hotel rooms for a select audience of media people. It didn't take long for the press to conclude that the Judds were without a doubt one of country music's best artists, a sentiment just about everyone else agrees with today.

Utility equals innovation in design and execution. If you own a health food store, how about giving away a fat-and-cholesterol counter guide? Do you run a sporting goods store? Hand out baseball or football schedules with your logo printed on the back. Do you manage an Italian restaurant? How about an attractive description of the various kinds of pastas printed up on giveaway cards? Then, all you have to do is let the media know about it. Apply the precept of utility, and you will make headway fast.

The second fundamental principle is juxtaposition. Woody Allen once said that this was the secret to comedy. I also think it's one of the secrets to many great ideas. Throwing together two disparate personalities, notions, styles, or concepts makes people see things in an entirely different light.

For my client, "Entertainment Tonight" host Mary Hart, I helped come up with the idea to have her gorgeous legs insured with Lloyds of London for $2 million. One of the brightest women I've ever met, Mary quickly realized the potential of such a plan. I brought together one of Mary's most attractive assets with the notion of insurability. Two disparate themes, one wild P.R. idea.

The female hard-core rap music trio BWP sought to bring attention to itself in a crowded field of sound-alike look-alike rap groups, and hit upon the idea of incorporating into their latest music video the notorious home video depicting the beating of Rodney King at the hands of a few L.A.P.D. officers. They brought together two distinct entities into one, and reaped enormous media coverage from it.

To demonstrate the severity of hunger in the world, a noted charity staged an elegant black-tie sit-down dinner, but the only thing served on the fine china was a tiny portion of rice and beans, representing the typical day's diet for most poor Third World residents. Again, the juxtaposition of upper-crust dining manners and starvation food rations made for a powerful P.R. message.

You too can devise two or more concepts and link them together, forming a similarly impressive synthesis. The alchemy you create by juxtaposing themes can work wonders for your business or your Guerrilla P.R. campaign, and you will find your creativity will be recognized and rewarded.

If done right, the third principle, humor, rarely fails. Ideas grounded in humor succeed because, frankly, they make us feel good. If you recall your favorite TV commercials, I'll bet at least half are of the comedic variety. Maybe the fast-talking Federal Express man tickled your fancy, or it was the Bud Light "Taste Great—Less Filling" debates, or perhaps the turbo-charged Friskies kitten. Clearly, the use of humor is the most disarming method for hooking others.

Dave Schwartz catapulted his used car business into the stratosphere by renaming it Rent-A-Wreck, a moniker that delighted everyone who came across it. The name alone brought Dave literally millions in media exposure and business dollars.

Personal fitness trainer Bill Calkins got his name in every paper in the country with his annual "Worst Shapes Hall of Fame." Patterned after Mr. Blackwell's "Worst-Dressed List," Bill's list teased those celebrities most in need of diet and exercise. Sample entries saluted such notables as Chicago Bears lineman William "The Refrigerator" Perry ("The Refrigerator is overstocked"), movie critic Roger Ebert ("Should spend more time 'At the Movies' and less time 'At the Snack Bar' "), and rocker Ozzy Osbourne ("The only man to find a rat in his fried chicken and eat it").

Art's Deli, an enormously popular L.A. eatery, has printed on its menus a Yiddish lexicon with hilarious translations, i.e., "A Farshlepteh Krenk," which actually means "a drawn-out disease," but according to Art means "filling out your own tax return."

When actors Rick Moranis and Dave Thomas sought press attention for their comedy album *Great White North*, based on their lunkhead Canadian characters Bob and Doug McKenzie, they staged a press conference, appearing as Bob and Doug. They even recreated the very set made popular on the original SCTV episodes. The press conference was a smash hit, attended by more than a hundred media people, and it brought them widespread coverage.

The chief danger in the use of humor, of course, is that humor is often subjective. What's funny to you may not be funny to others. I can't tell you how to be funny, but I do know that all people appreciate wit. My best suggestion is to determine precisely what makes you laugh, and see if it makes others laugh as well.

Finally, you may conjure up an idea based on image. This may be the most powerful kind of idea you create, because nothing is quite as searing as a well-constructed image. Consider some of the indelible images we've experienced in the last few years. The "Challenger" explosion; the Rodney King beating; oil-soaked cranes in the Persian Gulf; the Long Island barge of garbage with no place to dump its cargo; 3,000 unemployed people standing in Chicago's winter chill to apply for 50 jobs. All these images say far more on their own than any possible accompanying commentary.

We're all accustomed to advertisers using images, symbols, logos, and other graphics to convey messages. Months before the movie *Batman* opened, we were teased with the stark black image of the Batman logo. The now-famous Infiniti luxury car TV campaign depicted tranquil scenes of riverbanks and cherry groves, never once showing the car. Apparently, the emotional impact of the image is worth more than any intellectual appeal. Guerrilla P.R. practitioners would do well to harness the power of the image when creating ideas.

In one of her campaigns, M.A.D.D. founder Candy Lightner graphically illustrated the problem of teen drinking by displaying scores of beer cans at a press conference—every can of beer was purchased by her underage daughter with an illegal I.D. The message was brought home in a stark manner.

Anti-abortion activists sometimes bring the bodies of aborted fetuses to their press conferences and rallies. Pro-choice proponents carry coat-hangers to symbolize the old back-alley abortions— equally potent symbols for the opposite points of view.

To draw on the image principle for your ideas, reconstitute your thinking into a wordless language. You might even want to use your own dreams as a guide, as did Stevenson and Stravinsky. Dreams employ symbolic language, and often the emotional impact of dream images is as powerful as any experience we can have.

How do you determine if your ideas are worthwhile? Steve Fiffer, in his book *So You've Got A Great Idea*, makes two salient points. Though he primarily addresses inventors, his precepts apply equally well to Guerrilla P.R. Fiffer says the key questions to ask in evaluating an idea are:

1. Determine need. Is your idea beneficial to others? Does it serve a purpose? In terms of P.R., will it help you achieve your objectives by helping to link you and your project together with the media?

2. Is it original? Does it excite? Is it different? The media are always hungry for something new; does your idea fill the bill?

Pondering the answers to these questions will help to steer your ideas either into the development stage or the trash can; but it's up to you to make that determination.

Now, what do you do with your ideas? They can serve many purposes, as you will see. Your creativity will ensure intriguing and well-written press releases, can't-miss magnet events (i.e., publicity stunts), effective marketing tools, and articulate verbal pitches to media representatives. Your ideas will serve you in business, in your Guerrilla P.R. efforts, and elsewhere in your life as your springboard for action.

In later chapters, I go into greater detail on formulating ideas for specific areas, such as writing bios or concocting a magnet event. But part and parcel of the notion of Guerrilla P.R. is the understanding that creativity, not money, power, or influence, is the driving force behind any such campaign. It has been said, "The unexamined life isn't worth living." I would add, "The uncreative life isn't worth living either."

LOOKING VS. SEEING

I want you to try something. Take a pen and paper, and open today's newspaper. Select articles from the news, entertainment, or the business sections. Read carefully and note how often the reporter seems to adopt a particular slant on the article's subject. See if you can detect *when* the influence of a publicist may have entered into the proceedings. Watch for:

- Quotes from "spokespersons"

- Detailed statistics and interpretation

- Polls and surveys

- Information about place and time of an upcoming event

- Links to outside occurrences, such as a movie premiere, a sporting event, or a theme (like, say, "Fire Prevention Week")

- Politicians speaking out about innocuous subjects

- Op-Ed articles by guest writers from show business, sports, and politics who normally do not write for the media

- Anything at all to do with entertainment

Any of these should trigger a flashing sign in your mind: PUBLICIST AT WORK. Most of us read the paper or watch the news without giving a second thought to the sources. Yes, reporters regularly dig up their own information, but they often rely heavily on spokespersons and publicists for help, and you should begin noticing that influence. You can no longer simply look at the story; you have to see what's behind it.

Let's make a dry run with a hypothetical illustration. Read the following fictitious newspaper article and mark every sentence, phrase, or fact you sense may have originated with a publicist. Then check the next page to see if you hit them all.

CITY COUNCIL TO RULE ON OAK TREE PRESERVE NEAR HILLSIDE PARK

(City Hall): City Council President Ron Preston announced yesterday the Council will meet next week to determine the future of a centuries-old grove of oak trees outside Hillside Park where developers seek to build a shopping mall. It is also the location of the annual Country Bazaar, which brings crafts merchants from across the country to the area. "I've always sought a balance between protecting the environment and the need to create jobs," said Preston. "In this case, the Council has to make a tough call."

Dora Hutchins, director of Save The Oaks, urged the City Council to rule in favor of the trees. "The area around Hillside has been ravaged by developers for decades now. It's time for the city to take a stand and just say no to developers."

Equally vocal has been Jack Larsen, president of the Halo Corporation, which last year acquired leases to the disputed property. "Our environmental impact study showed Halo's proposal will not adversely affect the area," said Larsen.

"The Oakdale Galleria will revitalize the economy, creating 700 jobs while preserving the natural beauty of Hillside."

Councilwoman Jane Rogers, an outspoken slow-growth advocate, refuted Larsen's claims. Said Rogers, "He knows perfectly well his development will increase traffic, crime, and pollution in Hillside by 65 percent, as well as destroy forever one of the park's crown jewels, the ancient stand of oaks."

The matter was further complicated this week when several bulldozers arrived at the site to remove the trees. A dozen protesters from Save The Trees handcuffed themselves to the machinery, and were arrested only after hours of tedious sawing of the handcuffs. Said Hutchins, "We felt we had a right to commit civil disobedience."

Al Rojas of the Spring Bazaar issued his own comment on the controversy. "We hope to stage the Bazaar next May at Hillside, but if not, we will find a new location."

Said Buck Nelson, 14, a regular hiker at Hillside, "I like the trees, but a mall would be radical too. Either way, it's okay with me."

The matter will be resolved once and for all at next week's Council meeting, which is expected to be extremely contentious.

Now let's look at the story more closely. Both politicians have their own press secretaries, who keep their bosses' competing career interests uppermost on their agendas. Both the developer and the environmentalist employ publicists to issue press releases, gather statistics, solicit stories from the media, and cook up ideas like hand-cuffing protesters to bulldozers. Even the Spring Bazaar sought to keep itself in the public eye with a spokesman of its own. The only entity in the story who didn't was the fourteen-year-old kid, and maybe he ought to consider it.

Now scan a few real articles and see what you come up with. Try it again with your local TV news. You'll see the same forces at work. There's a lot of time and/or space to fill; something or someone's got to fill it. It might as well be you!

TIPS & TRAPS

1. *The media assume the public is easily bored.* By the time of the last *Apollo* lunar mission, the astronauts had to play a game of moongolf to keep earthbound TV audiences tuned in. The media's primary goal is to elicit attention. Clue into that.

2. In Guerrilla P.R., strategies are built on expediency and efficacy. *Making an immediate impact is paramount.*

3. *Keep up with the news.* Following current events is the responsibility of every aware citizen. Additionally, in Guerrilla P.R. you need to keep pace with the shifting winds of culture. Knowing what's hip, happening, and trendy gives you more credibility when you design your campaign.

4. *Money does not talk when it comes to P.R.* What matters is the idea and the presentation, neither of which need cost much.

5. *A Guerrilla publicist is not intimidated by media.* You must apply a certain amount of pressure on the media or you will not be heard.

6. *You don't have to be great.* It's sad but true: we live in a mediocre world, where good is great, competent is terrific. Be a little better than good and the world will open its arms to you!

TAKING INVENTORY

In order to be irreplaceable, one must always be different.

—"COCO" CHANEL

I'm surprised how often people believe themselves to be unimportant. Perhaps it's a consequence of our mass society that individuals downplay their own ability to affect the world. To those who wonder whether they make a difference, here's a helpful parable: according to an M.I.T. physicist using mathematical models, it has been shown that the beating of a butterfly's wings in Brazil can eventually exert enough influence on natural forces to cause a tornado in Texas. You may think of yourself as a tiny butterfly, but remember, you matter. What you do has profound repercussions on those around you.

This holds true in every area of life, personal and professional. To succeed at Guerrilla P.R., you must *retain a healthy and positive sense of self-importance.* Whether what you do is "important" or not, you will never convince others it is unless you yourself believe it. If you own a balloon store, you'd better believe you not only sell the best balloons in town, but that without them, life as we know it would cease.

I once heard a story about a mattress manufacturer who sought help from a respected P.R. man. At their first meeting, the publicist asked, "What do you sell?" The bedmaker replied, "Why, I sell mattresses, of course." Shaking his head, the other retorted, "No, you don't. You sell sweet dreams and good sex."

The Guerrilla Publicist always sees his mission in a wider context. There's a popular bumpersticker that reads, "Think globally, act locally." That's the attitude behind Guerrilla P.R.

I've made my position clear on the concept of perception as reality, but that does not excuse you from delivering substance. Ultimately, face value has no value, unless it's backed by something real. The first step toward image expansion, toward real depth, begins with self-inventory. You must assess your strengths and weaknesses, your skills and, most importantly, your uniqueness.

Uniqueness. Singularity. Distinction. These words must form your Guerrilla P.R. mantra. Nothing I ask of you will be as challenging as defining yourself and your product in wholly exclusive terms. What's special about your upcoming church carnival? What's different about your nightclub act? Why should I buy your donuts and not the guy's down the street? To put it bluntly, who the hell do you think you are?

This is not meant to antagonize. Self-examination should invigorate. But let's go about it in an orderly fashion. Start by answering the following questions (I use the word "product" generically to include every possible project one might seek to publicize). Write down your answers and then compare them with my subsequent analysis.

A G.P.R. TOP-TEN SELF-INVENTORY QUESTIONNAIRE

1. What attributes of your product are distinct from those of competitors?

2. Why should potential customers choose your product?

3. Precisely who comprises your targeted market?

4. What makes you personally qualified to launch this product?

5. List five reasons why your product *cannot* fail.

6. List five reasons why, despite your best efforts, your product probably will fail. (See it from the other guy's viewpoint.)

7. What three traits do other people find most attractive about your personality?

8. What three personality flaws most often hamper your success with others?

9. Complete the following sentence: "I am at my best when I _____."

10. On a 1–10 scale, rate your abilities on the phone, on paper, and face-to-face (1 equals "Complete Dweeb," 5 equals "Not So Bad," and 10 equals "I Should Have My Own Talk Show").

SELF-INVENTORY ANALYSIS

QUESTION #1: As is commonly believed, the media are indeed hungry for stories, but not just any stories. *To be newsworthy, there must be some distinctive quality to the subject.* Journalists sniff out what's different, not what's the same. Your aim is to dovetail with that thinking.

Ask yourself what separates your product from others. Is there something special about you or about the people who work with you? Anything unusual about your background? Does your product offer features not seen before? Do you provide novel services to your customers? Direct your energies toward originality and creativity. Those strains of uniqueness ultimately become the melody of your Guerrilla P.R. campaign.

QUESTION #2: This may sound like a marketing question, but it bears directly on your P.R. efforts. You need to crawl into the collective mind of the people you target and see things as they do. If you own a gardening service, what would your customers appreciate? How about a free health checkup on the backyard trees? Now you have something creative and desirable for customers that separates you from other gardeners. Potential customers would choose you because you offer more than just a manicured lawn. And that's something you can publicize.

QUESTION #3: If you know whom you want to reach, it's easy to select your media targets. But first you must decide whom you're going after. If you've just opened an All-You-Can-Eat Wine & Burrito salad bar, then your customers likely will be young, affluent, and educated. From there, it's a matter of cross-referencing the media outlets that appeal to such demographics.

QUESTION #4: Why you? This is important because the media will ask you the same thing. As a Guerrilla, you *are* your product, and if you look bad, so does your product. There's no hiding behind a corporate apron. Qualifications go hand-in-hand with an attractive media-ready personality. If that doesn't sound like you, don't worry. We'll fix it later.

QUESTION #5: I ask this because you need to get psyched up. If you present an original idea to the media, they will look for a hundred ways to shoot you down. It's vital you have a pre-planned strategy to quell their native skepticism. Determine here, in realistic but positive terms, why *yours* is the product to beat.

QUESTION #6: This question isn't meant to depress you. It's just a means of anticipating the slings and arrows of outrageous media. I assume you've already pondered the potential pitfalls you face launching your product. Return to that subject and explore the likelihood of failure. By doing so you'll be thinking just like an inquiring journalist. Turn the tables by formulating counter-arguments. You'll be like Perry Mason: you can't lose!

QUESTION #7: If you have a warm and inviting charm about you, then much of your battle is won. If you're less than warm and charming, but have a sharp sense of humor, that's a viable strong point. Perhaps you aren't the most articulate individual but you have a doggedly determined personality. List that. Highlight your strengths, because your Guerrilla P.R. campaign will be molded around them.

QUESTION #8: Similarly, it's critical to take an objective look at your weaknesses so they can either be turned into strengths or shoved so deep in the closet they won't have any impact. Of course, it's preferable to transform weaknesses into solid personality assets. It not only makes you a healthier, happier person, but it adds more ammo to your Guerrilla P.R. arsenal.

QUESTION #9: Close your eyes before you answer this question. Picture yourself operating on all eight cylinders, where nothing and nobody can stop you. You know that feeling of peak performance? That's the state-of-mind you want when implementing your Guerrilla P.R. campaign. Describe the conditions when you're functioning with optimum effectiveness. Once you spell it out, you can take steps to create that climate every day.

QUESTION #10: This is a question of simple self-examination. It's like Arnold Schwartzenegger eyeing his reflection in a floor-length mirror and saying to himself, "My biceps need a little more mass here, my deltoids a little more there." It's essential to maximize the basic skills of writing and speaking, so you can do the job right. Without a certain ability on both fronts, pulling off a successful P.R. effort will be difficult. Answer this question honestly, and then we'll work on ways to improve on both.

Now, take a look at your answers and see if a picture emerges. Do you see patterns of enthusiasm and inventiveness? Are the obstacles before you as formidable as you feared before? Have you gotten the sense that a P.R. campaign is more feasible than you once thought? I suspect after completing this survey you're feeling surprisingly good about your chances.

ONLY YOU

Let's focus a little longer on the uniqueness factor. It's impossible to overstress how important it is. Human beings are not worker ants. Our individuality is what makes each of us irreplaceable. The Talmud says, "If a person saves one life, it is as if he has saved the whole world." We would do well to develop a similar point of view in our business lives. It's certainly part of Guerrilla P.R. doctrine.

I encourage you to look long and hard at yourself and your project. Elevate those elements distinguishing you from all others. Don't hesitate to create some after-the-fact. When Shari Seligman started an L.A. mobile pet grooming service, she became just one of many similar entrepreneurs. But how many of her competitors thought to place a gigantic wagging dog's tail on the rear of their vans? Because of her inventive spirit, Ms. Seligman and her van became the stars of a national soft drink commercial.

Uniqueness, uniqueness, uniqueness!

WHAT WE HAVE HERE IS A FAILURE TO COMMUNICATE

There's an old story about the farmer who returns home after listening to a politician on the stump in town. His wife asks him, "Who spoke?" The farmer replies, "The mayor." Wife: "What did he talk about?" Farmer: "He didn't say."

Of the many failings of our national education system, one in particular strikes me as especially puzzling. A young person can ramble along from kindergarten through high school without learning a thing on the subject of communications. Yet communications is the No. 1 key to success in business.

Most of us learn this lesson too late, struggling for years playing endless catch-up. Some are blessed with an innate gift of communicating, while others study it in college or some other formal setting. Whether or not you have been trained, as a Guerrilla P.R. trooper you're going to have to get in shape as a communicator; otherwise you'll be forced to pay a heavy price.

I've personally known many people who—while they had a

measure of talent and a willingness to work hard—have never been able to rise as high in their professions as they would like. I feel certain the one overriding reason was their inability to communicate effectively with co-workers and superiors.

Studies show that, among America's most admired professionals, TV news anchors rank at or near the top. Most are little more than TelePrompter readers, yet they earn sky-high salaries because they are master communicators. I'm not suggesting your ideal role model should be the TV journalist, but you could benefit from adopting many of their tried-and-true techniques, even if you never go before a camera in your life.

The warm steady gaze, the apparent intelligence, the modulated voice, the sturdy posture and self-confidence—these are the components that make anchors so valued in society. Few of these traits come naturally to anyone, especially when staring into the lifeless eye of a TV camera. They must be learned, which means anyone can learn them, including you. Incorporating qualities such as these will make you more attractive when initiating your Guerrilla P.R. campaign.

The mysterious qualities that make one person charismatic and likeable, and another less so, have been contemplated by philosophers and businesspeople through the years. Dr. Lillian Glass, in her best-selling book *Say It Right*, identifies Seven Secrets of Great Business Communicators. Those secrets are:

1. They were confident and unafraid to ask for what they wanted.

2. They appreciated those that helped them.

3. They consistently nurtured relationships.

4. They were tenacious in going around obstacles.

5. They were excellent listeners.

6. They rebounded quickly and completely from rejection.

7. They were friendly and approachable.

These qualities, like all the positive traits I describe, are not only beneficial to the fledgling Guerrilla P.R. master, but also to anyone in any walk of life. On the other side of the coin, Dr. Glass describes Five Toxic Communication Personality Styles, all of which you should avoid like the plague:

1. The Instigator. One who communicates by trying to make trouble for others, verbally stirring up waters. In P.R., this manifests itself in making subtly destablizing remarks, and berating those that don't see things your way.

2. The Accuser. Hostile and intolerant, this style of practitioner reflects insecurity and self-hatred. One who ravages the competition or makes threatening remarks will get you nowhere in P.R.

3. The Meddler. An advice giver, often someone in no position to do so. You must approach media people with a measure of deference. Keep your confidence, but remember, they've been around the block a million times. Don't tell them what's best for them.

4. The Cut-You-Downer. One who, as Dr. Glass puts it, "will find a cloud in every silver lining." I doubt that anyone who wants to sell his own project via Guerrilla P.R. would stoop this low, but it's worth noting that chronic gainsaying is about the biggest downer I know of.

5. The Back-Stabber. This is communication by sabotage. Obviously, if you stick it to someone, they're going to try to stick you right back. Common sense dictates common courtesy.

Another highly regarded theorist, speech expert Bert Decker, in his book *You've Got to Be Believed to Be Heard,* describes "first-brained" communicators and "new-brained" communicators. The former are those who appeal to the more primal emotion-centered part of our psyches. This is good. Examples of first-brain communicators are Jane Pauley, Lee Iaccoca, and Ronald Reagan. New-brained communicators, such as Michael Dukakis and Walter Mondale, appeal largely to the logic- and decision-making centers. These two men were among history's biggest losers. We can all learn from their mistakes.

GUERRILLA P.R. EXERCISE

To practice your written and oral communications skills, take a moment to do the following exercises:

1. Recite a passage from a book, newspaper, or magazine into a tape recorder. Then speak extemporaneously on any subject for two minutes. Listen to the cadence of your voice. Is it sing-songy, flat, monotonal? Be objective in your assessment. Try it again, this time with your own modifications.

2. Tape a few of your telephone conversations. How do you interact with others? Do you interrupt, step on people's words, finish sentences for them? Do you utter nervous phrases like "ummm" or "you know"? Does your mind wander? Take careful note of observations. Your telephone persona is of maximum importance.

3. Tape or film a conversation between you and a friend. Are you stiff or fidgety? Do your eyes dart around the room? Do you smile too much? Not enough? Ask your friend for honest feedback on your ability to communicate effectively. Don't rely solely on your own impressions. (We're too hard on ourselves anyway.)

4. Write an essay on your project, thinking of it as your one shot to persuade others of your project's virtues. That's how important the written word is. Much of your campaign will be on paper; and if you free-fall there, your back-up chute may not open either. Think in terms of simple construction: a short opening paragraph with a punchy first line, subsequent paragraphs detailing your project's attributes, and a closing summary paragraph leaving readers curious and excited. Show your essay to as many people as you like, and listen to their criticisms. Rewrite it a few times until you've captured the essence of your endeavor.

TARGET PRACTICE

Earlier I mentioned the importance of determining precisely who your target audience is. Basically, there are two kinds of "audiences" you may pursue: active and passive. Appealing to each requires slightly different strategies.

An active audience wants to hear what you have to say. Subscribers to political or single-focus publications (e.g., the *Sierra Club News*, *NRA* monthly), sports magazines (such as *Ski*, *Muscle & Fitness*), and trade publications like *Variety* or *Adweek* constitute an active audience. They're predisposed to your message because they have a working knowledge of the subject and *have already incorporated the milieu of your project into their lives.* If you've designed the world's most comfortable briefs, the readers of *Underwear World* certainly want to know about it.

Conversely, a passive audience isn't looking for anything. John Q. Grump, sipping his morning coffee while flipping through the sports section, isn't necessarily ripe for your message. When he flops in front of the TV, clicker in hand, he isn't necessarily predisposed to hear what you have to say. Yet he and millions like him are your target. The passive audience is tougher to reach, though hundreds of times larger than the active audience.

In Guerrilla P.R. thinking, *there is no such thing as a mass audience.* Ultimately, you must reach individuals one at a time, which is why this method is effective on both the large and small scales. Keeping that in mind, any appeal to your target audience, passive or active, must embody the characteristics used to persuade individuals. *What works for one most likely works for many.*

Use yourself as a barometer. When was the last time someone convinced you of something? What kind of rationale was used? Did it play to your heart or your head? Your emotions or intellect? Think how often we hear about typhoons in distant lands that kill thousands, yet we usually feel nothing more than a momentary pang of horror. Compare that with well-orchestrated sympathy ploys, played out in the media, such as the frequent stories about the leukemia victim who needs a bone marrow transplant. Our hearts go out to such persons dramatically more than to the nameless victims of the natural disaster. Human nature dictates that we feel for other people one at a time.

Once you dissect your own responses, you'll see quite clearly the tactics used to persuade.

With a passive audience:

• *Lean toward a personal, more human approach.* When the late Jonas Salk invented the polio vaccine, his solicitation to the medical community was geared toward the vaccine's epidemiological applications. When it was sold to the public, all we saw were doe-eyed children and iron lung machines. You too must remember that most people appreciate being addressed on their own level.

- *Be broad and simple.* Assume readers or viewers of any particular mass media outlet are far less informed than those of an active audience outlet. Stress rudimentary points and wider connections, rather than microtechnical specifics.

- *Restrict your use of technical terminology not easily understood by passive consumers.* It's not only confusing to throw in a lot of ten-cent words, it also alienates you from your audience, which is obviously dangerous for your project.

With an active audience:

- *Emphasize the technical.* Active audiences derive pleasure from their possession of particular knowledge. Exploit that by underscoring the more exacting details of your project.

- *Try a harder sell.* Because an active audience is, by definition, more inclined to hear your message, you may present a stronger, more emphatic case. Because you and your target audience are on the same level of understanding, you probably won't be perceived as a flim-flammer.

GUERRILLA P.R.
MARKETING PLAN OUTLINE

Objective(s):
What do you want to achieve?

_____

_____

_____

Audience(s):
Who can best help you reach that goal?

_____

_____

_____

Definition of product or service: _____

_____

_____

Message:
Why your audience should want or could benefit by your product or service?

_____

_____

_____

Why are you better than the competition? _____

_____

_____

What else do you want your audience to know? _____

_____

_____

Media:
What vehicles should you use to get the message to your audience?

_____

_____

_____

Summary/Results:
How does the delivery of the above message to the targeted audiences via these media achieve your objectives?

_____

_____

_____

• *Narrow your focus.* Unlike a passive audience, the active audience doesn't require ancillary themes to develop an interest in your project. Astronomers may enjoy reading about newly discovered binary star systems, but down here we just want to know if anyone saw the ghost of Elvis up there cavorting with aliens.

Once you choose between the passive and active audience, you'll be able to tailor your Guerrilla P.R. campaign accordingly. But remember, you don't communicate with the audience directly. Your message is filtered through media. The newspaper editor and the radio talk-show producer are your conduit to the audience. Next, we shift our focus toward them, toward the media for whom you will soon be setting traps.

GUERRILLA P.R. EXERCISE

1. Consider whether you are targeting a passive or an active audience. Which media outlets serve that audience?

2. Just for fun, ponder switching from active to passive (or vice versa). How would you retool your media outlets? Which would work for you in this new setting? Why or why not this plan work?

3. Attached is a copy of the standard Marketing Plan Outline we use at my company. Although it takes a slightly different tack, examine it and fill it out.

TARGET PRACTICE TOO

You need not only to target your consumer, but likewise to target your media. But just who are these media folks, anyway? A study I read recently reported 95 percent of key media personnel were white, 79 percent male, 46 percent earned over $50,000 a year, 54 percent call themselves liberal, and 50 percent claim no religious affiliation. It certainly sounds like an ivory tower to me.

Actually, I've found reporters, editors, and producers to be an engaging lot overall, naturally curious and ever on the prowl for good stories. They consider their career a profession, but it most assuredly is not. Professions, that is, medicine, law, and accounting, are challenging fields of discipline, difficult to learn, all requiring state licensing. Ongoing education and re-certification are also required just to keep the shingle up.

None of that is true for journalism. Any glib wordsmith with a little luck and persistence can make it on-staff or as a freelancer somewhere. Some college experience helps, but even that isn't vital. Carl Bernstein of the famous team that broke the Watergate story joined the *Washington Post* as a cub reporter while still in high school. I'm not denigrating his skills as a reporter. However, I never met a surgeon who got his first job hanging out in front of the operating room looking for an opening in the scrub room.

Although, to be sure, there are some unsavory exceptions, I've found media people to be very much like the rest of us. They have likes and dislikes, as we do, and you can interact with them without worrying about offending their inflated sense of social standing. Believe me, they don't bite.

However, journalists do possess one useful human quality in abundance: intense skepticism. That old movie stereotype of the cynical, hard-bitten reporter has a basis in fact that lives on today. Journalists are born doubters. They presume guilt until innocence is proven, and even then . . .

Distrust is vital to their role. Journalists (at least the good ones) are trained to suspect official pronouncements from government officials and other spokespersons. Nobody scoffs like a journalist. They go to great lengths to look beyond the facade of the news and dig up a truer, albeit messier, reality.

That's why they're exceptionally suspicious of publicists. Even though I believe they need us as much as we need them, because we publicists are hired guns, reporters don't often put much stock in our pleas and arguments, at least not at first. I was told by one entertainment reporter from a large metropolitan paper, "Publicists don't believe in what they're selling. They're just paid pitchmen."

With Guerrilla P.R., that concern doesn't exist. You represent yourself. You believe in your project far more than any "paid pitchman" ever could. What you lack in seasoning, you more than make up for in sincerity.

And that pays off with journalists. They root for underdogs. They listen to "real" people, as opposed to us "unreal" professional publicists. Your very handicap of being unconnected may end up as your biggest asset, because the press will believe in your sincerity more than in mine. And I'm the most sincere person I know.

Above all, remember my Golden Tip regarding members of the media: *They want good stories.* They aren't paid to say "no." They're paid to say "yes" to the right stories. The principal aim of this book is to get them to say "yes" to you.

FROM THE GUERRILLA P.R. FILE

In Woodland Hills, California, one enterprising businessman opened the area's first combination chess club and exercise gym, so patrons might exercise both their bodies *and* their minds. Though the gym struggled financially for some months, the novelty of its appeal gained widespread attention, including a major spread in the *Los Angeles Times*. Not a bad way to checkmate the competition.

MAKING A LIST, CHECKING IT TWICE

Your first task as a Guerrilla P.R. recruit is to begin compiling a priceless possession without which you cannot function. It's the heart, the soul, the cosmic center of your P.R. universe. It's your mailing list.

A mailing list is far more than a mere collection of names and addresses. It's your media homing device. Having determined your target audience, you must amass a comprehensive list of key names from media and other areas that allows you to mold your campaign. Don't narrow your names solely to your specific target of the moment. The bigger your list, the greater your options. That doesn't mean you contact everyone on your list each time you send out a press release. You pick and choose who gets what, and block out long-term strategy as you go.

Your list should include not only media, but also potentially helpful organization types like chamber of commerce members, colleagues in your industry, government, friends and family, and anyone who might be of some help to you. However, in this section I want to concentrate on ways to put together your media list, since the assembly itself may prove to be the most daunting aspect.

Start by dividing your media list into three broad categories—national, local, and specialty—then further break these down by

medium, i.e., newspapers, magazines, radio programs, TV shows, etc.
Examples of what sort of outlets should make your list:

- National. These include network news organizations like CBS,
ABC, CNN, and their morning shows; national magazines like *Time*,
Newsweek, *Vanity Fair*, and *People*; national newspapers like *USA
Today*, *Wall Street Journal*, the *Christian Science Monitor*, and the *New
York Times*; wire services like AP and UPI; key syndicated TV shows
like *Donahue*, *Oprah Winfrey*, *Entertainment Tonight*, etc.

- Local. Includes daily newspapers; local TV news and talk
shows, like *A.M. Los Angeles*; local all-news or talk-radio programs;
weekly entertainment guides; local bureaus of the wire services;
public access and other local cable TV stations; city magazines, business newsletters, ethnic publications.

- Specialty. Magazines, trade publications, and other outlets that
relate specifically to your field of interest. If you're a musician, *Billboard* and *Spin* top your list; if you're a chef or restaurateur, then
Gourmet, *Bon Appétit*, and the food section of your local paper top
yours. Anything that appeals to that narrower active audience you
seek would come under this heading.

Compiling the list is like climbing a mountain. It starts out easily
enough, but may soon wear you out. Like most people, journalists
don't want to be bothered by unwelcome strangers, so finding comprehensive listings of media outlets isn't simple, although they are
available in one fashion or another for a price.

Many compilations, such as *Bacon's Publicity Checker* or *Editor &
Publisher Yearly*, can sometimes be found in the library. If you cannot
find them there, you might obtain older outdated editions free of
charge from established P.R. firms in your area. Most professionals
subscribe and don't need last year's copy once the updated edition
arrives, even though most of the info in the old volumes is current.
Check around. (I list additional sources in the appendix.) And of
course, you could shell out the hefty asking price and buy them new.

If you aren't able to find or afford these directories, roll up your
sleeves and get to work. Your first stop: the local newsstand. Peruse
carefully, pen and paper in hand. Write down the names of every
publication you think may be useful to you. Open the magazines and
newspapers, turn to the masthead (the page that lists the staff) and jot

down all key names, titles, addresses, phone and fax numbers.

Next, head back to the library. Go through the *Reader's Guide* and other resources that list names of newspapers and periodicals. If you can't locate them, ask the librarian. Start collecting as many names as you can, and begin shaping your master list.

Assemble your list in a way that's comfortable for you. I use a large alphabetized wheel rolodex. One of my friends puts his information on 3- × 5-inch cards stored in a shoebox. Others keep 3-ring notebooks with multiple listings on a page. The operative phrase is "whatever works." As time goes on, you'll want to update your list, so it's a good idea to write in pencil.

Remember, your list is a living organism. Don't write down merely the name, address, and phone number. If you list a TV station, make sure you include the names of pertinent news shows and segments, when they air, who hosts them, deadlines, area of coverage, and any other information that could help you comprehend the nature of the show.

Here's a sample listing:

> Bill Gonzo
> Anytown News
> 4444 Main St.
> Anytown, CA 90022
> 213-555-0000
>
> Home improvement columnist
> Column runs in Tempo section on Mondays
> Deadline for information prior Tuesday
> Prefers personal anecdotes from readers

For your list to work, you must find out which newspaper writers gravitate toward what subjects, since many tend to specialize. You do this simply by reading the publications. As I said above, you pick and choose whom to add to your list. Note that there aren't many general field reporters left; most are assigned a beat (city desk [metro news], business, entertainment, medical, sports, science, etc.). If you know who are the reporters for each beat at the outlets you care about, you can then direct your information accordingly, thus saving time and money. That kind of research pays big dividends down the line. Forewarned is forearmed.

Finally, be sure to keep your list as current as possible. This is the mobile society, remember? Nobody seems to stay put in any one place for long. You'll save a lot of money, time, and paper if you weed out the defunct listings as you go. Your list is like a garden; tend it well.

In the resource section of this book you'll find a substantial national list taken directly from my company's latest computer data banks. This will give you a healthy head start in compiling your media list.

MICHAEL LEVINE'S TEN COMMANDMENTS FOR DEALING WITH MEDIA

1. Never be boring. Never!
2. Know your subject thoroughly.
3. Know the media you contact. Read the paper, watch the newscast.
4. Cover your bases.
5. Don't just take "yes" for an answer. Follow up, follow through.
6. Never feel satisfied.
7. Always maintain your composure.
8. Think several moves ahead.
9. Be persistent, but move on when you're convinced you're getting nowhere.
10. Remember, this isn't brain surgery. Don't take yourself too seriously (like too many publicists I know). Have fun.

THE ART OF THE PITCH

Before you take on the media, you have to know something about The Pitch. *The way you pitch your project can have more bearing on your long-term success or failure with the media than the project's merit itself.*

How many times have you gotten in an argument with someone in which you said in a huff, "It's not what you said; it's the way you said it." The same principle applies when contemplating your pitch. With the right pitch, you'll get no argument.

This is where salesmanship comes in. The term is derived from the old "sales pitch" notion. It requires of you a substantial degree of self-confidence to pull off, but your belief in your own project will help you muster that. It also requires that you become the pursuer. Remember, as I said, nobody else will care as much as you care. It's your job to aggressively wake people up to the virtues of your project. That's what the pitch is all about.

The information about your project is objective, but your presentation is subjective. When your own subjectivity collides with that of the media, there's plenty of room for confusion, misinterpretation, and disinterest. That's why you must know precisely how to pitch before you make that first phone call or mail a press release.

The Pitch is your *selective oral mechanism for persuasion* (by oral, I mean the words you use and the way you use them). There are several styles of pitching, but all have two principles in common: they appeal *personally* to the individual being contacted, even if he or she is a stranger, and they rely on *logic* to make a case. How you pitch depends on what you're pitching and who you're pitching to. Time and practice will teach you which style to use.

"Personally" doesn't mean overly familiar or folksy. An ingratiating manner gets you nowhere fast. I'm talking about an undertone of humanity in your approach. As my friend Jane Kaplan, a staff producer on *Good Morning, America*, has told me, "It's a big turn-off to encounter people who sound phony, or too cheery and bright. It's like they've dropped out of Publicity 101."

No matter how impersonal the media seem, they're staffed by real people. Though they sift through hundreds of calls and pieces of mail every day, they invariably respond to what touches their emotions. Reach the *person* in the media, and, *voilà!*, you've reached the media.

The word "logic" has a cold and calculating connotation to it, but don't let that prevent you from employing logic when you pitch. Media people need to understand the sense behind anything they're asked to cover, so you have to be sensible. There must be reason along with your rhyme.

Say you own a video rental store, and you're cooking up a promotional campaign. Why is that worth a reporter's time? Because surveys show consumers prefer to rent movies rather than stand in line for them at theaters. And because "cocooning" is the social phenomenon *du jour*, your store is the only one responding with free popcorn on Friday and Saturday nights. Something like that will likely cause a journalist to prick up his ears. There must always be a method to your madness. Your pitch simply spells it out.

In all cases, one central overarching guideline when pitching the media (or dealing with anyone in business) is to employ the five F's—to be fast, fair, factual, frank, and friendly. These concepts speak for themselves, and they go a long way in gaining credibility for your project and in establishing a positive image for yourself as spokesperson.

Now, try it with the other sentiments, or choose your own. Keep uppermost in your mind the *underlying emotional component* to give your pitch sharpness and direction. Equally essential, you must steer your appeal toward one central message and remain consistent, at least in your first volley of pitching. If you say too much, or mix in multiple pitches, you diffuse your goal. You must give the media a pitch they can hit. Otherwise everybody strikes out.

You do not have to use the same pitch to all media. One size does *not* fit all. When contacting a consumer magazine, put a consumer-oriented spin on your pitch. If it's to a trade magazine, shape your appeal in a more technical fashion. But most importantly, always put yourself in the shoes of the person you're pitching to. Ask yourself what she's looking for, what he needs or wants. Generous empathy will take you far in Guerrilla P.R.

Some of the most common pitch styles are:

• FASTBALL. Direct, straight, factual. The fastball is most effective with national media. They're usually so busy, they have little time to sift through ancillary material. Remain polite and informative, but keep your focus on the basics of your message and the rationale

GUERRILLA P.R. EXERCISES

Complete the following to gain practice in thinking logically and personally:

1. You're the director of a local youth center, and have decided to stage a carnival to raise money for new equipment. Briefly list three distinct reasons why this event is necessary. For each of those three, spin off three other contributing factors, and so on. Carry it as far as you can, so that your final sheet resembles a pyramid-shaped organizational chart. You will see that every point has three substantiating bases, and each of those has three other bases. Of course, when you pitch the media on your own project, you won't inundate them with hundreds of "reasons," but you will have developed an unshakable foundation for your argument.

2. Let's keep the same example of the youth-center carnival. As I mentioned, when you make a personal appeal, you tug on human emotions. Take the following sentiments—excitement, sympathy, and joy—then write a brief paragraph making a case for the carnival centering on each of those emotions. For example, if the emotion were, say, fear, the paragraph might read:

> Without the Mid-Valley Youth Center, hundreds of teens would have nowhere to go after school. Many would turn to drugs and gangs without the positive influence of the center and its staff, and our streets would become more dangerous than ever. Next month's carnival will go a long way in raising desperately needed funds for new equipment. A successful carnival means our kids won't have to turn to the streets.

for media coverage. Don't offer extraneous details unless the person asks for them. What follows is a sample transcript. Don't start out a cold call like this—I'm only trying to impart a general approach. The same "feeling" can be imparted in a letter as well:

"Hello, is this the news editor of the *Daily Star*? Hello, Mr. Smith, my name is John Jones. I hope you aren't on deadline. Do you have a moment? Great, thank you. I'm calling regarding the upcoming carnival for the Mid-Valley Youth Center. Perhaps you saw the press release I sent a few days ago. I wanted to see if the *Star* would be interested in running a story on the carnival in advance of the event. Why should the paper do a story? Because our community's youth would easily fall prey to the scourges of society were it not for places like the Center. Because we have top stars from the sports and entertainment worlds coming down to lend a hand. The *Star* is known for its supportive coverage of community events. As you know, the Center could be shut down if we don't meet our financial goals. Perhaps you'd like to talk with some of our kids and learn firsthand how beneficial the center has been . . ."

• CURVEBALL. This approach appeals to the media's innate curiosity. Whereas a fastball stresses logic over emotion, the curveball stresses emotion over logic. This works especially well when you know something about the journalist contacted and the kind of stories he or she tends to do. You tie in other elements and paint a broader picture with the curveball. A sample fictitious transcript:

"Jenny James of the *Weekly*? Hi, Jenny, this is John Jones, and I wanted to talk to you about the Mid-Valley Youth Center carnival next month. You know, I think it would make a sensational story if the *Weekly* ran a story on the carnival the week of the event. That piece you did on unwed mothers last week was very powerful, and our Center is geared directly at kids just like those you wrote about. Most of our kids come from tough backgrounds, broken homes, drugs. We've been able to give them a sense of purpose and direction. The Center has been a positive influence in the community, and I'd love to have the participation of you and the *Weekly* . . ."

• SCREWBALL. Humor can often be effective, and with this style, it's emphasized. Appeal to the journalist's heightened sense of the unusual. Stunts, sideshows, ancillary themes are put to work here. A sample transcript:

"Is this Mr. Williams at Channel 6? Hi, I'm John Jones, and I'm calling regarding the upcoming Mid-Valley Youth Center carnival. Did you realize that we now have three bands set to perform, each one made up of former gang members, kids that have straightened out since they joined the center? Also, I just learned two members of the City Council will attend, dressed as clowns. I don't want to say which ones. We have a lot more surprises in store, and I'm wondering whether Channel 6 would like to do a story on the carnival . . . ?"

• SPLIT-FINGERED FORKBALL. Naaah, I'm not going to take this baseball analogy any further.

As you can see, there are myriad ways one can approach the same basic information. In Guerrilla P.R., you need to be prepared to attempt any one of them as the need arises.

TIPS & TRAPS

1. No matter how you pitch the media, please remember the five F's: always be fast, fair, factual, frank, and friendly.

2. Don't be intimidated as you design your pitch. The fact is nobody will come to you at first. You must be the aggressor, or you will not be heard.

3. If you are unduly nervous, turn it around: make your vulnerability an asset. There's no rule that says you must come across as a slick, polished professional. Openness, honesty, and a down-to-earth approach *will* work for you.

4. Whether writing or speaking, your objective is to be understood. It's of little use trying to impress others of your great intellect if they can't comprehend what you're saying. As I've said, avoid technical jargon unless you're *certain* the other person is qualified to understand it. Use vocabulary people are comfortable with. The smartest people I know speak simply and plainly.

5. Another excellent piece of advice from Dr. Lillian Glass: good communication is a give-and-take proposition. Don't think of your pitch as a short speech, after which you get a thumbs-up or thumbs-down. When you contact media people, or anyone in business, expect dialogue, negotiation, questions, and answers. Recapture the spirit of conversation. Remember, "con" is the Latin word for "with."

TRACKING

Before firing up your Guerrilla P.R. campaign, you have one last bit of essential paperwork to take care of: a tracking system. Every publicist has his or her own method for assessing the headway of a campaign, and a tracking sheet is designed to do just that.

Though there is no set format, most publicists generally follow a grid pattern, with one axis listing names of publications, TV, and radio stations, the other a series of columns with answers to questions like "date contacted," "materials sent," "comments," "results," etc.

Maintain your tracking system religiously over the course of your campaign. You use it not only to see where you are, but also where you've been and where you're going. No other document will better assist you in strategic planning. A Guerrilla P.R. tracking sheet is the only way to get a tangible picture of your progress. It's really like an X-ray of your campaign, and with it you can diagnose what's going wrong (if it is) without relying strictly on abstract feelings or opinions.

Let's say you've prepared a press release. On your tracking sheet list the media outlets you've sent it to, and when. A few days later you call the newspapers and TV stations to gauge their reaction. You should note the name of the person you spoke with. Distill his or her comments into a brief sentence or two on your tracking sheet. If the media contact wants additional material, ship it out, noting on the sheet what you sent, and when.

You can see that by maintaining a thorough log like this, you will always know exactly where you stand with any media target. You can refresh their memories, and remain a step ahead.

On the following page, I offer a sample of a tracking sheet I've used, but by all means feel free to devise one that works for you. As long as you have a tracking sheet form in place before you make that first call or lick that first stamp, you'll be in good shape.

GUERRILLA P.R. TRACKING SHEET

DATE OF CONTACT	PUBLICATION/OUTLET	CONTACT/PHONE NUMBER	MATERIALS SENT AND DATE	COMMENTS

GUERRILLA P.R. COMMANDO: CANDY LIGHTNER

When her thirteen-year-old daughter Cari was killed by a drunk driver, Candy Lightner felt devastated, broken, and angry. But she channeled her fury into forming a revolutionary organization that impacted America as few others have. Today we're all familiar with the work Mothers Against Drunk Driving (M.A.D.D.) has done, but not everyone knows the story of Candy's struggle to get her message heard. She did it through sheer grit and determination; she did it with Guerrilla P.R.

Back in 1980, when Candy first launched M.A.D.D., she knew nothing about public relations. But one sympathetic reporter helped Candy organize a press conference to introduce M.A.D.D. to the public. Though it was not well attended, Candy and her surviving daughter explained the harrowing consequences of drunk driving to the assembled media. A photo of the tearful mother and daughter flashed around the world, and suddenly the agony of death from a D.U.I. had a face and a name: Candy Lightner.

Over the years, Candy has undertaken many successful media crusades to spread her message of fighting drugs, alcohol, depression, and grief. She did it all without ever having to hire a slick P.R. firm. "I visited reporters personally, sat down, and talked with them," she recalls. This dynamic woman used the sheer strength of her character to forge a movement.

Along the way, she also picked up a few useful tricks regarding the media. "I'm convinced if we had hired outside P.R. in the beginning, we wouldn't be where we are today," says Candy. "We worked on gut instinct, not by training, as a P.R. firm would." At that first press conference, seeing the reaction to the photo, Candy comprehended how the media hone in on visuals.

"We hadn't planned scenes of crying," says Candy. "But instinctively we knew the media need something dramatic." In a recent campaign to pass a California bill requiring a five-cent tax on alcohol, Candy sent her daughter to purchase a six-pack with a fake I.D. She then held a press conference—with her daughter sitting behind a small mountain of beer cans she'd bought, illustrating just how easy and how enormous the problem actually was.

"You have to tell a story that will supercede other news," she notes, "because you're in constant competition with other issues."

Despite her flair for the dramatic, Candy also learned when to pull in the reins. "You can't beat an issue to death. You don't call them every time there's a drunk-driving death or every time there's a court case you're unhappy with. Make sure when you do contact the media, it's with something very important. Never cry wolf, or they won't come back."

It's hard to imagine Candy Lightner having enemies, but like any celebrity, some media people feel they haven't done their job unless they take an axe to society's high and mighty. In Candy's case, one reporter said to her, "Nobody's done a bad story on you, and I think it's time." Candy has since learned to avoid such traps. "I don't think the media are objective at all," Candy asserts. "They're in this for the money, like everyone else. The press tell me it's a matter of being honest with the public. But I've seen a lot of people get hurt by inaccuracies."

Her criticisms notwithstanding, Candy still credits the media for much of M.A.D.D.'s success. "For whatever reason, they took us on as the cause of the eighties," she says. "Thank God they did, because otherwise most of the auto accidents in this country would still be caused by drunk drivers. It was thanks to the media that public awareness was raised."

Her advice to prospective Guerrilla P.R. commandos: "First know your issue, your client, or your business thoroughly. Then, do as much research as possible so you speak intelligently. Next, find an angle that will appeal to the public, because that's what the media will want. Finally, use your gut instinct. You're a person first. What would you like to know? What would catch your eye? Answer that and you're home free."

A modern heroine who has truly changed the world, Candy Lighter, despite the tragedy in her life, is truly home free.

3

FIRST MANEUVERS

In human relations kindness and lies are worth a thousand truths.

—GRAHAM GREENE, BRITISH AUTHOR

WHO YOU GONNA CALL?

By now, you've pulled together a workable media mailing list. You have a phone, stamps, and an overflow of good ideas to promote your project. But hold on! You're not *quite* ready to launch your Guerrilla P.R. campaign. Before that first step, I want to divulge one of the secret weapons of your entire effort. It's not a wholly novel concept. Much has been written and said about it before, but not often in terms of public relations. I'm talking about networking, or the making and using of contacts.

It's an ancient custom in Australia when two aborigines meet on the trail, they must stop and talk. In the course of their conversation, they're required to discover a common relative. If they can do so, that must mean they're friends. If they cannot, it automatically means they are enemies and must fight each other. In several documented cases, the search went on for days. That's primitive networking at its finest.

Statisticians have theorized that any one of us is no more than six contact links away from anyone in the world. However, it's getting those first three that counts. In the course of my career, I've met thousands of people from various walks of life. Some turned out to be little more than sources of small talk at a party, but others have become valuable business contacts, clients, and friends. As you know, my philosophy is grounded in an expectation of opportunity. I find it not only in the media I absorb, but also—and most especially—in the people I meet.

Gerald Michaelson, writing in *Sales & Marketing Management* magazine, says, "If you desire high quality in your business, you must have a high-quantity network." Seventy percent of top management executives accept new jobs at pay levels higher than their previous posts *largely* due to their large networks of highly placed contacts. Networking will aid you not only in your own business, but in your Guerrilla P.R. plan as well.

A Guerrilla publicist is a provocateur. She engages people, draws reactions from them, makes them think. The more people within your sphere, the more powerful your message becomes. This is true in all realms of life. Even Jesus' message didn't take on transcendent power until hundreds, then thousands, and finally hundreds of millions of people heard it. Throughout the ages, there have been other enlightened individuals with compelling ideas, but none of them had Saint Paul, the greatest Guerrilla P.R. master in history, to get the word out.

Your story may not be of biblical proportions, but you do need to take it to the people, however large or small your target audience may be. So here are a few suggestions regarding networking, how to increase your own circle of contacts, and how to enhance your presence in the process.

First, you don't have to "join" a network—you already belong to one. I'm referring of course to your family, friends, and existing business associates. To increase your network, consider the following:

- Seminars

- School and college acquaintances

- Alumni organizations

- Church or synagogue

- Business groups like the Better Business Bureau, Rotary, Chamber of Commerce

- Political parties and organizations

- Hobby clubs

- Family

- Recovery groups

All these may bear fruit, but you should be on the lookout at all times. I've made contacts while camping in the mountains, at concerts, standing in line at the bank and grocery store, on airplanes, and even once while paying a parking ticket. I happen to be a fairly gregarious person, and find meeting new people fun. However, not everyone has such an easy time of it. If that sounds like you, listen up.

To expand your base, above all else you have to be likeable. As with any other muscle in your body, your personality also needs to be exercised regularly to stay fit. It would be impossible to calculate how important this is. When getting in the P.R. boxing ring, you fight two battles. One is to sell your product or project; the other is to sell yourself. This isn't news to anyone who has ever read a business magazine or self-help book in the past. But it amazes me how often such simple lessons can be lost on people. So let's take a refresher course.

A friend of mine recently bought a copy of Dale Carnegie's all-time best-selling classic, *How to Win Friends and Influence People.* She reported that a few colleagues chuckled when they saw her reading it. "A relic from the past," they called it. "Outdated and meaningless," they said. Those people don't know how wrong they are.

Carnegie's "Six Principles to Make People Like You" resonate as convincingly today as when he published them in 1936. They may seem obvious on the surface; but we all know how infrequently they're put into practice. In brief, they are:

1. "Be genuinely interested in other people."

2. "Smile."

3. "Remember that a person's name is to that person the sweetest and most important sound in any language."

4. "Be a good listener. Encourage others to talk about themselves."

5. "Talk in terms of the other person's interests."

6. "Make the other person feel important—and do it sincerely."

These are the fundamentals that make for good human relations on every scale and in every setting. But of them all, I find Principle No. 4 to be far and away the single most important. Ralph Waldo Emerson said, "Every man I meet is in some way my superior, and I can learn of him." The best way to be a better person is to be a better listener.

Listening is integral to our personal and professional progress. The owner of one small supermarket overheard a customer saying she would like fresh fish. He set up a fish bar on beds of ice and his seafood sales skyrocketed.

In this era of "time famine," people need to be listened to in a nondistracted manner. God gave us two ears and one mouth—as the expression goes—so He must have wanted us to do twice as much listening as speaking. I encourage you to develop the lost art of Shutting Up.

Other skills breed goodwill for those who practice them. Empathy, the ability to deeply feel where another person is coming from, is indispensable. Once you can see things from another's perspective, you not only develop compassion and tolerance, but you also will be a better persuader of your own point of view.

Don't forget, optimism is also a big turn-on. The world is so filled with whiners, handwringers, and complainers that if you show even a modest level of enthusiasm you're bound to stand out.

Equally important is a sense of humor, not only to your Guerrilla P.R. and business endeavors, but to your life as a whole. Am I mistaken, or are people a lot more serious today than they used to be? When I attend meetings these days, I see too many strained faces. There's a difference between taking your work seriously and taking yourself seriously. If you lighten up, your network will grow, because others will be attracted by the light.

YOU'RE PART OF THE PICTURE

What you are . . . thunders so that I cannot hear what you say to the contrary.

—RALPH WALDO EMERSON

There's one big difference between professional and Guerrilla P.R.: whereas the pro drives around all day in someone else's car, the Guerrilla drives his own. There would be no campaign if not for you, and to leave yourself out of the picture would be to sabotage your efforts. I said in the first pages of this book I wanted you to think like a publicist, and I hope you've begun to do that. Now I want you to start acting like your own client.

You are the best media point person for your project. Nobody else can speak with as much passion, knowledge, and insight. You cannot function merely as a funnel for press releases or act as ticket-taker for your own carnival. You must become the focus for the media's attention on your project. You must become their resident expert on whatever it is you do.

That means that anytime, anywhere, when asked to speak to the media—you're on call. Assume a pocket pager has been surgically attached to your body. That's how accessible you must be. So before I get to the chapters that relate specifically to individual media, let's spend some time preparing to become, as Tom Wolfe put it in *Bonfire of the Vanities*, a Master of the Media Universe.

Does the name Roger Ailes ring a bell? He's the astute media consultant who played a major role in Ronald Reagan's 1984 reelection campaign, and is nothing less than a modern-day Dale Carnegie. Nobody on earth understands media better than Roger. He's taught me a lot, and I'd like to share with you a few of his ideas.

Earlier in the book I discussed ways to be a better communicator. But Ailes goes one step further by spelling out the keys to effective communicating with media. As Roger states in his book *You Are the Message*, the four essential components of good media communication are: be prepared, be comfortable, be committed, and be interesting. It may sound simplistic, but often great ideas are very simple. Mastering these four is no easy trick. They all take practice.

Preparation is obvious. You must be thoroughly knowledgeable about your subject when you engage the media. But, as Ailes puts it, others must feel that *you* know more about your subject than they do. Facts, figures, and philosophy should come as naturally to you as breathing. Proper preparation requires ongoing study, whatever your field of expertise. Even the violin virtuoso Itzak Perlman still practices his scales. Granted he does so while watching the Yankees on TV, but he keeps his edge via continuous preparation.

It's not only important you feel comfortable yourself, but that others feel comfortable with you too. Relaxation is the key. This isn't a book on stress-reduction, but I suggest you acquire skills that promote relaxation. TV, radio, and newspaper interviews can make anyone nervous; yet nervousness is the most counterproductive emotion you can show. It smacks of uncertainty, the kiss of death. Watch the "experts" on TV. They always *seem* to know what they're talking about, even when they don't.

So stretch, breathe deeply, roll your head, close your eyes, astrally project to Tibet. Slow yourself down in order to pump yourself up for the media. Making others comfortable with you requires a sparkle, a gentleness, a light touch. This doesn't mean you have to totally rearrange your personality, but try to bring out those aspects of yourself that inspire confidence and familiarity. Humor, listening, and noticing will bond you quickly to your media counterparts.

Ailes' third essential is commitment. That's just another word for caring. As a Guerrilla, you already care. It's a matter of putting that caring into action and demonstrating it to the media. Every one of the Commandos profiled in this book exemplifies total commitment. You should model that kind of zeal. Maybe we envy it in others because so few people these days feel passionately about anything. The media never fail to pick up on this.

To be interesting is tricky. On one level, we're all interesting in our own way. But once you go toe-to-toe with the media, we're talking about a performance. I've told you how easily bored the media get. They're like a two-year old child—short attention span. You have to keep flashing new toys to get them to keep their eyes on you. Your ability to keep them focused makes the difference between being seen on the front page or being shown the front door.

One way to do that is to become conversant in the *zeitgeist*, a German term meaning "spirit of the times." Guerrilla P.R. masters collect phrases, anecdotes, punch lines, quotable quotes, and other *bon mots* to keep the focus on themselves and their message. Remember what I said about gift-wrapping? This is another form of it. Read tastemaker publications like *Spy, Details, Rolling Stone.* Watch "The Simpsons" or "Northern Exposure" once in a while. Check out the latest Almodovar film. I don't want you to become sickeningly hip overnight, but there's nothing wrong with clueing in to our culture.

In addition, put yourself on a mind improvement program. Commit to reading several classics of literature each year, and I don't mean the latest Stephen King thriller. Cultivate your aesthetic self. It'll make you more interesting.

America is becoming the land of the TV zombie, illiterate, uneducated, unaware. The trend can be reversed only one person at a time, and I say let it begin with you. Read a novel by Dickens, or plough your way through Plato. Have you ever discovered the joys of Mark Twain or Shakespeare, Steinbeck or Flaubert? Have you been enraptured by the late string quartets of Beethoven, Wagner's *Ring* cycle, or early Billie Holiday? Even if, God forbid, your project never takes off, the benefits of acquainting yourself with the great achievements in culture will stay with you always.

PERSONAL P.R. POWER

Now, let's put the pieces together. I've already defined Public Relations in both macro and micro terms. Establishing good relations with, say, your co-workers is just as noble a P.R. target as profiled by *Time* magazine, if it accomplishes your goals. I've spent time in this chapter exploring ways to make yourself more P.R. ready, and if you practice and refine these skills, that's exactly what you'll be, no matter what your aim.

Let's say your initial goal is to rise to the top of the corporate ladder in your place of work. To do that, you may not necessarily need to pursue media or widespread public attention. Your target audience may be no further than your colleagues down the hall, or your customers who walk through your door. Before I get into the meat-and-potatoes about press releases, talent coordinators, and city desk editors, let's explore how to harness your personal P.R. power to influence just those in your immediate space.

Personal P.R. invokes the same philosophy as engaging in a full-blown media campaign: you ultimately appeal to "the public" one person at a time. As writer Sara Nelson wrote in an article in *Glamour* magazine, "No matter what, people will judge (others)—so why shouldn't (we) harness and direct that judgment?" Sara is right on the money. Personal P.R. is a matter of controlling to the greatest extent possible the impression you make on others immediately around you. More than any other form of "marketing," this is the one we each have the greatest ability to steer. Over the years, I've acquired a few skills that have helped me in this regard, and I believe they can help you as well.

Mark Twain once said, "I could live two weeks on a good compliment." I abide by this statement. It's in keeping with the Golden Rule and all the other priceless precepts by which civilization has prospered over the years. As I've alluded, personal P.R. success depends on being liked and being perceived as a charismatic, powerful person. If you read the advice of mentors like Dale Carnegie and Roger Ailes, you will have the knowledge necessary to pull this off. But, like anything, theory and practice are often very different.

Let's look at the hypothetical example of the junior executive who wants to move up. The greatest lesson I've learned in business is that the most profitable thing you can do is to be altruistic. Giving begets getting, pure and simple. So beyond the smiles and attentiveness, our junior executive needs to take action. He should accept high-visibility assignments others may not wish to take on, and plunge into his work as though the CEO were personally looking over his shoulder.

The Japanese have put down the American worker as undermotivated, and perhaps in some cases this is true. But, by and large, I don't buy it. I think we *do* know how to work hard, and while some may feel work can be its own reward, I know it also pays off down the line. Our junior exec should ask peers and co-workers for advice, trade favors, or even do them "on the house," cultivating an image as a team player, not a glory hog.

I have seen many cases where someone in business attempts to become popular at work and ends up coming off like a sycophant, or, in common parlance, a boot-licker. This invariably stems from insincerity. While you engage in self-motivated altruism, you must prove to yourself that you mean what you say and you say what you mean. Otherwise you come off like a slick politician kissing babies.

You develop sincerity by establishing a link between what you do and say today with what you hope to achieve tomorrow. Why?

Because I believe self-interest is the guiding force of the human universe, even in cases of extreme compassion, caring, and giving.

Before you accuse me of being selfish and conniving, think it through. Ultimately, everything we do originates in self-interest. Even an anonymous donation to charity, with no apparent ulterior motive, results in a good feeling for the donor. His self-interest lies in the satisfaction of doing good. So, if you recognize that zeal, enthusiasm, and devotion, with no trace of cynicism and disdain, can help you, can boost you, can actually redeem you in your career, then you should have no problem working up a good attitude.

Here's a real life illustration. A good friend of mine happens to be a major entertainment business attorney. He's represented many top stars, brokered scores of million-dollar deals, and has established himself as one of the premier litigators in Hollywood. But he didn't start out that way.

For his first few years out of law school, he bounced around from job to job, working in a D.A.'s office for a while, and looking for a toehold at a few leading law firms. He knew he was smart, he knew he was ambitious, yet he couldn't understand why he was pushing thirty and still hadn't found his niche. Although he had always possessed a fine legal mind, his career didn't begin to take off until he made a few fundamental changes in his own personality and outlook.

First, he took the sound advice of legendary football coach Paul "Bear" Bryant, who once told an interviewer, "I've learned how to hold a team together until they've finally got one heartbeat. There's just three things I'd ever say: If anything goes bad, I did it; if anything goes semi-good, then we did it; if anything goes real good, then you did it."

By deliberately relegating his own seemingly selfish needs to secondary importance, my friend found that his colleagues were more and more frequently coming to him for advice and collaboration. He never came on like a wild tiger bucking for senior partner. He made others around him feel like *they* ought to be senior partner. In this way he cultivated trust, respect, and affection. His personal public relations benefited immeasurably.

This attitude he applied equally with his clients. Like any good lawyer, he rigorously pursued their legal interests, but he went one step further. His newly developed taste for empathy helped him step into his clients' shoes. He believed he was championing what was right. He only accepted cases he truly believed in, and thus became more than mere legal representation for clients: he became their friend in the truest sense. Of course he benefited financially as his career mushroomed, but I know my friend could look anyone in the eye and say he prospered while doing what he sincerely believed in.

Now, was self-interest his primary motivator? I'd say so. He wanted material comfort, professional status, the power and ability to bring his dreams to life. But none of this would have happened had he not consciously adopted that unique form of active selflessness that engenders personal P.R. power.

Most of this book teaches you how to work with media. But if your objectives are more narrowly focused, if you simply want to make inroads with those around you, then the principles I've outlined in this chapter are your main link to success.

TIPS & TRAPS

* Show interest in other people and subjects beyond your area of expertise.

* If you're a stranger at a function, go with an acquaintance who knows the people there. He or she can introduce you.

* When you meet people, tell them what you do, find out what they do, and get their phone numbers and addresses.

* Make friends when you don't need them.

* Trying too hard can backfire. Center yourself.

* Keep your temper in check.

* Emulate the Japanese: have business cards made and give them out like candy on Halloween. People do keep them.

* Don't hype your product too much while meeting people in social settings. You're there to make new contacts.

* When you meet people, ask questions about them rather than hog the conversation. Later on call or write a brief note to let them know you were pleased to meet them.

* As you increase your network, remember follow-up is the key.

* Remember to keep in touch: make thank-you notes, announcements, holiday greeting cards, and other notices a regular part of your mailings to your list.

* Always, always, always keep your promises.

GUERRILLA P.R. COMMANDOS:
BOB COLUMBE & PETER CRESCENTI

In a world where phenomena like Ninja Turtles and the Lambada captivate the media, clearly crazy ideas sometimes turn out wildly successful. Take RALPH (the Royal Association for the Longevity and Preservation of The Honeymooners). What began as a simple desire on the part of two college administrators to see their favorite TV show back on the air eventually evolved into a national movement with thousands of members, annual conventions, and enough media attention to make Madonna jealous.

RALPH co-founder Bob Columbe recalls his organization's origins in 1983: " 'The Honeymooners' had been off the air in New York for two years and we figured we'd lobby to bring it back." They wrote and called a local TV station for months, but got no response. "We came up with the name of RALPH to make us sound more official," says Columbe. "But there was no initial plan to take it any further than getting the show on the air."

But it did go a lot further. Once they succeeded in getting "The Honeymooners" back on the air, news media took note. "Everyone we talked to in the media was a fan of the show," notes Columbe. "They looked for reasons to cover us." The pair would send out press releases via the office fax at C. W. Post College where they worked. Since "The Honeymooners" had national appeal, their releases were picked up all across the country.

RALPH's biggest break came when Peter and Bob appeared on the "Joe Franklin Show." After lobbying for months to get on, in their brief guest shot they reached millions. Membership ranks swelled to many thousands. RALPH grew so big, the founders incorporated. Annual conventions were packed events, and the media flocked to cover anything staged by RALPH.

"We did everything ourselves," says Bob. "We learned to capsulize everything of interest into two or three minutes." Bob also caught on to the benefits of visuals. Both he and Peter wore their official Raccoon uniforms whenever they appeared in public.

The two developed a keen sense of what the media liked. When Jackie Gleason donated his original Ralph Kramden bus driver uniform to RALPH, Peter and Bob invited the media to attend the arrival of the package via Federal Express. That morning, Peter and Bob's front lawn was jammed elbow-to-elbow with TV cameras, reporters, photographers, and even satellite dishes.

After five great years, the pair folded the organization because they had accomplished everything they'd set out to do. Jackie Gleason, Art Carney, Audrey Meadows, and Jane Randolph became close friends of theirs, but with Gleason's death, they felt it was time for RALPH to hang it up too.

Throughout the experience, Peter and Bob became wise in the ways of media. "You need to know your market," says Bob. "You also need to be available to media, even when it's inconvenient. Whenever any of them needed something on 'The Honeymooners,' they called us." Bob also cites his personal passion as a key. "You can't be enthusiastic about something unless you love it. If someone wanted us to promote 'The Brady Bunch,' we'd know what to do, but we wouldn't have the enthusiasm. We were successful because we truly loved the product. We sold our enthusiasm as much as we sold 'The Honeymooners.' "

Though the dizzying world of media fame has faded for Peter and Bob, they have no regrets, only fond memories. "I have three books of press clips seven inches thick," says Bob. "And I wouldn't trade the experience for anything." To the moon!

4

FANNING OUT: EXPANDING YOUR GUERRILLA P.R. TOOLS

Writing is easy. All you have to do is cross out the wrong words.

—MARK TWAIN

LETTER PERFECT

It's very likely the first shot fired in your Guerrilla P.R. campaign will be via the U.S. mail. Before you send out a press release, you may wish to contact some media by letter. By writing directly to an individual, you are far more likely to hear back from him or her, or get the person on the phone with a follow-up call. Letters are a form of direct one-to-one communication and demand a direct one-to-one response.

In addition, a letter is a great way to introduce yourself and your project. Guerrilla P.R. is a personal system, and a letter personalizes your project in a non-threatening way. Cold phone calls can be intimidating to both parties on the line. Press releases usually get mailed en masse. Letters are much warmer because they ideally go to one particular person. Still, like everything else, there's a right way and a wrong way to go about letter writing.

If you're one of those people for whom the word "write" causes unutterable distress, here's some advice. The best way to write is just to start writing. Let the words flow like water; get your thoughts on paper without editing yourself. Later you'll switch to a stingier mode, thinking of press releases or letters as Western Union telegrams with each word costing a buck. But for now, pour it on. Believe me, it's easier to edit out then add in, so don't hold back on your first draft.

If you need more savory analogy, think of writing as making a stew. Start with a full pot and cook down to richer more concentrated fare. The stew won't be as tasty if you keep your batch small and if you add too many seasonings after you've cooked it, and neither will your writing. So, bearing all that in mind, put on your chef's hat and let's return to your letter.

Begin by writing to *someone*, and not to Dear Sir, Madam, or Editor. If your list is worth more than the paper it's typed on, it will contain individual names and job titles. Use them. Secondly, don't write long letters. Nothing over a page. If you do, you'll lose the attention of the person you're writing to faster than an Olympic sprinter on steroids. Shakespeare said, "Brevity is the soul of wit," and at this point in my life I am unwilling to argue with him.

In any written or printed material you send out, appearance is important. Use quality bond paper here—letterhead if you have it—and *always* type. This book is designed to save you money, but if you don't have a typewriter or word processor, spend the money and get one. You flat-out will *not* be taken seriously by anyone if you hand-write. Here's a sample query letter, followed by analysis:

Mr. Bob Smith/City Editor
The Daily Life
Anytown, CA 90099

Dear Bob:

As director of the Mid-Valley Youth Center, I've seen firsthand the perils kids face today. Drugs, gangs, broken homes, illiteracy, and other social ills threaten the nation's future. Yet many of these problems can be overcome. I know because I have seen the way out.

At the Center, we help teens who might otherwise be lost to the streets. Our success stories include many now-productive members of society who credit the Center with giving their lives direction.

But we're in trouble. A budget crunch may soon spell the end of the Center. With no government funding, our only hope is public support. I can think of several good news angles: How can a facility doing so much good work be forced to close? How did a middle-class white man like me end up working with inner-city black and Hispanic teens? With our remarkable success rate in getting teens off the streets, what are we doing right that nobody else has yet picked up on?

I hope you'll consider running a piece on the Center. Our upcoming Carnival will provide a new infusion of money, but it will take even more to get the job done. I'd like to tell you more about the Carnival, and I hope you'll take a moment to read the enclosed material about the Center.

Looking forward to speaking with you soon.

Regards,

John Jones

As you can see, I wrote "Dear Bob" and not "Dear Mr. Smith." I tend to address journalists on a first-name basis. It's safer to be familiar in a letter than in person or on the phone, especially if you never contacted the person before. Don't be afraid to create a climate of friendliness. However, the same caveat is in order. Not every media person appreciates excessive familiarity at first. So keep your interpersonal antennae up.

In the first two paragraphs, I gave a thumbnail sketch of my project and injected a brief description of my role as well. In the third paragraph, I introduce the conflict, the angle, the central reason for contacting the media. Remember, they're looking for a story, so you have to give them one. But don't blatantly tell the person that you "need publicity." Journalists are not in the publicity business; they're in the news business. So your objective is to provide news.

In closing, I mention my news item—in this case, the carnival—but I don't overemphasize it. My intention is not to sell per se, but to increase awareness, to prime the media for a press release later. The letter is a teaser to increase the likelihood the journalist will respond to my appeal down the line. I also mention "enclosed material." It's a good idea to attach brochures, previous clips, or some other supporting materials. It gives extra weight to your claims. For a nice personal touch, I often add in a hand-written postscript. Try it!

With letters, as with nearly everything you send to the media, don't count on everything being read word-for-word. Most people are too busy to carefully scrutinize all of your written materials. They're looking for the basics, which you have to impart succinctly. If you can crystalize your message, you will not only have grateful media people to deal with, but, very possibly, receptive media people as well.

TIPS & TRAPS

* Think in terms of summary. Be brief and to the point, always keeping in mind what a story on your project can do for the media outlet, not what the story can do for you.

* Although you need to be concise, emphasize a few interesting details. After all, the story will come alive via details.

* You need to walk a fine line between offering helpful news angles and writing the story for them. Professional pride comes into play, and editors do not appreciate being instructed on how the story should be written. I suggest you err on the side of brevity and allusion.

* This is a lesson that took me a long time to learn: the best kind of writing, especially in letter form, is to write it as you would say it. Gaudy phrases like "as per your request . . ." or "This serves to inform you . . ." are examples of dark-ages writing, and do nothing but clutter the page. What I do (and I did it writing this book) is imagine I'm actually speaking to someone when I write. Ask yourself as you type, "Is this how I would put it if I were talking to someone?" That's not to say you can't attempt to write well, but if you follow this suggestion, what you write will always be within another's grasp.

FROM THE GUERRILLA P.R. FILE

To show its solidarity with Americans reeling from the recession, Domino's Pizza launched an unusual marketing campaign in 1992. The "Eat Your Rejection Letter" project idea was simple: just bring your employment-rejection letter to your nearest Domino's and get $1 off the price of a pizza. Lay-off notices work too, and you can even show it to the delivery man for your credit. Is this a great country, or what?

THE PRESS RELEASE

A recent *Wall Street Journal* report noted that 90 percent of its coverage originates with companies *making their own announcements.* Most of the time, those announcements begin with a press release. As I've said, no matter how we perceive the world, news is—and will always be—what somebody else says it is. If you feel your project is newsworthy, and are able to persuade the media to go along with you, then your project *is* news. Period! The press release is the basic vehicle of news, and with it a Guerrilla publicist taps into enormous power.

Many books attempt to teach press release writing, but there is no single absolute approach. I've marveled at elegantly crafted releases from amateur do-it-yourselfers, and I've held my nose reading releases from top corporations, written so poorly as to defy belief. Though there are as many styles of press release as writers, there are some characteristics shared by all good releases. The basic format is as follows:

• Type your release double-spaced on 8½-inch × 11-inch paper, preferably white, with one-inch margins on all sides. Be sure to use only one side of the paper (although two-sided would be more ecologically sound, most editors unfortunately don't like this practice). Some publicists I know use eye-catching colored paper, and a few journalists tell me colored paper can be effective. I find it both hard to read and silly, but you should go with your own taste. If you have a letterhead, use it.

• In the upper right-hand corner, type FOR IMMEDIATE RELEASE, or, if you prefer to have your release held until a certain date, type, for example, FOR RELEASE SEPTEMBER 15.

• Always date your release, either in the upper right-hand corner or below the words FOR IMMEDIATE RELEASE. Some place it at the end of the release in shorthand: 091892 for September 18, 1992. It doesn't matter which style you choose, but it's important to note when material is sent out.

• Be sure to include a contact name, phone number (daytime *and* nighttime), and an address. Place it under the date, or turn it into a final one-sentence paragraph at the end.

- It's best to keep the length to one page, but this isn't always possible. If you have a large amount of information, subdivide it into several shorter pieces, i.e., a biography on you and/or other principals, a one-page news release, a history of the project, etc. (I address this later). The key is to break up your information so it's easier to read and so the media won't feel inundated. If your release ends up being more than one page, do *not* staple the sheets. (In the interests of saving trees, you may want to type your release on 8½-inch × 11-inch paper, if you have a bit more than a page of material.)

- Keep the message simple, and paragraphs as short as possible, no more than two or three sentences. Try to begin your paragraphs with action-oriented verbs.

- If you're sending your release to TV and/or radio, phonetically spell out difficult names for easy pronunciation.

- If you go longer than a page, use a "slug" or identifying word or phrase at the upper left corner (e.g., <u>MID-VALLEY YOUTH CENTER</u>). Don't hyphenate or carry over a paragraph to the following page.

- Factual, or spelling, or grammatical errors are *totally unacceptable*. When I spot these in other releases, fairly or not I tend to write off the entire content. I'm sure that's true for journalists as well. Get it right. *All* of it.

- Where applicable, use bullet points or asterisks, and leave as much white space on your release as possible. An uncluttered page indicates an uncluttered mind. It's easier to read and will make a better impression on reporters.

- Finally, at the bottom, type three hash marks—# # #—to signify the end of your release. Don't write "30"—it will counterproductively date you.

Once secure with the format, you're then faced with the task of writing coherently and effectively, which is far more important, but not as hard as you may think. Remember, your release is designed to entice while at the same time convey a news sense. It's a delicate balance. So observe the following guidelines related to content:

• The single most important advice I can give you about press releases, and anything you write, do, or say when it comes to media, is this: be honest. Do not fabricate information, do not blatantly stretch the truth, do not omit pivotal details. If you do any of the above, you will be caught, you will be vilified and written off by the media. Beware. They know where you live.

• You're ostensibly presenting "news," so make sure you include in the first paragraph the five W's of journalism: who, what, when, where, and why. Nothing else is more vital. Because your release is supposed to be akin to objective news, save the editorializing for your quoted material. That's when you have a chance to voice pointed opinions.

• Your message should be structured in descending order of importance, i.e., most critical information at or near the top, and the lesser points following.

• Use strong action-oriented language and clear sentence structure.

• Never overestimate an editor's understanding. That doesn't mean talk down to people or patronizingly spell out basic information. But make sure your message is understandable to anyone at any level of education, about the nature of your project. Someone writing about jetliners should write in language comprehensible to someone unfamiliar with aviation.

• Be careful about hype. We all have a tendency to trumpet our wares, but the media are cynical and do not warm up to overkill. Don't claim your greasy spoon diner has the best burgers in the world. That's best left to the world's burger eaters to decide.

• While I'm on the subject of hype, beware of overhype in terms of presentation. My friend Trisha Daniels, the talent booker for "The Maury Povich Show," told me about a publicist who sent a one-sheet press release in a box the size of a microwave oven; and another who sent his release enclosed with a carton of grapefruit. Both ploys caught her attention, but neither worked. One was a pointless gimmick, the other a flat-out bribe. Trisha didn't hesitate for a second to send the grapefruit back.

Here's an example of a press release I wrote not too long ago for one of my clients. Analysis follows:

FOR IMMEDIATE RELEASE   February 15, 1991

CONTACT: Michael Levine
213-659-6400

IMPROV FOUNDERS FRIEDMAN AND LONOW
DEMAND OSCAR COMEDY CATEGORY

Calling comedy "the step-child of the Motion Picture Academy," Improvisation Comedy Club founders Budd Friedman and Mark Lonow are calling on the Academy to bolster industry recognition of comic films and actors by formulating new Oscar categories. Beginning today through April 15, Friedman and Lonow will place petitions in all Improv clubs to collect signatures of film fans urging Best Comedy and Best Comic Acting Performance categories. The petitions will then be forwarded on to the Academy.

Over the past thirty years, few statuettes in the Best Film and acting categories have gone to comedic productions. "*Annie Hall* and *The Sting* won back in the seventies, and Kevin Kline won a couple of years ago for *A Fish Called Wanda*," notes Lonow. "And that's been about it for a very long time."

Friedman and Lonow cite several highly successful films over the past several years—including *Ruthless People, Big,* and *Back to the Future*—all of which, they say, are clearly Oscar-worthy films. "It's an old adage by now that comic acting is far more difficult that dramatic acting," says Friedman. "Besides, comedy can be just as instructive, inspirational, and offer as much insight into the human spirit as drama. I wish the Academy would take all this into account."

The Improvisation Comedy Clubs are the first and most successful chain of comedy nightclubs in America, with clubs in several major American cities. They have long served as the proving ground of the nation's top comics.

This release kicked off a successful campaign for the Improv I mentioned earlier in the book. As you can see, the headline is short and clipped. I often see headlines with three or more clauses, but that's poor form. Faced with a choice of simplicity or complexity, *always choose the former*. Headlines should be no more than one clause, leading off with the protagonist. If you're pushing the church chili cook-off, write "First Community Church to Stage Chili Cook-Off . . . ," or something like that, keeping it short by deleting articles like "the," "a," "an," etc.

Even though the chances of your own headline being used verbatim by the press are virtually nil, your headline has two purposes: to summarize the gist of your story, and to grab the attention of the reader. Notice in the above example I led with the name of my client. That's important in establishing the protagonist of the release. In describing the content, I used the word "demand." Now, of course my clients weren't in a position to demand anything of the Motion Picture Academy. But use of strong language gave the entire release the desired spin.

The first paragraph paints in broad strokes the essence of the release; the second, third, and fourth paragraphs provide support, with historic examples and quotes. These add substance. Quotes aren't always required, but can be very effective in both personalizing the release and for sneaking in subjective commentary otherwise inappropriate in a journalistic setting. Let me hammer this home once again: press releases mimic actual newspaper stories, so you must appear to put forth a modicum of objectivity if you want to gain the interest and respect of journalists.

For your opener, distill up to three key points into two or three sentences. Be simple, direct, and present your information like a news story. If you like, use language that captures the flavor of your project, e.g., "The city's hottest chili chefs battle appetite burn-out at First Community Church's Annual Chili Cook-off." This opening paragraph should contain answers to the five W's.

In your next paragraphs, introduce supporting information. One way to do this is to pull out strains introduced in the lead, and expand on them. No more than two "strains" per paragraph. "Strains" in my example above would be references to the Improv (which I expand upon in the very last tag paragraph), the Oscar's dearth of comedy awards, and the Improv's willingness to do something about it.

If you are the main person involved, quote yourself. Make your quotes cogent, concise, and snappy. Break them up into two sections by pausing at the end of the first clause, as in the final two sentences of the Improv/Comedy press release.

Everything publicists do requires a *framework of veracity.* I couldn't just say, "There ought to be a Comedy Oscar" without explaining why. Everything you write has to have a reason. You must beware not only of dangling modifiers but also of dangling contentions.

But what do you have to write about? Are you announcing the opening of a store? A sensational new kitchen tool? Whatever it is, your main hook is your focus. Ideas for subjects are all around you. If you're not sure you have a real news hook, how about a survey? Concoct a question like that florist who asked his customers who they'd most like to send a bouquet to. Tally the results and turn them into a release. You can do releases on business predictions. Although prophecy is a dubious activity, the media eat it up.

If you're a retailer of some kind, cook up some poll or series of questions you can ask your customers. Take as large a sample as you can and write a press release on it. It's unscientific, but that would never stop the papers from reporting it. Let your imagination run wild with these surveys.

One of my former clients ran a traffic school. I suggested he conduct a survey on whom his students would most like to bump into on a crowded freeway. His release ran in two local papers. It was an utterly meaningless fluff story, but the press had fun with it, and my client reaped enormous exposure for his school.

How's this for an idea? I often arrange for the Mayor's office to declare "So-and-So Day" in L.A. for one of my clients. It's a minor favor the city provides almost any citizen for almost any reason (not too long ago we woke up to "Freddy Day" for the latest *Nightmare on Elm Street* movie). You get both the certificate and a good excuse to send out a release.

Once you feel comfortable writing, you can begin to stretch out. No single release may be right for every media outlet. In Guerrilla P.R., flexibility is your strength. If you need to tailor a release for one or more particular targets, by all means do so. Keep the following additional concepts in mind:

• Tailor to Audience. Ultimately, you must consider the reader, listener, or viewer of the media outlet you're contacting. Feel free to alter your wording to best suit the targeted audience.

• Tailor to Outlet. The needs of TV and print journalism are different (much more on this later). For TV, think visually. Your release should entice TV to videotape. For print, that's not as critical. Some publications are more irreverent than others. Some more newsy. Point your release in the appropriate direction.

• Tailor to Location. Geography plays a role too. If your Guerrilla P.R. plan includes a wider area than your immediate vicinity, shape your words to reflect the interests of the region you're contacting. For example, I don't pitch the media in Birmingham, Alabama, the same way I pitch San Francisco. You need to be sensitive to various community mores.

GUERRILLA P.R. EXERCISE

Okay, I've given you a lot of information. Take a moment to digest it all. Now, it's your turn. Write a press release announcing your project, or describing your service. Remember, lead with your most important information, and unveil the rest in *descending* order of importance. (In a newspaper, for example, space may become tight and they'll need to lop off the last couple of paragraphs of your story.)

Once you're done with your first draft, take a good look at your release. Read it aloud. How does it sound? Does it have a conversational ring? If not, have another go at it. In editing, follow the other Golden Rule: when in doubt, cut it out. There is no piece of writing in existence that couldn't have benefited from the blue pencil. Be merciless. Cut until you can't cut any more. Then cut again. Don't worry. English is the most versatile language on earth. Have fun with it!

TIPS & TRAPS

* Timing is important when sending releases. If you are announcing an event, obviously you have to send your release some time in

advance. If you are looking only for a mention, ten days should suffice for a daily newspaper; three weeks in advance for a weekly tabloid. Magazines, of course, require longer leads, but they rarely run press releases.

* Try mailing them to arrive on slow news days, like the day after a major holiday, or the odd fifth week of the month (many competing companies send releases regularly on the first, second, third, or fourth week of the month).

* If you're announcing an event, you may provide a summary at the end of your release, i.e., WHO: Mid-Valley Youth Center; WHAT: Annual Carnival; WHERE: Reynolds Park; WHEN: August 3, 12:00 Noon.

* Follow-up is key. Wait one day after you feel the press release arrived, then make your call (more on phone skills later).

* If your release is picked up, send a thank-you note to the reporter or editor responsible. Build bridges wherever you can.

On the next few pages, I've reproduced several more real press releases that were serviced by my firm on behalf of clients. Each illustrates a different objective, but you will notice that all adhere to the basic rules I outlined.

This first is an example of a straight announcement, with the five W's clearly detailed in the opening paragraph.

FOR IMMEDIATE RELEASE   December 2, 1990

Contact: Michael Levine

LARRY THOMPSON ORGANIZATION TO PRODUCE *I LOVED LUCY: THE LUCILLE BALL AND DESI ARNAZ STORY* FOR CBS

(Los Angeles) Larry Thompson, veteran producer and personal manager, will produce an original two-hour film, *I Loved Lucy: The Lucille Ball and Desi Arnaz Story*. It will air this fall on CBS, Lucy's network home for much of her spectacular career. Acclaimed biographical dramatist William Luce—whose credits include such films as *The Woman He Loved* and *The Last Days of Patton*, as well as *The Belle of Amherst* and *Lillian* about Lillian Hellman for Broadway—is writing the teleplay. Production begins in the spring.

The film's storyline opens in the 1940s at the time Lucy and Desi first met, and ends with the broadcast of the premiere episode of "I Love Lucy," the series that revolutionized television and launched the couple into superstardom.

Though they were beloved by millions around the world, the off-screen life of the couple was often tempestuous, and the film also examines that side of their relationship. Says Larry Thompson, who serves as the film's executive producer, "Lucy and Desi have been entertainment icons for forty years. We will tell the truth in our film, but always remain sensitive to the great esteem we all hold for Lucy and Desi. They were unique in the history of television."

According to Thompson, the leading roles will be played by unknown actors. Said Thompson, "In our initial consultations with CBS, it was decided to cast unknowns for the roles of Lucy and Desi. This will give some up-and-coming young actors and actresses a tremendous opportunity. It will allow us to present Lucy and Desi's story in a fresh manner."

The Larry Thompson Organization, a feature film and television production company, and one of the largest personal management agencies in Hollywood, is responsible for over 100 hours of high-quality TV programming and numerous motion pictures. Among LTO's productions are the acclaimed CBS movie, *The Woman He Loved*, the story of the Duke and Duchess of Windsor starring Jane Seymour, Anthony Andrews, and Olivia de Haviland, *Little White Lies* starring Ann Jillian, and *Original Sin*, starring Charlton Heston.

Next is a release designed to affix an impression on the media and public regarding a client. There's no real "news" here, but because it centers on a controversial topic and a well-known figure, this story was readily picked up by the press:

FOR IMMEDIATE RELEASE

MICKEY ROONEY CONDEMNS "CANCER" OF DISCRIMINATION ON U.S. GOLF COURSES; VOWS TO PRESSURE SEGREGATED CLUBS

An avid golfer for over 62 years, legendary entertainer Mickey Rooney has spoken out forcefully against country clubs and golf courses that bar blacks from membership. The issue recently came to light with the controversy surrounding a PGA tournament held at Shoal Creek Country Club in Birmingham, Alabama, a facility that never before admitted blacks.

"Of all the major sports, golf is the test of sportsmanship," said Rooney, who has played on every major course in the world. He added, "There's no place in sports for discrimination. Racism is the cancer of America."

Most major sponsors of the Shoal Creek tournament, e.g., Delta Airlines, IBM, and Toyota, pulled out of the event. Rooney applauded the move. "The best way to strike back is to hit them where it hurts: in the pocketbook," said the actor. "We have to mount continuous nationwide public pressure to guarantee that this sort of travesty never occurs again." Thanks to the loud public, commercial, and media outcry, Shoal Creek finally changed its policy, and recently admitted its first black member.

As for his personal involvement, Rooney stated, "I will refuse to play on any course that discriminates against minorities. Golf should not be a game just for the privileged few, but should be open to anyone. It's good that this issue has finally come to light so that the sport of golf, and the nation as a whole, can address it properly, and wipe it out."

Here's a tongue-in-cheek release concocted over lunch when my client, comedian Robert Schimmel, and I were feeling a little silly. This release is complete fiction, and the media knew it. But they love a good chuckle as much as anyone, and the release got tremendous coverage:

FOR IMMEDIATE RELEASE

ROBERT SCHIMMEL PROVIDES VITAL NEW INFORMATION FOR U.S. CENSUS

(Los Angeles): They advertised on TV and radio, they sent information through the mail, they tried everything, but the U.S. Census Bureau still failed to get nearly a quarter of Americans to respond to this year's Census questionnaire. So, as a public service, comedian Robert Schimmel has been surveying his audiences recently with census questions of his own. The results are quite surprising:

• 84 percent of Schimmel's audience respondents expressed that they would be willing to have oral sex with Mike Tyson for a million dollars.

• Conversely, the same 84 percent claimed they would pay a million dollars *not* to have oral sex with former British Prime Minister Margaret Thatcher.

• An astonishing 97 percent admitted having erotic fantasies about Robert Schimmel.

• Only 1 percent of respondents claim to have ever been unfaithful to their spouses.

• 99 percent admit to being pathological liars.

• Schimmel's audience is split down the middle, 50-50 percent, on whether peace will ever be achieved in the Middle East.

• Virtually all (100 percent), however, believe the Mid-East peace process would move forward if Shamir [now ex-job] and Arafat could get together at the Hefner mansion, drink a few mai-tais, and party with Miss May, June, and July in the Grotto.

• The most-often reported sex fantasy for women involved rubber sheets, Dan Rather, and reduced calorie Miracle Whip.

• The most-often reported sex fantasy for men involved a *menage à trois* with Mrs. Fields and Jenny Craig.

• Not a single respondent (0 percent) can recall having engaged in sexual intercourse with any member of the Brady Bunch within the last five years.

• Bucking conventional wisdom, most people surveyed (87 percent) claimed their favorite musical artists to listen to during lovemaking were not Johnny Mathis or Frank Sinatra, but rather Grand Funk Railroad, Weird Al Yancovic, and Menudo.

• 85 percent feel pornography to be a blatant form of sexual exploitation and a severe blight on society, and all felt so strongly against it, they would henceforth restrict their personal use of pornography to absolutely no more than three times a week at the most (not counting holidays).

• 63 percent have had affairs with co-workers, employees, and clients, not so much for the romantic thrill, but for the tax benefits.

• 75 percent believe sex is over-rated.

• 75 percent believe themselves to be under-raters.

Schimmel will present his findings to the U.S. Census Bureau, the National Institutes of Health, the U.N. World Health Organization, and *Penthouse* Forum. He hopes his survey will both foster better understanding between the sexes, and result in a few inexpensive dates.

#

This next release was fashioned while I was promoting my earlier book, *The Address Book*. Having spent several years closely studying fan mail patterns, I'd learned quite a lot, and the facts that comprise this release merited attention. Though it doesn't relate precisely to my book, it helped foster the impression of my expertise in the fan mail field.

FOR IMMEDIATE RELEASE

MACAULAY CULKIN OF *HOME ALONE*
AMERICA'S NEW FAN MAIL CHAMP

America has a new No. 1 fan mail heavyweight champion: *HOME ALONE's* diminutive child star, Macaulay Culkin. The underage actor is now receiving more than 35,000 pieces of mail every month, eclipsing the previous fan mail king, superstar Tom Cruise. This is according to noted public relations executive, author, and fan mail expert Michael Levine.

The wide-ranging letters have included dozens of marriage proposals (with most wedding dates set in the twenty-first century), offers to baby-sit, invitations to dinner, dates, proms, Disney World vacations, and adoption requests.

HOME ALONE, which to date has grossed over $250 million at the box office to become the fourth highest grossing picture in film history, made a star out of Culkin. In the film, Culkin portrays an intrepid little boy left to fend for himself after his vacationing family inadvertently leaves him behind. The success of *HOME ALONE* has made Culkin the highest-paid child star in movie history, with a new salary of over $1 million per picture.

# # #

The press release will be the bread-and-butter of your campaign. Unlike unwanted phone calls, poorly attended press conferences, botched publicity stunts, and other potential nightmares, you can't go wrong with a press release. If it's well composed, contains useful or intriguing information, and passes the media test as a legitimate news piece or feature story, you *will* have success. *A press release can never ruffle anyone's feathers. A reporter will either be hooked or he won't.*

To prove it, I'll close this section with a story about persistence. An author doing his own P.R. for a book he'd just published ardently desired to get a review in an important regional paper. He sent a press release and copy of the book to the paper's editor, who thought it presumptuous for the author to promote himself. The editor threw the package away. The next month, an identical package arrived on the editor's desk, which was also tossed.

This went on for eighteen months straight. A press release would arrive, and the overworked editor would trash it. Finally, out of sheer exasperation and admiration for his tenacity, the editor met with the writer, and found that he loved the man's ideas. A big story ran in the paper and the author sold a great number of books. If he can hang in there, so can you.

SNAP DECISION

You furnish the pictures and I'll furnish the war.

—WILLIAM RANDOLPH HEARST

When Paul "Pee-Wee Herman" Reubens was arrested inside a Sarasota adult movie theater in the summer of 1991, he may have felt his reputation was over. Not true. It didn't truly suffer until a few days later, when the indelible image of his mug shot blanketed newspapers and TV screens across the country. Nothing said more about Reubens' misfortune at that time than those searing images of his scruffy, forlorn face.

At some point during your Guerrilla P.R. campaign, photographs will likely play a part, but you need to understand a few things about their use before you send them out. Pictures can become an expensive and wasteful enterprise, and since I want you to save money, pay close attention.

First of all, if the pictures don't look good, don't send them. There's nothing more pathetic than a press release with a fuzzy Polaroid print, out-of-focus black and white, or a 3- × 5-inch color snapshot attached. The media cannot use these. They serve only to assure the sender of either a chilly or a disinterested reception when he contacts the media with a follow-up call.

Photos can tell a story. Boris Yeltsin standing atop a tank during the abortive Soviet coup said everything about his courage and the Communist collapse. But, most often, photos do not tell a whole story. Their primary use for P.R. purposes is adjunct illustration. If you send a picture to a magazine, there is no guarantee it will run, even if it's a good shot, and even if they run a piece on your project. Space requirements and editorial taste loom much larger in the decision-making process.

Photography can jack up your costs. So you have to know what pictures offer you in a Guerrilla P.R. campaign. Your photo can do one of several things:

- Make more concrete a hazy news angle.

- Put a face to a name.

- Persuade one publication to run a story, if the photo is granted as an exclusive, that is, for its use alone.

- Reinforce an image in the public mind that advances your P.R. objectives.

- Further legitimize your project with a more elaborate presentation.

- Provide an emotional counterpoint to the story (as Candy Lightner did with her M.A.D.D. photo).

How do you determine if your release merits an accompanying photo? Just answer "yes" to either of the following questions:

- Is there a central photographable "object" in your news angle, such as a new invention or product, or a recognizable building such as a restaurant, mall, corporate office, etc.?

- Is your news story about an individual, such as a significant new hiring, or the appearance of a performer at a local venue?

If you can answer "yes," then by all means consider sending a photo. If the answer is "no," save your money and forget the pictures. It's not worth the expense because the chances of your photo running are practically nil.

If you've made the decision to send a photo, there are a few things to keep in mind. For one, don't expect to get the picture back. Most news organizations keep massive files, and that's the likely resting place for any material sent to them. If you send a picture of a person or persons, avoid the standard head shot. It's boring. Flip through your local newspaper and study the pictures. You rarely see static head shots. Put some action in your photo. And don't be afraid to use well-composed pictures with atypical angles. Arty no, interesting yes.

Always attach a caption to the picture, but never write directly on your print, either front or back. I type the caption on a separate piece of paper and tape it to the back. Keep your caption brief, describing what is in the shot and who, left to right. As an example:

FOR IMMEDIATE RELEASE

PHOTO CAPTION

John Jones, Director of the Mid-Valley Youth Center, is pictured above with Mayor Jones at the Center's May 5th Spring Carnival, which raised nearly $5,000 to support anti-drug programs. Pictured above from left to right: John Jones Levine, Mayor Jones, and President Bush.

Another way to help increase the odds that your photo runs is to offer it as an exclusive to one particular news outlet. If you do this, write "EXCLUSIVE TO THE *DAILY TIMES*" on the caption, and *make sure the editor is aware of the exclusivity.*

TIPS & TRAPS

* Polaroids, Instamatics, and other cheap cameras just won't do. Your picture must be taken with a 35mm camera. If you don't own one, borrow one.

* Your photo should be in black & white. Even though many publications run color these days, you stand a better chance of success with a black and white shot, which reproduces better in print. B&W is less expensive film both to buy and to develop. However, some papers *do* run color, and encourage its use. Study your outlet before you send.

* Make sure your exclusive shot is distinct from the others.

* It's best to submit 8 × 10 photos, but 3 × 5s are acceptable and far less expensive.

* Don't send in "mob shots," i.e., photos of a big crowd. Identifying everyone is difficult, they're uninteresting pictures, and they won't run.

* If you're pitching to a print medium, why not see if they'll shoot the pictures themselves? It guarantees quality and it makes it far more likely the newspaper will run the shots. You have nothing to lose by suggesting.

* In terms of photo quality, especially for a shot you hope to see reprinted in newspapers, make sure the print is not too dark. Sheldon Small, who owns Multiple Photo, a top photography lab in Los Angeles, tells me this is one of the most common blunders. Pictures always reproduce darker, and if your shot is dark to begin with, you're in trouble. So lighten up!

THE PERFECT PRESS KIT

A press kit is a package of materials to assist the media in comprehending a story. Whether it's for a movie star, a chic boutique, or the Jerry Lewis Telethon, a press kit distills the important features of a story, and makes them clear to the media. As I said before, you often have to do much of the media's work for them, and the press kit is one of the best ways to do that.

It's a common misconception that better press kits are necessarily expensive. That's not true. Good press kits embody two central elements: they tell a clear story about who or what they represent, and they display some originality in their presentation. And that doesn't necessarily mean bells and whistles. It may mean simply that they're well written. If these elements are missing, it won't matter how much was spent—the press kit will stink. Generically, most press kits contain the following (although no single one is required):

• A biography on the principal individual or individuals involved

• A photo of same

• A history of the person, place, or thing described

- Reprints of newspaper clippings, if available

- A timely press release, if applicable

Some publicists add such materials as a quote sheet (a collection of quotes from critics, colleagues, commentators, etc., extolling the virtues of the project); canned features (self-written "articles" suitable for reprint in newspapers and magazines); logos; promotional audio-cassettes; vital statistics sheets; and even sample products, such as the little box of raisins I found in one promo giveaway, or the 3-D glasses I found in another. (The most phenomenal I ever saw was the one a major record company sent out to promote a new band. Each kit contained not only lavish printed materials, but a micro-cassette machine with a personalized message to me à la "Mission Impossible." It must have cost tens of thousands to produce and distribute.)

In a perfect world, where you're the richest person in town, you could afford large quantities of fancy embossed press kit covers, with inner pockets to hold lavishly produced materials. But you're not the richest person in town, so our aim is to devise good press kits on a Guerrilla budget. It can be done, but like everything else in Guerrilla P.R., most of the capital required consists of your own imagination.

First, let's define terms by breaking down the main components of the kit.

Bio

To write a good biography, you don't need the skills of a Hemingway. Unlike fiction, bios are quite formulaic in structure. If you follow the formula, you can generally produce a serviceable bio. That doesn't mean they're a piece of cake to write—all good writing requires thought and effort—but it does mean you have at your disposal clear guidelines to steer you through.

In some cases you may only want to write a short-form bio, which would be akin to a somewhat expanded version of those brief biographies on the back of book jackets. This short-form version may prove useful as a paragraph in an initial press release. But when it comes to press kits, you will want to include a more extensive long-form bio.

Here's the formula: no more than three double-spaced pages in length (try to limit it to 1½ pages if possible). Don't begin with "Mr. Smith was born in a log cabin in Manhattan." Instead, your lead should encompass the salient features of the person *as they relate to your project*. Make it catchy, but not cute.

The next paragraphs should remain current. Describe recent achievements of your subject, especially those the media will tie to your project. Then insert a transition sentence to segue into the person's history. The next couple of graphs describe highlights of his or her past, leading up to the present. Recap place of birth, interesting aspects of childhood, how the person entered his/her particular field, and provide a summary of pertinent career achievements. Tell the story narratively but succinctly.

Wrap it up with a brief but upbeat concluding graph, catchy but not cute. Remember, this bio will be read, or more likely scanned, by media people unimpressed by hype. If you're too adulatory, the media will scoff. How can you impartially claim something is great when it's you you're talking about? Let the facts speak for themselves. The following are two bios I wrote for clients recently which give a good illustration of the formula.

JASON SCOTT LEE

As Avik the Eskimo in Miramax's epic film, *Map of the Human Heart*, actor JASON SCOTT LEE portrays a simple man grappling with overwhelming change. Ironically, his performance in the film, shot near the North Pole, may soon have Jason himself grappling with change. For with the release of *Map of the Human Heart*, the world will discover a major new star in JASON SCOTT LEE.

Although he's landed several significant roles in the last few years, from *Born in East L.A.* to the acclaimed CBS feature, *Vestige of Honor*, in which he played a Vietnamese Montanyard warrior, Jason Scott Lee took on the role of his life in *Map of the Human Heart*. Written and directed by Vincent Ward (*The Vigil, The Navigator*), the film spans thirty years in the life of an Eskimo villager and his lifelong love affair with a Cree Indian. The film also stars John Cusak, Patrick Bergin, and "La Femme Nikita's" Anne Pariaux.

"My character is about sharing, giving, and following his heart," notes Jason. "It may seem naive from a Western point of view, but coming from the Arctic, it makes sense that he lives so far out on the limb in both love and war." That describes Jason himself to a degree, although as a native Hawaiian, life above the Arctic Circle couldn't have been more strange.

"No one would want to vacation there," he says, "but it's one of the most amazing places I've been to. The land is constantly melting and developing. Shooting was quite difficult at times." Perhaps most memorable for him was a scene in which Jason stood alone atop a twenty-square-foot chunk of ice that started floating out to sea while the cameras rolled. Eventually, Jason was out in the channel in rough frigid water. With his ice raft breaking apart, he was rescued just in time.

Most challenging of all was aging his character from sixteen to forty-five. "I would get up at 3:00 A.M. to begin the four-hour make-up process," recalls Jason. "I used that time to bring myself to a slower rhythm and prepare." All in all, the making of *Map of the Human Heart* and playing such a demanding role fit right in with Jason's natural sense of adventure and inner exploration.

Raised in Hawaii, Jason Scott Lee grew up playing sports. He was an excellent surfer and gymnast, and for a while delved deeply into Hula, which he found a powerful form of expression. While in high school, he became interested in drama, but didn't study acting until attending college in Orange County, California. There he met acting coach Sal Romeo, then in the process of launching a new theater in Los Angeles. Jason had shown much promise in acting class, and was invited to join the theater.

Not long after moving to L.A. he connected with an agent. Jason successfully won his very first audition for a small comic role in *Born in East L.A.*, the 1986 hit by Cheech Marin. "I play one of the vatos," says Jason.

Later roles included that of a hoverboarder in *Back to the Future Part II*, and the lead in the moving after-school special, *American Eyes*, in which Jason played an adopted Korean youth searching for his roots. When time permitted, he also performed on stage at Sal Romeo's Friends & Artists Theater, which he found enormously gratifying.

"If you seek certain truths in acting, it's a never-ending adventure," says Jason about his profession. "It takes on both a spiritual and technical aspect, and teaches you to be honest." As for his approach to a role, Jason has no absolutes. "There is no 'method.' I use anything and everything within my reach," he says. "All the world's a stage."

As for the future, Jason eagerly looks forward to more film work, as well as returning to the theater when time permits. He is a talented artist, and he sketches whenever possible. Writing and directing are other dreams he also expects to realize one day. As for now, he has his hands full nurturing an acting career. Yet he sees a strong parallel in his work as an actor and his larger role as a human being. "By being honest in your life, you can transfer that onto the screen," he notes. JASON SCOTT LEE: a star of tomorrow with feet firmly planted in today.

LYNN MONTGOMERY

The most common advice to writers is, "Write what you know." That's just what Lynn Montgomery did in creating "The Torkelsons," a Buena Vista production from Michael Jacobs Productions, which premieres this fall on NBC, airing Saturday nights at 8:30 P.M. Unlike most half-hour comedies, "The Torkelsons" draws its humor from real-life situations . . . literally. Millicent Torkelson, the matriarch of the Torkelson family (played by Connie Raye) is actually based on Lynn's grandmother, a proud Oklahoman who raised thirteen children.

"Millicent is a real survivor," notes Lynn. "She's in her late thirties, poor, and yet instills in her five kids a genuine joie de vivre." Reflective of Lynn's Southern-influenced sensibility, "The Torkelsons" is very much a character and language-driven show. If William Faulkner or Tennessee Williams had ventured into the world of the sit-com, they might have come up with something like "The Torkelsons."

As creator and writer of "The Torkelsons," Lynn Montgomery crafted a uniquely personal vision of a quiet Southern world. "The show was born out of the folklore from my mother's early life in Oklahoma," says Lynn. "I grew up in southern California, but spent every summer in Oklahoma on my grandmother's farm."

Though "The Torkelsons" takes place in the present day, the show's humor and characters are timeless. Millicent's fourteen-year-old daughter, Dorothy Jane (played by Olivia Burnett), struggles for independence and understanding. Millicent, whose husband left the family one day, balances loneliness and the pain of abandonment with love for her children and a powerfully positive outlook.

"So much of TV is mean-spirited," observes Lynn. "I hear over and over from people, 'Why isn't TV written for us?' " With "The Torkelsons," Lynn Montgomery has sought to remedy the situation, bringing to the television screen a large measure of simple human values and gentle humor.

Lynn Montgomery herself shares many of the same values. Born in the L.A. suburb of Ontario, Lynn recognized at a very early age her own gift for storytelling. She grew up in a close and loving family which supported her creative endeavors. A graduate of U.C.L.A., Lynn worked as a fashion model in Paris for a year before returning to the United States to launch a writing career.

After serving as a writer of syndicated radio specials for Westwood One, she began writing screenplays in the early eighties. She sold "In Sorrow, In Secret" to Columbia, "Oklahoma Christmas" for CBS, and "Crucible" for Jon Voigt, yet none of her scripts were produced. Then in 1984 she wrote and produced "Child Abuse: The Day After," a documentary on the failings of the child protective custody system. It won a local Emmy for Best Documentary that year.

Lynn continued writing short stories, poetry, plays, and scripts, and finally her persistence began to pay off. In 1988 Disney Studios contracted with her to write and develop TV pilots and films after they read "Queen for a Day," Lynn's screenplay based on her Oklahoma past. Recalls Lynn, "I never had a doubt from the moment I first wrote it, that this material would sometime be seen by a large audience." Several incarnations later, a half-hour four-camera version, dubbed "The Torkelsons," was presented to NBC. "When Brandon Tartikoff read the script, he said to me, 'Lynn, I read this at a time in my life when I needed something life-affirming, and "The Torkelsons" was it.' "

As writer and creator of the show, it would seem Lynn has her hands full, but she is currently completing several other pilots, a movie for television, and other works in progress. Despite the load, she's not at all a Hollywood fast-tracker. Lynn owned a bed-and-breakfast inn near Big Bear, California, for a time, and also formed a poetry workshop at a shelter for homeless children in Santa Monica. "I'm not just writing," she points out, "I'm living too."

Together with her artist husband Richard Kriegler, Lynn makes her home in Los Angeles, and looks forward to having a family of her own in the near future. In the meantime, she'll continue creating memorable characters and valuable stories. "I've always been a storyteller," says the softspoken writer. As Americans will soon learn watching "The Torkelsons," she also happens to be one of our best.

As you study these two examples, notice a certain flow. I've written a lot of these, so it comes rather easily to me. But with practice, you can do it too. As an exercise, write your own bio following the suggestions described. Strive for flow. After you've composed a first draft, cut at least 25 percent of what you wrote. Tighten it up as much as you can. It's really not hard to nail it down.

Photos

My previous comments about photos don't uniformly apply with regards to a press kit. If your press kit contains a bio of an individual, you may wish to include a photo, preferably an 8 × 10 black & white head shot. If your subject is an event, a product, or a place, a photo can be helpful in making your project more concrete in the minds of media people. But a photo isn't always essential. If you play your cards right, you'll make the media come out and photograph or film you, rather than having to run the expense of printing photos yourself.

Clips

Obviously, if you've never mounted a press campaign before, you probably haven't amassed a collection of press clippings on your project. But it ain't necessarily so. It's possible there have been stories on your project, or closely related projects before your arrival on the scene. Even if there are no such articles, it's perfectly legit to include reprints of stories that simply pertain to your subject.

For example, say I wanted to include some clips in my press kit for the fictitious Mid-Valley Youth Center. I would include recent hard-hitting articles from the national or local press on gangs or community efforts to help troubled teens. These would add ballast to my pitch. Reprints from other publications tend to legitimize your project by showing journalists that other media felt the subject worthy of coverage.

If you do include reprints in your press kit, paste them up as precisely as possible and photocopy them on one sheet of paper, two-sided if necessary. Avoid more than one sheet for any one article, because media people are usually too busy to do any more than glance at what you send them.

Canned Feature

A canned feature is a newspaper article you write yourself. Many small papers and magazines lack the staff to report on every subject that interests them. A canned feature can significantly help the media help you. However, they aren't so easy to write. Unlike a bio, which is written by the numbers, a feature doesn't always follow as strict a formula. And if you're already nervous about your writing ability, composing a full-fledged article may spook you.

Not to worry. Though I've never worked as a journalist, I know a few of their tricks. First, keep paragraphs brief. Newspapers are well aware of the short attention span of most readers, so you need to make your piece scannable. Next, pack your article full of quotes. Reading the newspaper you'll notice most light features contain an abundance of quotes. That's because usually a reporter would rather have the subject tell his own story. This fulfills the journalist's need to remain objective.

So, for example, if I wanted to write a canned feature on the Youth Center, I would first select a theme: "Financially struggling center helps troubled teens despite adversity." With that premise, I'd write a brief headline and lead paragraph, recap the center's history, then let the quotes speak for themselves. Thread quotes together with a narrative to lend continuity, and always end your piece with a quote. Lace in new words to say the same thing, i.e., "He says," "He comments," "He notes."

Here's my own attempt at a canned feature:

YOUTH CENTER THRIVES DESPITE ONGOING BUDGET BATTLES

While gang wars claim young lives in the streets, many lives have been reclaimed at the Mid-Valley Youth Center, now in its fifth year of operation. But today, the Center faces its biggest fight yet as it struggles for solid financial footing. It's a fight the Center may not win.

Center Director John Jones has his doubts about the future.

"We're really being squeezed right now," says Jones. "Many of our funding sources have dried up, including half of our government monies." The Center had been 50 percent funded by the county until earlier this year, when the Board of Supervisors voted to slash programs like the Center.

"With only private funding, we cannot offer the same kinds of activities for the kids as we used to," notes Jones. The Center has provided not only sports and recreation facilities, but has an on-site job counselor helping teens find summer work. In addition, the Center has sponsored drug rehab and anti-gang programs, encouraging inner-city teens to avoid self-destructive patterns.

"Our success rate has been higher than many other similar centers because our staff came from the neighborhoods and really cared about the kids," commented Jones. "Some of them are volunteers who give more than 100 percent to this effort."

In order to stay afloat, the Mid-Valley Youth Center is preparing to launch long-term fundraising. A carnival, rummage sale, candy drive, and other projects will be scheduled throughout the year. Says Jones, "We need the community to give back to a place that has given so much. These fundraisers could go a long way to keeping us going."

Launched five years ago, the Mid-Valley Youth Center was the first self-contained center of its kind in this part of the city. With gang and drug activity dominating the neighborhoods, the arrival of the Center was met with initial skepticism. But soon, the comprehensive program brought results. According to local police statistics, violent crime in the area was down 23 percent within a year.

Despite the success, the Center faced continual budget crises. But Jones remains confident. "We've stared down guns, crack, murder, and despair, and we've triumphed. I'm sure this budget battle is one we can win too."

Any canned feature you write will echo your own leanings. But such features can be useful in presenting your case in a more impartial setting. And it's always a hoot to see your own self-congratulatory words gracing the pages of your hard-hitting local newspaper.

Vital Statistics and Quote Sheet

In many ways, you have to play midwife to your own media success. Spoonfeeding information to the media and doing their work for them not only endears you to them, but increases the chances they'll go to bat for you. A quote sheet or vital statistics sheet typifies the kind of visual aid the media love.

On one sheet of paper, can you list fifteen informative statistics about your project or about your subject in general? If you don't think so, think again. Go to the library, delve into research. You can quantify almost anything. If you own a retail store in an exciting growth industry, find out how many similar stores have opened nationwide in the past year. If you are a divorce attorney, cite the latest numbers showing the percentage of marriages that end in divorce. Find ten similar facts and you've got yourself a vital statistics sheet.

Here's a sample fact sheet I received from a local homeless-shelter network recently. Notice, it says nothing about the shelter program itself, but by recitation of these stark facts, it reinforces the need for such a program:

SAMPLE FACT SHEET ON HOMELESSNESS

• Los Angeles County has the dubious distinction of being the homeless capital of the nation. Conservative estimates place the number of homeless persons in the county from 100,000 to 160,000.

• Prevalent estimates place the number of homeless Americans at three million.

• Families with children present the fastest growing sector of the homeless population.

• 28,000 to 32,000 children are homeless in L.A. County.

• Since 1980, budget authority for all federal housing assistance programs has been cut by more than 75 percent.

• 1.1 million children use free food pantries each month in California.

• More than one in five people in the county will seek food assistance this year.

A quote sheet consists of statements by individuals directly bearing on your project. Don't include epigrams, such as those I've sprinkled throughout this book. Rather, use only those that pertain specifically to your project or field of interest. If you have a collection of reviews of your product, excerpt the best of them.

If you can collect several quotes from well-known people commenting on your area of expertise, use them. For example, if you're an inventor marketing a new skin care product, perhaps you can find *recent* quotes from dermatologists, government experts, movie stars, anyone talking about skin care. This augments your pitch by expanding the arena beyond yourself and your project.

Backgrounder

You may want to include a backgrounder if your business or project is based on highly technical knowledge, requires an understanding of its history, or is in any way tied to complicated subject matter. A backgrounder is simply a document, of any length, that thoroughly explains the "background" of your business. It is rarely quoted, but will serve to properly educate the media people as to the nature of your project.

Video Press Kit

I debated whether to include video press kits in this book because of their cost. Most Guerrilla P.R. budgets cannot encompass a video press kit, but I felt I should at least give you the information and let you decide for yourself.

The VCR explosion of the last ten years revolutionized not only consumer lifestyles, but the business world as well. I recently purchased a laser jet printer for my computer, and included with the instructions was a video on assembling the thing. Actors routinely submit to casting directors' video compilation reels along with 8 × 10 glossies. Most corporate offices today have VCRs, and probably most of us wonder how we ever entertained ourselves at home without them.

Video has become important in P.R. as well. Nothing is more searing than an image, and video provides that in ways prose or still photos never can. However, as with everything in this game, perception is the key, and if a video presentation appears cheaply made or poorly thought out, it could do more harm than good.

A video press kit provides much of the same information as a written press kit, but tells the story visually. It is *not a home movie.* Even if you own a top-flight video camera, think twice before you decide to make a promotional video on your own. If you aren't a film maker, you won't have a refined sense of editing, pacing, and cinematic composition. Not everyone can do this.

But, if you think your project would benefit from video, find out if there's a film school in your town, or a local college that teaches film. You may snag an ambitious film student willing to help you at no cost. He or she may even be able to provide film, camera, editing facilities, and actors. If there's a grade at stake, you'd be surprised how enterprising students can be.

Once you've decided to go ahead with a video press kit, remember a few key precepts:

• Don't make the video too long. Unlike written material, scanning a video is a chore.

• Combine movement with static shots to lend visual variety.

• Combine voice-over (i.e., off-screen narration) with on-screen presentation of information.

• If you are going to be the chief spokesperson for your project, put yourself in the video. If that makes you nervous, see the section in subsequent chapters about media coaching and appearing on-camera.

• Insist on quality. No shaky hand-held cameras, no fuzzy sound. Even if it only cost you a few hundred bucks, make it look like a million.

• The video press kit is meant to inform. In your script (and you *will* need to write a script), make sure the important points are covered. But remember, this tool shouldn't be used in lieu of a written press kit, only as an adjunct.

• Duplication costs can run you into the ground. If you have hired a film maker (student or otherwise), he or she may have access to video duplication machines. Don't go overboard and make scads of copies. Once you send them out, you'll probably never see the videos again, even if you request them back.

I won't say any more on video press kits, because they really aren't congruent with the Guerrilla P.R. mentality. They make you spend money instead of making other people spend money on you. But, if the opportunity arises, seize it, because as a Guerrilla, that's what you do.

MAGNET EVENTS

One afternoon ten years ago, five L.A. businessmen met at a local coffee shop. Though they'd established careers in diverse fields, they were brought together by a common passion: a love of chocolate. These five chocoholics decided to form an organization of like-minded zealots, and the Chocolate Lovers of America was born.

They struggled at first, sending out newsletters and releases, trying to get press attention. But what put them in the national limelight was an appearance in the annual Doo-Dah Parade, Pasadena's loony alternative to the Rose Parade. The perennial brief-case drill team and a squad of cop-slapping Zsa Zsa's are typical entrants in this marching madhouse.

The Chocolate Lovers of America entered the Doo-Dah Parade dressed as chefs throwing chocolate kisses to the onlookers lining the street, who literally ate 'em up. After that, the CLA was at last in with the in crowd.

When the Mel Brooks film comedy classic *Blazing Saddles* opened, the publicist in charge staged a screening of the western spoof at a drive-in. Only horses were allowed in, each tied by his reins to the speakers stand. Horse d'oeuvres were served, and a horsepitality suite was available as well. Oh, and of course, the press was invited.

Staging a magnet event like that is one of the best ways to draw attention, and for my money, it's a most appropriate alternative tactic in the Guerrilla P.R. arsenal. We used to call them publicity stunts, but that term has fallen into disfavor. In some ways, I prefer it because it smacks of daring. Like anything you do with the media, there should be some semblance of a news angle, but as you already know, the media cover the ridiculous as often as the sublime.

The key to conceiving magnet events is thinking tangentially. Of all the components to Guerrilla P.R., this one allows the most freedom. Dream up anything you want as long as, somehow, in the end, it ties into your project. The Planet Cafe, a faceless little restaurant in Chicago, landed a feature on the NBC Nightly News for cooking up Pajama Night: show up Sunday evenings in your sleepwear and get 10 percent off your bill. How wacky! How effective!

I've mentioned how Bob Columbe of RALPH made news when he called out the media to witness the arrival of Jackie Gleason's "Honeymooners" bus driver's uniform which the Great One shipped from Miami to Long Island. It was just a coat in a box, but Columbe's front lawn was so packed with media, the delivery man had trouble making it to the front door. As another example, one business author hired people with sandwich boards strapped to their bodies to promote his book in the financial district.

To devise your own magnet event, ask yourself the following questions:

• How willing am I to toy with my image? Magnet events sometimes involve unusual, sometimes absurd, escapades and this might clash with a more decorous reputation. As an example, I think it unlikely that either a Republican or a Democratic Senate Majority Leader will ever cruise the D.C. Beltway on a wheat harvester combine in order to push his farm bill. But if the nature of your project allows for some spirited fun, then proceed.

• Can I inject some sort of theme into my magnet event? Zany for the sake of zaniness is useless. The media don't have time for that. You must concoct something that tells a story. M.A.D.D. launched candlelight marches in several cities commemorating the many dead and injured victims of drunk driving. Find a way to symbolize some aspect of your project through the magnet event.

• Is my magnet event visually compelling? Whatever you do has to be photographable. When ACT-UP, the radical AIDS activist group, interrupted Catholic church services and poured blood on the sanctuary steps—offensive as it may be—it made for indelible images. ACT-UP was on every newscast in America that night. I'm not suggesting you in any way break the law, but if you develop an outlaw imagination, you'll grant yourself the freedom to come up with all kinds of ideas.

Once you've selected an event, plan not only the details of the event itself, but also the media attention you hope to solicit. Use the same basic tools of phone, press release, fax, and network, but, to retain an element of suspense or surprise, couch your wording with a touch of secrecy. Build suspense, cultivate curiosity. A magnet event is one circumstance where you don't give the whole story. Entice the media, and they may just go for it.

TIPS & TRAPS

* Remind the media to send a photographer.

* Budget carefully. You don't want to run up a big bill staging a fancy event.

* Magnet events can be time-consuming. Make sure you allot enough of your own schedule to planning, organizing, and staging yours.

* Walk through the event on-site beforehand. The more you know about the terrain, the fewer surprises await you.

* You may want to invite more than just media. Perhaps the public at large can join in. Youth, church groups, or any other organized group might add the right populist touch.

* For something like this, get help from family, friends, or colleagues.

MICHAEL LEVINE'S TOP TEN ALL-TIME P.R. STUNTS

1. In 1809, writer Washington Irving staged his own kidnapping to promote his book, *Knickerbocker's History on New York.*

2. John Lennon and Yoko Ono's infamous 1969 week-long "bed-in" honeymoon at which the ex-Beatle and his wife donned pajamas for peace.

3. A publicist for Frank Sinatra implanted a concert audience with bobbysoxers paid to fake hysteria. It caught on!

4. In 1962, a national campaign was launched to clothe naked animals. God knows why, but the effort received national press.

5. During the contentious 1968 presidential campaign, the anarchistic Yippie party ran a pig for chief executive.

6. Mel Brooks' comedy classic *Blazing Saddles* was given a P.R. send-off with a horses-only-transportation premiere at a drive-in theater.

7. Rock star Richard Marx, to promote the release of a new album, performed short concerts in five cities across America in one day in 1991. Unfortunately the album stiffed, but the concerts were terrific.

8. Malcolm Forbes throws himself and one thousand of his closest friends a seventieth birthday party at his own Moroccan casbah. Reported cost: over $1 million.

9. Hands Across America: in 1987 millions joined hands ostensibly to raise money for the nation's hungry, but ultimately for no better reason than to stop traffic in the middle of the street.

10. The relay of the Olympic torch across America in 1984. Thousands participated, from children to wheelchair-bound athletes, and many more thousands cheered along the path. It set the stage for the most watched and most exciting Olympiad ever.

MORE WRITE STUFF

A canned feature is a piece you write to include in a press kit, and to be honest, that's often as far as it gets. But you can generate first-rate clips for your press kit by writing articles for print media as a sideline. If they run in the paper, you get not only clips, but credibility, stature, and a potential audience of thousands or millions. Best of all, with your byline adorning the piece, you establish yourself as an expert in your field, which means the media will come to you for information and analysis from here on out.

A letter to the editor of your local paper is one great way to get started. News articles that relate in some way to your project, even obliquely, offer a golden opportunity to write in. Newspapers always need well-composed letters responding to the issues of the day. You may not get much response from such a letter but, included in your press kit, it shows you have a style that grabs the attention of editors.

Still, the editorial section does get read. Perhaps it's not the most widely read in the paper, but it's the best read. Devotees of the op-ed pages are often intellectual, highly educated, and influential. Op-ed pieces (op-ed stands for "opposite the editorials" or "opinion and editorials") are another excellent way to make you and your opinions known. Although these pages are largely comprised of syndicated columnists, every newspaper on occasion runs unsolicited essays by local citizens. The general guidelines are:

• Keep the piece short, no more than 400–500 words (about 2–3 typed pages, double-spaced).

• Write in the first-person. This is the opinion section after all, so allow your personality to run free.

• Even as you strive to make your piece flow, make each paragraph unique. Begin with an overriding theme, presenting that theme in the first two paragraphs, then cite several supporting examples. Read twenty op-ed pieces, and you'll see what I mean.

The following is an example of an actual op-ed piece I wrote that ran in several publications. Notice how I build on my theme from paragraph to paragraph. Though this piece wasn't directly about me or my business, it served to augment my standing within the P.R. and business communities.

THE CASE FOR INTERNSHIPS
by
Michael Levine

America may be the Land of Opportunity, but this is also the Land of the Big Trade-Off. Sure, you can have that nice house, but you're going to have to become a mortgage slave to keep it. You can drive that fancy sports car, but you'll have to fork over an insurance premium as hefty as the GNP of some Third World nations. In the Bible it says, in life, if you want honey, you get bees with stingers. For anything worth having, there's a price to pay.

It's the same with a career. Most professional positions require experience, but in this classic Catch-22, how does a young college student or graduate gain that experience? Well, it's just as Mark Twain said, "Never let school interfere with your education."

I believe the intern programs in place at companies like Coca-Cola, Procter & Gamble, CBS, and mine provide the best chance for young people to enter and grow in many professions. Although the work is demanding, with little or no immediate financial return, interning is a textbook example of a win-win situation.

When a young student comes to my public relations company and tells me he's willing to intern, a distinctly modern social contract is entered into. Though he is not a servant, and I am not a teacher, if he does some unpaid work, we'll do some teaching. The company gets the opportunity to observe eager and smart young people who energize the company. Like a farm team, interns are prospective employees, and we get to watch them in action. For the intern, the rewards are far greater.

Firstly, most interns are college students, and nearly all receive valuable college credit for their services. Beyond that, interning teaches the neophyte how to function in a complex, real-life adult business environment. Mike Tyson could have studied boxing manuals his whole life, but he would never have become the Champ if he hadn't stepped into a real ring. No classroom can substitute for visceral, palpable learning in an authentic setting.

Problem solving, initiative, creativity, and cooperation are all fostered as the intern struggles to carve a niche for herself. To make it as an intern, one must embody the qualities of any effective worker, and the rewards go far beyond the merely educational. Many interns go on to highly successful careers.

Interning is practical. In an ever-tightening job market, it provides career preparation, enables a young professional to develop marketable skills and demonstrate potential to a prospective employee. But beyond the practicalities, there's a bigger picture that needs to be addressed.

For too many, America has become the Land of the Freeloader and the Home of the Lazy. People seem to want it all, right here right now, with a minimum of effort. Dreams of winning this week's Lotto game have supplanted that dream of building a life built on Freud's twin peaks, "Lieben and Arbeiten," love and work. The old-fashioned work ethic is, if not dead, then surely on the critical list. America says it wants to be No. 1, but many refuse to expend the effort to get there. We can do it, but there's only one way, and that's simply to work for it, and work hard.

For centuries, apprenticeship was the equivalent to today's technical college. The spirit of apprenticeship is still alive in interning. If America's work force whined a little less, and had a little more of the initiative of my highly motivated interns, maybe this country could find a semblance of its former glory. Yes, they do not get paid. But as my interns have so brilliantly demonstrated, nobody works for free.

Don't just limit yourself to the editorial page. You should strongly consider writing your own articles for trade and consumer publications too. I've done many, and I don't think anything has proven as beneficial in establishing my personal credibility with the public.

If you aren't sure what to write, try a "list article." That would be something like "Ten Things You Can Do to Improve Your Sales Right Now," or "Eight Secrets to Better Lawn Care." Equally feasible is a Q&A-style piece, which would address similar concerns. Just pose five to ten of the most commonly asked questions regarding your business or project, and then answer them in the same punchy style described above.

Whatever line you're in, I'm sure you can concoct a list or a series of questions like this. They're easy to write and very easy for readers to grasp. Best of all, editors love them.

The key to dreaming up subject matter is to think not in terms of your own benefit, but of the benefit of the reader. Of course, you're out to promote yourself and your project, product, or service, but editors and readers don't care about that. You must think altruistically if you want to reap rewards.

Op-ed pieces to newspapers can be freely submitted as unsolicited articles. But before you write any *other* kind of article, for magazines, for example, you must first write a query letter to the editor, as detailed in the last chapter. I don't care how wonderful your piece is, most unsolicited manuscripts get thrown away without being read (unless the publication has a published policy of accepting them).

So write a short letter first, introducing yourself and your concept for the piece, giving maybe a two-paragraph taste of what you plan to write. The letter shows you're professional, respectful of the editor, and, most importantly, that you can indeed write.

If the editor likes your idea, he'll request the full article, and you will have thus established a permanent rapport with an important media player. And don't underestimate the shelf life of these pieces. Unlike newspapers, which wind up on the recycle stack the next day, magazines may stick around a long time. A friend of mine still gets inquiries for his business based on short pieces published up to five years ago in a trade magazine.

A few suggestions when preparing to write: take an inventory of all you know about your chosen topic, but also include what you *don't* know. This will determine what, if any, research you need to do. You can get the ball rolling by coming up with a catchy title or opening line. Check into books and magazines, and, if you have access, use your modem to link up with the vast computer information sharing network. Keep track of catch phrases and buzzwords to lend an authoritative tone to your piece; but remember, you don't have to be the ultimate expert. Your goal is to present a crisp, thoughtful article that benefits the reader first of all, and, with a little luck, will benefit you too down the line.

One other tip: editors like to give things away to readers, especially if they're free. If you can include in your piece an address where readers can obtain a no-charge premium, say a newsletter, a product sample, or additional information (with your name or your business name on it), all the better.

GIVING GOOD PHONE

Conversation is the art of never appearing a bore.

—GUY DE MAUPASSANT

I wonder sometimes how business was transacted before the invention of the telephone. Of all the technological pillars that hold up our civilization, the phone is the most intrinsic. Without it, the foundation would collapse. I could live without the internal combustion engine, MTV, and the Cuisinart. But not without the telephone.

Neither could any Guerrilla P.R. plan. While professional publicists may travel to Hollywood movie premieres or tag along on cross-country interview junkets, the Guerrilla variety is primarily housebound. Your wings of freedom are found on the telephone lines, so you must use the phone wisely—and often—if you are to succeed.

P.R. people have a reputation for being abrasive, hyper, and cynical on the phone. I keep all of those traits in my arsenal, but they are not the sum total of my phone persona, and they certainly shouldn't comprise yours. As is true in all aspects of life, you catch more flies with honey than with vinegar. Civility is the lubricant in the machine of human interaction, and you should always be your most polite when dealing with media.

I've mentioned how busy journalists are. *Be sensitive to that.* I always begin a conversation, even with reporters I know well, with "Do you have a minute to chat?" If they give their okay, I'll press on, but I make sure I obtain their permission first. Then I know they have consented to participate in the conversation.

Let me remind you once again of the importance of listening. Too often, conversations aren't true dialogues as much as a pair of monologues, with one party pondering his next point while the other speaks. Pay attention. Listen to the other person and trust yourself to think on your feet. People like to be listened to. They like people who listen to them, and the more people like you, the more inclined they'll be to help you out.

Now, as for pitching by phone, I assume some or all of the following have been done:

• You have sent a press release in advance of the call. (Sometimes, cold calls are necessary, but do your best to avoid them.)

• You are *thoroughly* familiar with the media outlet you're contacting, including personnel, style, audience, etc., and you are reasonably familiar with the work of the reporter you contact.

• You're speaking with the person you intended to reach. Not an assistant, not a colleague, but the real McCoy. (I know this isn't always possible, and you may at times have to deal with underlings. Don't be insistent; go with the flow for a while.)

• You are prepared to answer any questions. This is something to take seriously, and you won't know if you're ready unless you practice first. Conduct a mock conversation with a friend. Have the friend pepper you with all sorts of questions, even hostile ones. You have to be ready for anything.

Once in contact on the line, begin by summarizing the central point of your release. Even if the reporter received it, he/she may not clearly remember the content. After your summary, repeat the reason for your call, that is, you're looking for an advance story on your project, coverage of the event, a calendar listing, etc.

What you say next depends on the reply you get. If the reporter shows some interest, offer a new tidbit of information not included in your release. Give reasons why his or her publication should *want* to cover your project, all the while keeping in mind the lessons from before: they need news angles and they seek to serve their audience.

Take your cues from the person you speak with. If you detect irritation or impatience, say something like, "I won't take any more of your time," or "Give me just a minute more." You can press the journalist somewhat for an answer, but if she says she can't commit just then, accept it and ask when to call back for a definitive answer.

If you are met with utter indifference, ask leading questions that require a response. For example, "Have you found that the paper has done stories like this in the past?," or "Would additional news angles help you?," and then provide them. If the journalist still isn't biting, offer to send more material (if you have it) and say you'll call back in a few days. Gentle persistence erodes stubborn resistance.

Of course, record everything on your tracking sheet.

These suggestions are generic to all media. Getting what you want by phone involves careful manipulation of the call. You must feel in command even as you behave deferentially to the person you speak with. As the saying goes, you get no second chance to make a first impression.

TIPS & TRAPS

* Call from a quiet place. Background noise is distracting to both you and the party you're calling.

* Modulate your speaking voice to avoid a monotone.

* Don't come off like a Boy Scout, but do speak with enthusiasm and vigor. If you don't believe in your message, nobody else will.

* Never show anger or frustration with the person you call. Even if they're behaving abominably, you have to keep your cool to keep your connection.

* If the person you're trying to reach isn't in, don't always leave a message when you call. Sometimes media people rely on their voice mail to screen calls. If you leave two dozen messages, you will probably *never* hear from the reporter. Call with the intention of speaking to someone, but leave only a tiny handful of messages.

* If you still have trouble contacting the person, call his or her editor and explain your circumstances. Surprisingly, editors and managers are oftentimes more easily reached than those they supervise.

* I can't think of anything worse for your business than being unreachable or missing important calls. If you don't have a phone answering machine, get one today. The phone company now offers message center service for a nominal monthly charge.

JUST THE FAX

The fax machine is another one of those modern contrivances some wonder how we ever survived without. You can get a fax for the home, office, and even the car. I imagine soon some fast-tracker will install one in his shower. Anyway, I have a love-hate relationship with the fax.

On one hand, they are amazingly useful. What once had to be sent slowly by mail or expensively by Federal Express can now be delivered in seconds for the cost of a phone call. The written word can now travel literally at the speed of light, greatly expediting business. And because of their relatively low price, there are now more than three million fax machines cranking out over eighty-two million pages each day.

On the other hand, the fax is a tremendous invasion of privacy. There's something about having lengthy documents sent unasked for that makes my skin crawl. If you've never had someone fax you a twenty-page document, especially when it's on uncut thermal fax paper which you have to tear into sheets yourself, then you can't imagine how truly irritating it is. I know I'm not alone in this sentiment. There's something presumptuous about a faxed document.

If you decide to fax material, I urge extreme caution. It may not necessarily be read and considered any more quickly or seriously than anything sent by mail, and it could have the opposite effect of annoying the media recipient. Having said all that, here's some more advice:

• If you don't plan on making extensive use of a fax machine, don't blow the family fortune buying one. Use a machine at your place of business, or a friend's. Many convenience stores, pharmacies, and supermarkets now have fax machines available as well; most charge a service fee, so shop around.

• Never fax anything over four pages. Because most fax machines don't cut paper, anything more than four pages becomes one long unwieldy mess. Also, use black ink in your document; it transmits best.

• If you must send a long fax or multiple faxes, and you're paying for it at a local shop, ask the manager for a volume discount. Some places offer up to 25 percent off for long faxes.

• Reporters who work with tight deadlines appreciate speed. Army Archerd of *Variety* says, "Faxing is immediate. Besides, if it's down on paper, it's likely to be more accurate."

• Because faxes can sometimes be illegible, write out all numbers, e.g., "six-hundred," to avoid misinterpretation.

• Most machines send only standard letter-sized paper. If your original is larger, reduce it in the copy machine first.

• If your message is urgent, phone ahead to let the receiving party know the fax is on its way.

• If you send by fax, make sure you're reachable by fax. Don't send unless you can receive faxed material somewhere, and make that fax number clear to those you contact.

So far, you've been brushing up your communications skills, writing skills, and have been preparing your plan of attack. Now, it's time to move out. Basing an entire campaign strictly on press releases and phone calls is certainly possible, but it's like dining in a Chinese restaurant and ordering only a bowl of rice: it's authentic all right, but as long as you're there, why not try the moo-shu pork?

PEOPLE GET READY

I imagine at times you've been miffed by my commanding you to "be interesting" or "perform" without some instruction as to how. Let's start with some basics I've gleaned over the years. My theory about "perception as reality" holds true on every level. So, in your dealings with media and the public, you want to make a good impression every time. This section is meant to help you prepare for in-person interviews, TV appearances, and gladhanding of all kinds.

Research has shown people form strong opinions about others during the first seven seconds of meeting someone. Non-verbal signals are critical in determining the impressions individuals make on others. Appearance, dress, body language, attitude all contribute.

Consider the famous Nixon–Kennedy debates in 1960. People watching on TV overwhelmingly felt Kennedy, with his easy manner and good looks, was the hands-down winner. Those listening on radio felt Nixon won, based on the content of his answers. That historic series of debates was a defining moment in establishing the immutable power of the mass media to influence events.

Peggy Klaus, a media readiness consultant and an astute observer of human behavior, assists actors, news anchors, and corporate leaders with what she terms "physicalization," or ways in which the body moves. She emphasizes that our gestures should involve the least amount of stress. One should present oneself with ease and fluidity, seeking and finding a comfort zone.

This holds true not only for the body but for the voice. Former British Prime Minister Margaret Thatcher's voice dropped five notes after her election, some feel because she was trying to sound more "mannish." As a result she was constantly hoarse. Later, she reverted to her natural speaking voice. She had found her comfort zone, and so must you.

Clearly, even on your level, the right signals must be sent from the start. So, when you are gearing up to meet with the media, observe the following:

- *Once again, do your homework.* This goes for any contact you make with media reps. Know as much as you can about the newspaper, magazine, radio or TV show in question. Know who the anchors are, what section the reporter writes for, when the show is broadcast. If they perceive you as knowledgeable about them, they'll be more likely to treat you with respect.

- *Be on time or even early* for interviews, staging events, or anything else involving media. Punctuality is a sincere form of courtesy, tardiness a dire form of disrespect. This is especially true with TV. They're on extremely tight schedules, and you could throw a king-size wrench in the works if you waltz in late.

- *Dress appropriately.* Despite the title of this book, you shouldn't dress like a Guerrilla. I don't suggest you rush out and order a closetful of Armani suits, but dignified dress is a sign of self-respect, something you always want to convey. When on TV, dress is paramount. Unless your project is tied into the art world or counterculture, make sure your attire is neat, well-tailored, and on the conservative side. It will pay off.

- *Use open body language.* In Guerrilla P.R. you're a walking billboard. Everything you do communicates a message, including your body language. Look at yourself in the mirror. Are you expressive with your hands? Do you shift around? Do your eyes dart? Study yourself as if studying a lab animal, and be just as analytical.

- *Listen attentively.* Listen to the questions asked and read beyond the question. Media people are diggers. Why do you think they call a hot story a "scoop"? Because they have an insatiable desire to get below the surface. You have to be ready to provide that, but you can only if you pay attention. By listening, you'll be able to steer the conversation your way.

Until now, you've been assembling all the parts of your Guerrilla P.R. machine. Now it's time to throw the switch and put your machine in gear. In the next chapter, we reach out to the various media, making your vision a reality.

GUERRILLA P.R. COMMANDOS: SI FRUMKIN

There was a time when the term "Soviet Jewry" usually made people think of diamonds from Moscow, but that was before Si Frumkin came on the scene. A Holocaust survivor, the Lithuanian-born Frumkin arrived in America in 1949 as a young man anxious to start a new life. He built a successful business, earned an M.A. from the University of California, and started a family, but his real passion became the Jews he left behind in the Soviet Union.

In the late 1960s and early 1970s, along with a small band of supporters, Frumkin embarked on a true Guerrilla campaign to increase awareness of the plight of Soviet Jews. Over the years, he evolved into a media master, and almost single-handedly rallied the public around his issue with his tactics.

Nothing was too dramatic for Si. He spray-painted the words "Save Soviet Jews" on the side of the first Russian tanker in L.A. harbor. He hired a helicopter to fly over the Super Bowl trailing a banner reading "Save Soviet Jewry." When Brezhnev visited Nixon at San Clemente, Si released 5,000 helium balloons with the words "Let My People Go" emblazoned on them. Wherever and whenever he could, Frumkin and his cohorts appeared at Soviet cultural events dressed in their indigenous Soviet costume, handing out literature, creating a stir, and making people feel uncomfortable.

His creativity brought constant media attention. He launched a campaign to have Americans send their unused holiday cards to the Soviet embassy in Washington, pleading to release Soviet Jews. He staged a musical at synagogues around southern California. He even jokingly contemplated a "Martyrs for Soviet Jews" campaign wherein he and his friends would break their legs skiing at Mammoth. "We wanted to have bathing beauties stand before City Hall with signs, but we couldn't get enough pretty girls," he says.

Si's prankish wit helped him survive the long days of struggle, but his instinctive understanding of the media made him a natural Guerrilla P.R. genius. "The first thing we wanted was to get the media talking about us," he recalls. "In many cases the publicity we received was because we were confrontational. We never did anything overtly violent, but the media love confrontation. If we annoyed people, too bad."

Si made a distinction between his P.R. goals and those of others. "It was not a question of winning people over," he notes. "Normally the aim in P.R. is to get people to like you because you want them to buy your product. That was not true for us. We wanted to convince the world of our strength and the rightness of our cause. My feeling was that those people hostile to us because we picketed a basketball game would never be sympathetic anyway, and they didn't matter."

Working with next to no budget, Si relied on street smarts. He set up a darkroom to develop his own photos of magnet events and rush them to the papers. And he understood the needs of editors. "The average planning desk at a TV station or newspaper has about 300 items every morning," says Si. "They have to decide where to send the five or six available crews and reporters. We tried to make things 'sexy.' We poured blood and excrement in front of buildings, burned Soviet flags, whatever was visual."

His activities made him the reigning "expert" on Soviet Jewry, so the media called him whenever comment on the subject was needed. "They didn't call me because I was wonderful, but because I had the information." Today, with so many Jews departing the former USSR, Si feels vindicated and ecstatic. "It's a miracle," he says. "Ten years ago, if I were told a million Jews would be leaving with many more to come, I wouldn't have believed it."

His advice to other Guerrilla publicists: "Believe in what you're doing. Be totally dedicated, and be ready to work eighteen-hour days. Learn enough skills to check up on the professionals who supposedly know better. Chances are they don't know any more than you do."

5

FIRST ATTACK: THE PRINT MEDIA

*To a newspaperman, a human being is an item with the
skin wrapped around it.*

—FRED ALLEN

DEALING WITH NEWSPAPERS

Picture the newsroom: a hangar-sized warehouse of cramped cubicles,
clacking computer keyboards, ringing phones, and human bodies in
perpetual motion, racing to meet unforgiving deadlines. Now picture
the overworked reporter juggling three or four stories at a time. The
phone rings. It's you on the line, pitching your project to this harried,
disinterested grouch. If you think taking your call is his idea of a good
time, think again. But don't let that stop you.

There's a widespread notion out there, mostly fostered by journalists themselves, that reporters have no need for publicists. Don't
believe it. Reporters need sources. If you become a source for a story,
then you're what the reporter needs, and that puts you in a position
of considerable power. How you exercise that power is what counts.

To score with newspaper reporters and editors, you have to
comprehend their requirements. First, news value is central to their
thinking. They aren't interested in hype. Fluff is fine, but hype isn't.
Everything Michael Jackson generates in the press may strike you as
hype, but because it's *his* hype, it's transformed into news. You aren't
yet in as fortuitous a position.

As for whom to contact, there's a wide array of job titles at a
newspaper: Executive Editor, Managing Editor, City Editor, ad in-

finitum. You'd be best served trying to reach those on the front lines, such as section editors, features editors, and general or beat reporters. The higher-ups in management don't have much to do with day-to-day reporting. Thankfully, newspaper writers and editors are far more accessible than their TV counterparts. If you call the switchboard and ask for someone by name, chances are good the very person you want will pick up the phone.

That's not always true, especially if you're calling writers at major papers. Hurdling the heavily defended lines of voice mail alone is enough to put off many hardy souls. There's no getting around the fact that large daily papers in the Top Fifteen markets, such as the *Los Angeles Times* or *New York Times*, run differently than do smaller town papers like the *Des Moines Register*. But it's only a matter of scale. The smaller papers are in many ways more effective: though not as high a number of people read them, they tend to have more impact in their given communities. Besides, they tend to have nearly as much access to news sources as their big brothers in the big cities.

Rebecca Coudret, a reporter for the *Courier* in Evansville, Indiana, is quick to note that her paper is a link in the Scripps-Howard chain of more than 300 newspapers across the country. Any story she writes goes out on their wire, and has a potential reach of millions. So, if you live in a small city and fret that your audience would be limited if you stayed parochial, relax. If your local paper hits your target audience, then that's the paper you want to be in, and it may reach out further than you guessed.

When you contact a newspaper, keep your news angle uppermost in mind. Most likely you've already sent a press release and/or press kit. So, once you've got a reporter on the phone:

• *Avoid the hard sell.* Saying "You *have* to cover this" just won't work. My reporter friends uniformly claim their disdain for pressure from outsiders. You must be willing to bend, even to the point of losing. Better to miss out this time and keep a friendly contact, rather than go for broke in an obnoxious manner and lose out permanently.

• *Be friendly, but not ingratiating.* Nobody likes to be sucked up to. Your manner should steer clear of the sickeningly familiar.

• *Know the reporter's work.* I say this over and over. You will genuinely flatter a writer if you let him know you're acquainted with his work. Don't fake it. If you refer to a piece that ran a week ago, you'd better have read it. Aside from the goodwill, you can make more sensible suggestions as to the nature of the reporter's coverage of your project.

• *Be sensitive to deadlines.* Most newspapers are dailies. That means that every day the herculean challenge of putting out a newspaper is met by these individuals. Give them credit. Reality for newspaper writers is the deadline. Like an ever-moving wall of molten lava from a Hawaiian volcano, deadlines are unstoppable. So if you're pitching an event, make sure you give the writer plenty of time to work with your request, and don't call when he or she is under the gun. Morning papers have late afternoon deadlines, so call in the late morning. Conversely, afternoon papers should be contacted in the late afternoon, after they've gone to print.

• *Remember that many journalists have an inflated sense of self-importance.* There's a reason why so many people out there distrust the media. Many media people believe they're on a mission from God, and they can be unbearably arrogant at times. You could be the next victim of a cynical writer spoiling for a fight. Counter with a professional attitude, quiet enthusiasm, relentless cordiality, and an iron-clad pitch.

When it comes down to negotiating a story idea, there are several options to go after. They include:

• Feature. A full-length descriptive article on you, your project, or related topics. These tend to be the most beneficial to you because of their length, prominent placement in the paper, frequent use of photo-illustration, and prestigious journalistic cachet.

• Q&A. A simple question-and-answer interview. These can be reprinted in entirety or condensed into much shorter pieces. Either way, they make for excellent coverage.

• Round-up. When you or your project fit into the scope of a larger piece a writer is working on, a round-up story may be your best bet. Say you own a computer dating service. A writer may be working on a "Love in the 90s" think piece, and your insights may dovetail nicely. Take it if you can get it.

• Column item. Some journalists write regular columns for the paper. Perhaps you can interest one of them to devote one of their columns to you. These articles tend to be more emotional and subjective, which can be a real boon to you and your project. Other columnists report on upcoming community activities and events. You may benefit greatly from such a column mention. Usually local columnists focus only local issues.

• Calendar. This is nothing more than a line item notice in a calendar of events. But you'd be surprised how well-read these pages are. At the very least, make sure your event is listed.

It's okay to suggest to the reporter what you feel might be best. He or she may then direct you to another writer or editor. Make sure everyone you talk with has received or will receive press materials. Sometimes, reporters pass them on to editors, and vice versa. Determine that before you send along another package.

What if your pitch works and the reporter wants to do an interview or story? Congratulations! But being on the receiving end of an interview requires preparation. Properly handling interviews can make or break your Guerrilla P.R. campaign, so let's lay some groundwork.

First of all, even though the reporter seems to hold all the cards (after all, he will ask the questions and write the story), you do have a considerable role in shaping the tone of the interview. The reporter may frame the questions, but you frame the answers. You'll probably sense right away if the writer is sympathetic, skeptical, or downright hostile.

No matter what, you need to concentrate on positive responses. Do not get defensive or evasive. Keep your language and decorum on a high level, because a reporter will pounce on anything he or she senses might be controversial.

Here's a fictitious interview that shows how to gently deflect tough questioning:

Q: "The Mid-Valley Youth Center seems to be a black hole for public and private funds. Why are you once again turning to the public to pump more money into a losing proposition?" (This question is hostile, full of loaded terminology like "black hole" and "losing proposition." Reporters often goad subjects into giving more info than they intended to reveal, and this is one effective way of doing that. Don't duck the question, but deflect hostility by absorbing it into your own agenda.)

A: "I understand why some people may get that impression, but it's more important that people understand how our budget process works. I have for you a complete financial audit conducted by an independent accounting firm, which shows how prudently our funds were used. We're seeking new funding now because the current economy has made it tough to keep existing programs going."

Steering the conversation hinges on telling reporters *what you want them to hear*, not what they hope to hear. To do this, never lose sight of your objective. Of course you should respond to skeptical or tangential questions, but your challenge is to return to your main points without coming off like a snake oil salesman.

In essence, the interview is like a game of tennis, of give-and-take. What you give depends on what the interviewer serves you, and the same goes with him or her. Anticipating their questions, rehearsing (but not memorizing) your answers, and amassing a collection of transition lines ("What you said reminded me of . . ." or "I should also mention that . . .").

Another tip. Unlike TV news, print media find detailed statistics useful. Provide as many as serve your case. But avoid appearing to blow a smokescreen made of numbers. Reporters are trained to question everything, so be sure your case is airtight and your statistics relevant.

If the reporter interviews you at your place of work (assuming your workplace is the location of your project), be open. Show him or her around; offer as much information and access as possible. They will draw their own conclusions no matter what you do, so you may as well expose the reporters to everything germane.

The process doesn't end once the interview is over. If later you think of other points you failed to mention, call the writer immediately. Make sure you get his phone number before you part company. Don't pester writers too much as to when the story may run. Most reporters have little control over this, and frequent calls will only alienate the writer.

After a story does run, if it's positive (or even if it's constructively critical), you may wish to call or write the reporter with your thanks. But here again, reporters' pride comes into play. They usually don't feel they did you any favor by running a piece about you, whether positive or negative. It was a simple matter of news to them; so sometimes "thank-yous" can be insulting. Use your own judgment.

Remember, there's no scientific definition of news. It's whatever people are talking about. You want to become news, so get them talking!

GUERRILLA P.R. EXERCISE

In a mock interview, have a friend ask you a few general questions, and see if you can navigate the conversation entirely in your own direction.

TIPS & TRAPS

* Although it's common practice, avoid doing interviews in restaurants. They're noisy, distracting, and it's hard to make a good impression with a piece of steak stuck between your teeth. Meet in an office or other work setting.

* To whatever extent possible, see that the reporter tapes your interview to ensure accuracy. I don't need to tell you about the pitfalls of being misquoted.

* Yes, an interview is business, but it's also human conversation, and not an interrogation. I find it effective to lock into the other person's humanity. Liveliness, friendliness, openness all have an impact, no matter what the reporter says about keeping his or her journalistic distance.

* Pause often; reflect on your words. You're on the record now (unless you tell the reporter otherwise), and you want your words to reflect your truest and best sense of yourself.

* Don't forget to ask the reporter to send you a clip. For one reason or another, you may not always have the opportunity to obtain one.

FROM THE GUERRILLA P.R. FILE

Kraco Enterprises, one of the nation's largest auto detailing and accessory companies, together with publicist Alex Litrov, cooked up a scheme in 1988 to find America's long-distance commuter champ. Word of the contest spread throughout the media, and finally they found their winner: Rod Conklin of Darien, Connecticut, who commuted a total of 408 miles each day from his home to Boston and back. The story was picked up on CNN, *USA Today*, UPI, as well as many local newspapers and TV stations. Kraco was mentioned several times, and the whole campaign was a raging success. Now if only someone would help poor Mr. Conklin find a job closer to home.

DEALING WITH WIRE SERVICES

At every press conference held by every president since Franklin D. Roosevelt, the privilege of asking the first question goes to the reporter from the Associated Press, America's most important wire service. The reason is simple. AP is picked up by every newspaper in the country, and most of the world as well. The wires provide eyes and ears to papers too small to cover the world. In fact, despite what ABC says, more people get their news from the wires than from anywhere else.

There are other wire services besides AP. UPI, Reuters, Gannett, and syndicates like King Features, New York Times Syndicate, and Los Angeles Times Syndicate are a few of the largest, although some, like the New York Times and L.A. Times Syndicates send out only those stories that have appeared in their newspapers. But all wires furnish members and subscribers with reams of stories covering everything from the White House to the local five-and-dime. Like other news media, wires hunger for stories and scoops, and they could play a significant role in your Guerrilla P.R. campaign.

Wires differ most markedly from newspapers in that they produce nothing printed. They service subscribers electronically (in the old days it came over a teletype "wire," hence the name). Though the large wires have bureaus in most major cities, their inherent anonymity may make them a little harder to find. However, you generally need look no further than your nearby metropolitan white pages.

Once you locate them, proceed with caution. Unlike your local paper, which serves and is beholden to the community, the wires serve a much larger constituency, and can be much less inclined to jump on your story than the daily down the street.

Whereas daily papers often assign beats to reporters, such as city desk, entertainment, sports, etc., most wire service writers are general reporters covering everything under the sun. As busy as newspaper journalists are, wire reporters are unbelievably overworked, usually juggling four or more stories at a time. Everything I said about sensitivity to the journalist's workload goes double for wire reporters.

Ironically, though, unless they're covering major national stories, most wire reporters are not subject to the crushing deadlines of the dailies. They have more time to labor over detail and give their stories a little more scrutiny. So, pitch them *solely* on the merits of your story. Wire stories tend to reflect a more universal nature, so that they can run in any paper anywhere. A proposal with too local an angle is likely to be turned down. Pitch accordingly. Think broader.

And while I'm on the subject of wires, don't forget to consider America's syndicated columnists. I'm sure you read a few of them regularly. Although it's a long shot that Art Buchwald or Erma Bombeck will do a story on your project, they shouldn't be ruled out, and they are by no means the only fish in the sea. There are dozens and dozens of important columnists in this country, writing on everything from gardening to politics to child rearing. If you write a well-composed letter to one of them, either in care of the paper you read or directly to the syndicater, you just may have a shot.

The key is knowing the writer's work and style. Many tend to use parables and personal illustrations to make their points. That's where you might fit in. In your letter, suggest a column idea or theme to which your project may apply. With a good angle to dangle, there's a chance you'll hear from the columnist.

TIPS & TRAPS

* Never blanket a bureau, i.e., pitch to other reporters in the same office if the first one has already said "no." Word will get out and your name will be permanent mud.

* Your story will be best served by the nearest bureau. Though it might seem like you're closer to the nerve center if you contact the New York or L.A. office of UPI, stay close to home. If you live in Pittsburgh, call the Pittsburgh bureau.

* Wire reporters tend to work closely with member and subscribing papers. They read them carefully and know what's going on in the communities. They pick up stories from the papers just as the papers pick up stories from the wires.

* You should be careful with columnists with respect to time. You may not hear from them or their staffs for quite a long while (imagine the volume of mail they must receive), and you shouldn't put too many eggs in this one basket.

MEDIA FACTS

• There are 1611 daily newspapers in America.

• 863 newspapers have Sunday editions.

• There are approximately 7,000 weekly papers in America.

• There are over 5,000 trade publications in the United States.

• 156.3 million U.S. adults read one or more magazines each month.

• The circulation of U.S. dailies is 62.3 million.

- The *Hartford Courant* in Hartford, Connecticut, is the oldest daily in America, founded in 1764.

- The Top 10 newspapers in America and their circulation are: (1) *Wall Street Journal* (1.85 million); (2) *USA Today* (1.34 million); (3) *L.A. Times* (1.19 million); (4) *New York Times* (1.1 million); (5) *New York Daily News* (1.1 million); (6) *Washington Post* (780,000); (7) *Chicago Tribune* (721,000); (8) *Newsday* (714,000); (9) *Detroit Free Press* (636,000); (10) *San Francisco Chronicle* (562,000).

- *Reader's Digest* reaches over 48 million people each month.

DEALING WITH TRADE PUBLICATIONS

Whatever line of work you're in, there are trade publications covering it. In my business, *Variety* and the *Hollywood Reporter* fit the bill. In the music industry, it's *Billboard;* in the fashion world, *Women's Wear Daily;* and for Madison Avenue, *Adweek.* Trades can be micro-specific. Out there right now you can find avid readers of *Footwear News, Banking Software Review, Travel Agent Magazine,* and *Water & Waste Digest.* We all enjoy reading about our own business. It makes us feel connected to our own special industry or service.

A recent study conducted by the Opinion Research Corporation found 40 percent of business customers rated trade publications as their chief source of information about their particular product or service. That's a significant number. Even though a favorable trade story may seem like preaching to the choir, once your peers think you're hot, soon the public will too.

Trades can be dailies, weeklies, or monthlies, and many of them run special annual or bi-annual editions. Each requires different lead times, so be cognizant and act accordingly. Trades function much like consumer publications. They like scoops, exclusives, and breaking stories. But you'll discover right away that trade reporters are true experts in their fields. They possess refined knowledge in order to communicate to a rarefied audience. When you pitch them, address them as absolute equals in terms of comprehension of subject matter.

As with some consumer publications, trades are advertiser-sensitive. Many times I've seen businesses "buy" stories in the trades by purchasing ad space. This is unethical, and I would hope you never find yourself in such a position. If you're ever told bluntly that you must buy an ad to get a feature, walk away. Your dignity isn't for sale. Some may call this a naive attitude, but I've become successful without having to resort to such a stratagem. You don't have to either.

If a trade publication decides to do a story on you, make sure the reporter has *all* the facts. Send her as much additional written material on your project as possible, including information that has nothing directly to do with your Guerrilla P.R. campaign. If a personal interview and/or tour is in order, roll out the red carpet. Remember, this is a person who ostensibly knows as much about your business as you do, so don't even think about trying to embellish the facts. The trade journalist is one reporter who will see through it.

In addition to pitching trades for stories on you and your project, you may offer to submit your own article or guest editorial, just as we discussed for consumer press. I would say the trades are much more likely to run your piece than a daily paper because you're coming from an insider's position of strength. Make sure you speak with an editor before you set pen to paper, though. You could set yourself up for disappointment if you go to the trouble of writing a piece, and then get no response from the trade publication. Or, they might already have a competitor's piece in type.

With anything you write, observe the following guidelines:

• Don't offer any written work for publication by more than one trade. That violates the honor code of exclusivity.

• Try to keep your piece on the shorter rather than the longer side. You'll make a greater impact, and keep the attention of your audience.

• Seize on one or two (at most) simple themes. Marketing expert Bob Serling, in a short article he wrote for a leading marketing journal, made his points using the term "leverage" as a hook. Every paragraph heading used this term to make its points.

• Remember what I said about writing, in the previous two chapters. Good writing is good writing, no matter where it ends up, and everything you write should come off polished and well-thought-out.

Because they're supported almost entirely by advertising from within the industry they represent, trades are industry's cheerleaders. Unlike their counterparts in the newspaper world, trade reporters aren't generally out to get anyone. They prefer to be viewed as boosters. Thus, if your angle is upbeat and positive, you stand a good chance of making it in the trades. Trade stories make excellent clips and can really get a Guerrilla P.R. campaign off and running. So give the trades your best shot.

DEALING WITH MAGAZINES

I don't know about you, but I have a hard time throwing away magazines. Whereas the daily paper is hurled on the "recycle" stack at the end of every day, year-old copies of *Time, Newsweek,* and *Rolling Stone* keep popping up in different corners around the house. There's something permanent about a magazine. If it's inscribed in the pages of *Life,* it lives forever.

In my experience, magazine editors are more selective in what they choose to print. Perhaps because most magazines are monthlies, editors' jobs are on the line with every issue. Each story is make-or-break.

Magazines and legitimate tabloids like the *L.A. Weekly* or the *Village Voice* have longer lead times than newspapers, up to five months, and more if you're new to them. There's less space in magazines than in newspapers, so every word counts more. For the news-oriented weeklies, like *Time,* summary and analysis are the watchwords. Their editors assume a high level of astuteness on the part of readers.

Just because you have a Guerrilla P.R. approach doesn't mean you don't belong in *Newsweek.* You simply have to "nationalize" your pitch. If you recall the section on pitching, I urged you to create variations on your pitch to apply to different media. For national magazines, you have to broaden your concept.

To use the Youth Center as an example, instead of pitching the magazines on the reduction of crime in the area, I would stress how America can turn its troubled youth around with the right mix of compassion and dedication; one of President Bush's thousand points of light—you get the picture.

Keep in mind that many well-known magazines occasionally run special issues (also called "one-shots"), such as *Sports Illustrated*'s swim suit edition, *Life* magazine's year-end issue, etc. Some are far more esoteric or accessible than those. When you speak with editors, find out if any such specials are being planned. You might fit in.

Much more than newspapers, magazines are graphics-conscious. Editors agonize over who or what goes on the cover, while teams of designers labor over each issue's layout. As we saw with *Vanity Fair*'s celebrated cover of the nude and pregnant Demi Moore, this obsession is understandable. Keep this in mind when you pitch.

Not that you'll have any impact on layout, but if the writer or editor senses your awareness, you'll gain stature. Don't be afraid to offer suggestions here and there on ways to illustrate your story. They may not accept them, but they'll respect your involvement.

Phoning is not as effective as writing when contacting magazines. Not all writers are on staff. Many are freelancers whom you can't reach by phone anyway, but they can always receive forwarded mail. Fire off some letters to writers you find particularly intriguing. Not every newspaper article has its writer credited, but practically all magazine pieces have an accompanying byline. All writers have editors and all magazines have mastheads, so it's pretty easy to figure out whom to contact.

Weekly tabloids catering to individual communities have slightly different requirements. Though they don't encompass the global scope of *Time*, they often emphasize analysis, investigative reporting, and expanding the range of local stories. So if you want a meaty feature, you have to present to them a bigger picture. Say you own a small business in a revitalized area of your community. Suggest a round-up story idea focusing on the rebirth of the local economy, using your shop as an example.

Magazines can frustrate you. Because of limited space and their paranoia about what goes in, you may find yourself up against a wall much of the time. But keep trying. A good magazine lends credibility to a project. The writers tend to write at a higher level than their newspaper counterparts (primarily because they have more time to turn in their pieces).

Besides, most magazines, in order to be profitable, usually enjoy a far wider circulation than almost any metropolitan daily paper. Even if circulation isn't great, magazines get passed around. Statistics show that the average copy of a magazine reaches 4.8 readers. The moral is: do your best to make magazines a part of your G.P.R. diet.

FROM THE GUERRILLA P.R. FILE

Columbia University research fellow Harold Zullow made the papers across America with his unusual sociological studies. Zullow theorized that the pop charts are good predictors of the overall direction of the national economy. The thesis states that either pessimistic songs or truly awful songs make it to No. 1 just before an economic downturn. His proof: "Escape (The Piña Colada Song)," "Keep On Truckin'," and "The One That You Love," all utter treacle, and each hit the top spot just before a recession. Just goes to show that if you concoct a weird-enough theory, you'll attract the media like a moth to a flame.

OTHER PRINT POSSIBILITIES

The world of print journalism doesn't end with the daily paper, the trade publication, and the weekly edition of *People*. Entire forests are devoured every year to feed our insatiable appetite for print. As a Guerrilla publicist, your m.o. is to cover every base, especially those the pros tend to downplay.

If you live in a college town, there's probably a college paper on campus. They're usually student-run; and you'll find college kids enthusiastic and open to new ideas (unlike their jaded counterparts at the daily). True, most of the articles are campus-oriented, but once in a while they jump on atypical stories. They are by nature very accessible, so give your college paper editor a call.

Don't neglect community ethnic newspapers. There are hundreds of important newspapers across America that serve the African-American community, such as the *L.A. Sentinel* and New York's *Amsterdam News*. Obviously, these papers cater to the needs of their readership, but they are almost always open to important stories, interesting side bars, or announcements. Spanish-language papers, like *El Diario* in New York, or *La Opinión* in L.A., all have English-speaking staff reporters who will cover your story if it has merit for their readership. You can reach a vast audience by tapping into these kinds of papers.

Many organizations and businesses distribute in-house newsletters, and are often open to outside stories. Check with large companies in your area to see which have such a program. Also, every pastime has a specialty publication to call its own, e.g., *Car & Driver*, *Ski*, *House Beautiful*, etc. Do you fit in with any of them?

Many churches and synagogues have newsletters too. If you're a member, perhaps there's a way to contribute a piece to your in-house publication. Write a letter to the editor of the newsletter, or submit a short piece on how your project is helping the congregation.

Think political. Your local or state Democratic, Republican, or third party committee probably has a publication. Once again, you may be able to create a piece that relates your project to your political activities.

LAST WORD ON PRINT

It's said we're becoming a nation of illiterates. Fewer and fewer people read anymore. Daily papers are dropping like flies; SAT scores are down; kids know more about the latest Madonna video than what's happening in the Middle East. The future looks bleak.

But our society remains glued together by the printed word. Our institutions, our economy, our entire society is welded to the written word. As high-minded as that sounds, it most definitely trickles down to the Guerrilla P.R. level. If you were to get on TV and not in print, you wouldn't last. The account of our civilization ultimately will be told in the written record, not the video, even in the short-term.

I placed my chapter on print before the one on TV because I believe it to be the most important. Yes, you will be seen by more people if you appear on TV, and perhaps your project will gain a greater lift by a guest shot on "Donahue" than from a piece in the *New York Times*. But perception is reality. If you are canonized by a *New York Times* article you will have achieved a level of legitimacy far greater than any TV stint can deliver.

Go for it all, but by all means, go for print.

GUERRILLA P.R. COMMANDO: ANGELYNE

She's as much a part of the Los Angeles landscape as the Capitol Records Tower and the Hollywood Sign. For nearly ten years, billboards of the pouty-lipped, platinum blonde Angelyne, perched atop her pink Corvette, have dotted the boulevards and byways of the city, creating a pop culture heroine the likes of which we haven't seen before. Most people have wondered who the hell she is, but over time, the ubiquitous billboards of "the girl on the Corvette" have become a true southern California icon.

The Angelyne mystique arose out of L.A.'s preoccupation with fame and image. For no reason other than her striking appearance on the billboards, Angelyne became a symbol of L.A.'s fast-lane mentality. Her fame has spread throughout the world, though most people aren't quite sure who she is or what she does. Many would guess the doe-eyed vixen to be a first-class bimbo. They should guess again.

Angelyne happens to be a supremely intelligent businesswoman wise in the ways of self-promotion and Guerrilla P.R. Without ever hiring a publicist, she turned herself into a permanent part of the city's persona. But how?

"I'm a rebel," she told me, "very much into being original. I detest clichés." The former rock singer claims a lifelong devotion to achieving celebrity. "When I was three I knew I would never feel right until I became famous," she says. "Fame made me feel more normal." To achieve her goal, Angelyne embarked on a campaign to get her image before the public.

"I started with posters," she recalls, "then bus shelters. Next, we put out small billboards, then larger ones. We finally painted my picture on a ten-story wall at Hollywood and Vine. After that, the media were all over me." Angelyne estimates she gained $10 million in free publicity because of the massive media exposure from the billboards. Her posters included her management phone number, which hasn't stopped ringing since Day One.

Thanks to her innovation and perseverance, Angelyne's movie and personal appearance career has taken off, more than paying for the cost of the billboard campaign. Her chief advice to others hoping to entice the media: "I relate to the media the same way I relate to men. Never touch anybody. Tease them until they come to you. I have never had to call anybody for anything. They called me."

As special as she feels herself to be, Angelyne is convinced everybody has within him or her the makings of a star. "We canbecome free agents unto ourselves," she says. "In the future, I think everyone will be able to make the most of their artistic side." Angelyne has certainly made the most of her abilities. She won the fame she wanted, paid nary a penny for the media exposure, and today, she's probably having the last laugh. That's life in the big city.

6

SECOND SALVO: ELECTRONIC MEDIA

Local (TV) news has always been more ukelele than sym-phony.

—HOWARD ROSENBERG, *L.A. TIMES*

TELEVISION

In the last ten years, the "vast wasteland" got a whole lot vaster. The proliferation of cable TV opened up grand new vistas for viewers, with more choices available now than ever imagined just a few years ago. Upstarts like CNN, Fox, MTV, and HBO have taken their place at the table of mega-profits alongside the shrinking networks, while public access and UHF channels continue to mushroom. Answering the old question "What's on tonight?" isn't so simple anymore.

For the Guerrilla P.R. strategist, TV is essential. TV is power; if you get yourself on the tube, power passes to your hands, and success in your efforts is almost guaranteed. Yet despite the many similarities of the various media, TV is a breed unto itself.

For one thing, a newspaper exists in the realm of space, TV in the realm of time. One involves imagination, the other image. Even on talking-head news shows like "Face the Nation," the image is what counts. The congressman rambling on about third-quarter housing starts may be a womanizing blowhard, but if he looks and sounds good up there, his most important message—"Re-elect me!"—comes through loud and convincing.

Because of TV's time constraints, practically every moment on the tube is scripted down to the millisecond. TV is not so much a marketplace of ideas as it is a big show. Even news programs—local and national—are just shows. To make it on the air, your project must become part of the show, a part people will want to watch. If not, no matter how deserving you may be, the only TV you'll appear on is the one in the department store with the camcorder trained on you.

To be part of the show, you have to know how TV works. For Guerrilla P.R. purposes, let's divide the medium up into its constituent parts:

• News. This includes everything from Tom Brokaw to the goofy weatherman on Channel 6. News programming has diversified greatly over the last decade. The advent of CNN, the expansion of local news, cable, and a plethora of prime time shows originating with the network news divisions (like "60 Minutes," "Prime Time Live," "20/20," etc.) have dramatically increased the broadcast hours devoted to news.

• Public Affairs. Although public affairs programming has decreased since F.C.C. deregulation during the Reagan administration, it still constitutes an important outlet for varying points of view on issues of public interest. Most network affiliates in major markets have their own Sunday Newsmakers shows which usually cover local political subjects.

• Infotainment. These shows, more than any other, have flourished in the last few years. There are two types: the town meeting and the simulated news show. The town meeting variety started with Phil Donahue back in the seventies, featuring a charismatic host and an inquisitive studio audience. Now, we've got Oprah, Geraldo, Maury, Sally, Montel, and Jerry Springer, to name a few. They cover two basic catch-all themes: real life, and Hollywood. You'll tune in either to find Warren Beatty pushing his new movie, or three recovering alcoholic Satan worshippers in love with the same paraplegic transsexual. Like I said, real life.

Sim-news shows are among the most reviled and most watched in the country: "A Current Affair," "Hard Copy," "Inside Edition," and "Entertainment Tonight," are among the best known. These shows thrive on sensationalism. Sex, scandal, and sin are their stock in trade. But once in a while, they cover more wholesome subjects . . . like you perhaps.

• Morning shows. NBC's "Today" is the grand-daddy of morning shows. CBS and ABC have "This Morning" and "Good Morning, America." Nationally syndicated shows like "Regis and Kathy Lee"—as well as the many local outlets, e.g., "Good Day New York," "Home," and "Today in Minneapolis"—provide invaluable exposure opportunities. All stories run on these types of outlets have some national or universal significance.

TV is a much bigger deal than print. A newspaper reporter need bring along only a pad and a pencil, sometimes a tape recorder, to ensure accuracy. On the other hand, a TV news crew includes a reporter, a sound technician, a camera operator, a producer, and a driver. An appearance on the set of a news broadcast or talk show involves dozens of people, from make-up artists to assistant directors to videotape editors. In a word, TV is *complicated.*

TV news, like print, has an inflated sense of journalistic scruples. Though few news stars have come up in the realm of hardnosed print reporting, TV journalists like to believe they represent the same grand tradition of news coverage as, say, the *Washington Post.* Despite a few isolated instances where that is indeed the case, basically comparing the two is pure horse bleep.

With the average report lasting somewhere around a minute, local TV news is a sham. It's sports, weather, and the nightly murder and fire report. It's headlines read by ex-beauty queens and pretty boys, and woe to him or her that doesn't look the part. There's little analysis or in-depth reporting; and come Sweeps Month, we're likely to be deluged with five-part series on lesbian nuns or fifty ways to tell if your wife is cheating on you.

Yet despite its deficiencies, TV news can be more dramatic and memorable than any other shared experience. From the death of a president in 1963 to the explosion of the Challenger in 1986; from Watergate to Contragate, the Gulf War to the crumbling of the Soviet Union to the burning of L.A. after the Rodney King verdict, television news has given shape and meaning to the events of our time. I wouldn't trade it for anything.

Your main task is *knowing whom to contact.* Don't worry about getting yourself on the "CBS Evening News" (though I hope that's part of your long-term game plan). Instead, concentrate on local outlets first. You may have a wealth of choices before you, especially if you live in one of the Top 25 U.S. markets.

Most cities have affiliates of all three networks. Each has its own news division. Many independent stations have their own news programs as well. In L.A., we have the big three (CBS, NBC, ABC), Fox News, three independents, PBS, and several UHF channels with news programming, including two in Spanish, and others in Korean, Japanese, Farsi, and Chinese.

Most news programs run credits at the end (especially on Fridays). Look for the names of assignment or planning editors. Those are your initial contacts. Send them your written material. All newsrooms have "future files," and everything sent gets looked at, considered, and put in the file. If the station has full-time medical, business, or consumer reporters, and your project applies, you may contact the reporter directly, but generally it's prudent not to call a reporter. He or she would have to check with the assignment editor anyway, who might be miffed if bypassed.

Be current with the station's format. Know the anchors, the reporters, the weather and sports staffs. Once you make the call, proceed much as you would with a newspaper editor. The assignment editor handles that day's schedule; the planning editor looks ahead to the subsequent few days, so depending on when and what you're pitching, you'll know whom to ask for.

Reiterate the main points of your press release, make your pitch, and remember to keep *visuals uppermost in your mind*, because that's how TV tells its stories (and, of course, record everything on your tracking sheet). The editor will not promise you anything. Crews are always scarce, and even when editors say they'll be there, all it takes is one apartment fire and the crew meant for you is off on a new assignment.

Because TV news, especially local news, is unable or unwilling to delve into thoughtful analysis, its coverage tends to be shallow. Because it emphasizes image, it tends to cover stories based on their photogenic appeal rather than their intrinsic news value. Given all that, TV news is much more open to the influence of publicists than are newspapers.

Station personnel may ask themselves, "Are we being used?" when contacted by publicists. Sometimes even when the answer is "yes," they'll cover the story anyway. That exclusive videotape of the world's largest pizza is just too good to refuse. They may acknowledge on the air that it's a promotional event they're covering, but cover it they do.

That doesn't absolve you from trying to pitch a genuine news angle, much as you would the newspaper. If you are the author of a book on, say, work stress, and you need a news peg to hang your pitch on, tie it into a broader subject like increased lawsuits stemming from on-the-job stress. You relieve the station from crassly promoting your book, you've given them a news angle, and you'll be the "expert" they interview on the subject.

I mentioned the overwhelming impact of time on the newscast. It's a real concern. Commercial breaks come when they're supposed to come, and any interview, no matter how compelling, will be dumped in a second if the floor director mimes a knife slicing across his throat. However, in another way, time has opened dramatically in television.

Not many years ago, the TV news day lasted at most ninety minutes, from 5:00 to 6:30 P.M. Now, it often starts at 6:00 A.M., continues until 9:00, reappears at noon, breaks until 4:00 P.M., then continues until 7:00. In L.A., one independent station begins its nightly newscast at 8:00 P.M. and ends at 11:00 P.M. Taking the entire day into account, that's a lot of time to fill.

Even though TV news limits the amount of time devoted to one subject (other than "Nightline" or "MacNeil/Lehrer NewsHour" on PBS), the impact is great. As one news director for a local network news operation told me, "Five minutes of undivided attention is better than a distracted glance at a newspaper."

If TV news decides to cover your event, make sure you have the proper contact names at the station, and get direct phone numbers. Going through a main switchboard is like trying to get through to the pope. Make sure your times are synchronized, and meet the crew at the appointed hour.

Escort them where they need to go, but don't be too pushy. These people have done this sort of thing a million times before, and they know what they're doing. Help them get started, then get out of their way.

If you're the one being interviewed, you can finally pat yourself on the back as a full-fledged Guerrilla: you set up your own campaign and made yourself the focal point. But being on camera is an art unto itself, and I address that in detail later in this chapter.

TIPS & TRAPS

* Never call a TV news department in the afternoon. Everyone is getting ready for the broadcast. Always call in the morning.

* Avoid calling during sweeps months (February, May, and November) unless you have something that either feeds their ratings mentality or is genuinely significant news.

* Stunts, like sending custom coffee mugs or showing up at the station dressed in a silly costume, don't work anymore. News personnel are far too busy to watch the parade go by.

* Here's a tip from a news director: the best times to get on TV news are weekends, holidays, and the day after holidays. Business and government offices are closed, making these invariably slow news days. Try to arrange your coverage on those days.

* Weathercasters often mention upcoming local goings-on in their reports, especially charity-related events. Consider that as an option.

The national morning shows are among the crown jewels of desirable publicity outlets. Their audiences number in the many millions, and in some ways the big three—"Today," "Good Morning, America," and "CBS This Morning"—set the tone for the news day around the world. They, like the national network news programs, are also among the most difficult to get on. But as "Good Morning, America" entertainment producer Jane Kaplan notes, "We have two hours of programming each day that must be filled. We're open to anyone who has a good idea."

Approaching the morning shows is not much different from your appeal to any other outlet. Write first, follow up with a call, and get right down to business with the producer you speak with. The key here is framing your story with that universal theme anyone can relate to. If you own a retail outlet and you're offering something unusual to draw customers, tell the morning shows you're demonstrating what one small businessperson can do to combat the recession. If you sell electronic equipment, tell them you're levying your own voluntary symbolic tariff to protest unfair foreign trade practices. This is your chance to go for something grandiose.

What also works for the morning shows, and anyone for that matter, are stories that pack an emotional wallop. Touching medical miracles, odd animal escapades, and gripping scenes of urban violence will always wind up on any news program, morning, noon, or night. If you have some way of pulling on heartstrings to pitch your story, that will help your chances immeasurably.

Public Affairs is a relatively small segment of TV programming, but a significant one. Most licensed television stations devote a percentage of their broadcast time to public affairs. If your project in any way serves the community at large as a social service or local improvement effort, look into P.A. programs as an outlet. They may not devote an entire show to you alone, but as part of a round-up or overall theme, you can be included on a panel.

Regarding cable and public access, many new shows are popping up all over. If you receive cable, study your TV guide for news, infotainment, and public access programs. Watch them and see how and where you might fit in. Small shows are more willing to take chances on lesser-known guests. They aren't always seen by large audiences, but they make for excellent video press kit clips for future use, and they give solid practice for the big time, i.e., the national talk shows. Public access TV is so wide open, you can create your own show and book yourself as sole guest on every segment. Of course, that may be too ambitious for you, but you'd be amazed how many people watch P.A. cable.

As for the infotainment and talk shows, these outlets could turn out to be the most important aspect to your TV campaign. And they're not as hard to get on as you might think. Twenty-five percent of the themes for Sally Jesse Raphael's show come from viewer mail, and I'll bet that statistic holds up for most of the talk shows. You *can* suggest yourself as a guest, and by doing so with artful persistence, you'll be remembered and called on when the theme for the show is right.

One author of a book on men and women wrote to the "Oprah Winfrey Show" with the intriguing hook, "Contrary to popular belief, men do not discriminate. They are equally unethical to both sexes." Soon after, she was kibitzing on the air with Oprah.

As with any other media outlet, before you contact a show, study it. Tape a week's worth. Get a feel for the interests and moods of the host. Read the credits to learn key staff names. Then, contact them the usual way: send a press release and kit, wait a few days, then make your call. I give a few phone numbers in the index, but for a local show, get the number from the broadcasting station. Let me reiterate: don't call them cold. These people are far too busy to talk to strangers, and you will kill your chances of making it on the show if you call before you write.

Once you have sent the material and you're ready to make that call, ask for the producer, assistant producer, talent coordinator, or talent booker by name. These people put together the show and its guest list. Of course the host has input, but he or she usually comes into the process later on. Your first hurdle will be the producers.

By now you know to vary your pitch depending on the outlet. The talk shows need something spicy. I'm not saying you have to falsely inject sex appeal, but you need to find a theme that works for them. If I were pitching the Youth Center, I'd stress the sensational issue of drug-related gang violence. That's an electrifying subject, one that will spark discussion, and can be developed into a theme for a show.

A friend of mine once represented an author of a book on movie flubs. He pitched Geraldo at Academy Award time for a show based on Oscar's greatest goofs. The producer loved it, and the author did the show, selling many books as a result. The key was shaping a theme to fit both the show and the project. But keep in mind, these shows are highly competitive. If Donahue books you, don't expect to appear on Sally the next day. That goes for local shows as well.

If you persuade the producer to book you, your next hurdle is the pre-interview. This is akin to a trial to determine whether you'll prove an interesting guest. As Trisha Daniels of "The Maury Povich Show" says, "The entire on-air segment is based on the pre-interview. I've seen segments canceled because of a bad pre-interview."

Remember, the talk shows don't care about your project; they care about producing a watchable show. If they determine you're not watchable, you're not going on. If they decide you fit the bill, and your project gets a plug, so much the better for you, but it's of no consequence to them. So you have to *pull out all the stops* on the pre-interview.

Whether by phone or in person, imagine your pre-interview is the real thing. Muster all the charm, charisma, eloquence, and insight you can when talking with the producer. Stay focused on the merits of your project or issue. Use every great line in your repertoire. Show humor, intelligence, and, if possible, controversy. They love controversy. If you own a restaurant and you're militantly for or against smokers' rights, let them know. If you're an entertainer and you feel strongly about censorship, express yourself. Don't be afraid of your own convictions. They serve you well on talk-show TV.

IMAGE AND ESSENCE: A TV GUEST PREPARES

Self-improvement books overflow with cute little phrases to help readers remember the authors' infinite wisdom. I begin this discussion with a cute little phrase: SOCO, or *single overriding communications objective.* When discussing your project on TV—or anywhere for that matter—you'll be home free if you boil your message down to its SOCO.

TV is about image, the visual image we see and the intuitive image we sense. Your message should be concise to the point of *haiku* when conveying it on television. Practice by writing two paragraphs defining your project and its aims. Now, cut that by 50 percent. Cut it again by another 50 percent. Continue cutting until you're left with two sentences. Using correct grammar, combine the two into one. That's your SOCO. Everything you say to an interviewer should emanate from this central theme.

With TV, it's not what you say, but how you say it, and how you look when you say it. Ninety-five percent of communication on TV is non-verbal. So demeanor and appearance play an enormous role in communicating your message. When Christine Craft was fired from her anchor position at a local TV news outlet simply because of her less-than-glamour-queen looks, many people were outraged by this seemingly crass and sexist move. I, however, was not. Anchors are paid to read news and attract viewers. If they turn viewers off, they have failed. Usually, in this country, that means a pink slip. I don't condone it; I merely recognize it as a matter of immutable fact.

Not only must the message be compelling, but so must the messenger: you. Most people's analysis of their own social abilities is much too harsh. They perceive deficiencies within, but go overboard in self-criticism. The trick is not to add unfamiliar traits to your

TV personality, but to keep at bay those traits that don't work for the camera. We all conjure this perfect person in our heads, trying to look and sound like Diane Sawyer or Johnny Carson. But we never measure up. I implore you to remove the judgments.

Are you shy and funny? Outspoken and contentious? Serious yet insightful? Don't change who you are. Just withhold the negative traits while accentuating your strong points. Observe TV personalities you admire. They share one common quality: they're relaxed. That's because they're comfortable being who they are. They're settled in. I've met many of them, and off-camera they're remarkably similar to their on-camera persona. Their image mirrors their essence.

All well and good. But how do you then translate that to the experience of being on TV? Keep in mind a few simple rules:

• *Know your material.* How many times will I say it? You should be so prepared—if Regis Philbin woke you in the middle of the night and asked you an obscure question about something remotely connected to your project, you'd immediately be able to answer intelligently! And don't talk in jargon! Speak in plain English.

• *Seek congruence with the interviewer.* The interviewer is the boss, so you have to quickly get a feel for his or her rhythm and direction. Think of the interview as akin to riding a horse. As equestrians adjust their bodies to match the gait of their animal, so should you adjust your attitude to the temperament of the interviewer. If he's rapid-fire, couch your answers in a compatible fashion. If she's probing and antagonistic, appear understanding and forthcoming.

• *Slow down.* If you want to appear edgy and unsure, speak fast. If you want to sound confident and intelligent, speak slowly. I know this is hard to do, because I remember in my early interviews I tended to speak much too rapidly. You have to consciously will yourself to decelerate. If you do, I guarantee you will not only sound more relaxed, you will also feel more relaxed.

• *Be succinct.* The worst thing you can be on TV is a bore. Long-winded answers to questions send viewers running for their clickers. We live in the world of the sound byte, and any answer you give exceeding thirty seconds hasn't been honed properly. That doesn't mean you can't tell a good story or that you should carry a stopwatch, but do practice brevity. By the same token, one- or two-word responses don't work either. You have to be articulate as well as to the point.

• *Emphasize the positive.* Whether you espouse a controversial view or not, be upbeat. Find areas of agreement with the interviewer, the panel, and the audience. Don't let them put words in your mouth, and don't oversell your project; but look for ways to stay on the bright side. If asked negative questions, answer the question you would rather the host had asked.

• *Don't panic.* If things become nasty, stay calm. Avoid talking over your host, but if he is really going for the jugular, go ahead and lay it on thick. Talk back, talk over him, give 'em hell. The host knows the audio track will sound hopelessly scrambled if two or more people talk at the same time. I promise you, to avoid viewer tune-out he will eventually shut up, and you can have your say. But, if all else fails, and you're being unfairly abused, walk off. Society is built on mutual respect, and if someone refuses to offer that, what are you doing there?

• *Relate to the audience.* Barring white supremacists, adulterers, and murderous babysitters, I find most talk-show guests generally win the sympathy of the audience. Overall, the audiences don't have the heart to attack guests as the hosts can, although they will if provoked. Look the audience in the eye, and be forthcoming with answers. You can win them over. Confidence is a must, but a spoonful of humility doesn't hurt either.

• *Go with the flow.* As carefully scripted as these shows are in theory, once the cameras roll, anything can happen. My friend Randi Gelfand, the talent coordinator at "The Joan Rivers Show," tells the story of a guest appearance by Angela Bowie (ex-wife of rock star David Bowie). Apparently, Angela was less than forthcoming about her wild life in the world of rock and roll. New York DJ Howard Stern, who was a guest earlier in the hour, spontaneously came back to the set, and showered Angela with shocking tabloid-style questions, getting her to open up about her sordid past. Angela was ready for anything, and so should you.

A WORD ON COACHING

Media coaching is a rapidly growing industry. Entertainers, corporate executives, politicians, clergy, and regular folks are lining up to learn how to behave in front of the camera. A friend of mine in this business prefers the term "image consulting" because her advice is applicable in any public situation, not just with the media.

Although image consulting can be helpful, it's often beyond the scope of Guerrilla P.R. The cost can run into the thousands, though some offer one- or two-hour make-overs for considerably less. They usually entail a quick diagnosis of the subject's personality and an audition on videotape. If you have the money, one of these sessions could prove valuable. Otherwise, use your own camcorder or even the mirror, and do your own "image consulting." I think you can objectively size yourself up, and make the necessary adjustments. Here are a few pointers:

TIPS & TRAPS

* Wear soft dark colors, minimal patterns, monotone outfits, but never whites, which "bleach" out skin tones. Avoid shiny accessories or clacking earrings and bracelets. The rule-of-thumb is "mirror your audience," meeting the dress standards of the group before whom you appear.

* Acknowledge your nervousness before you go on. If your shoulders are up above your ears, it's time to do some shoulder rolls. A certain amount of nerves is good, because it gets the adrenaline flowing, but you shouldn't focus on your jitters.

* Once on-camera, sit straight, hands folded in your lap, but don't be frozen in one position. Small movements are indeed exaggerated on the tube, but withholding movement, hiding, takes an enormous amount of energy. Relaxation is the key.

* Look at the interviewer, *not* the camera.

* Never interrupt unless, as I said before, you're being unfairly dominated or talked over.

* There are no bad questions, only bad answers.

* Shape your answers to sound personal rather than dry and technical. You really don't have to impress anyone with your intellect.

* Nervous before you go on? Try visualization of serene settings or deep breathing. Once you're on, imagine the set is your own living room and you're just having a conversation with an acquaintance.

Guerrilla P.R. means selling yourself as well as your project. The two are inseparable. TV offers you the best chance of cementing the connection. A successful TV campaign will set the stage for enticing future opportunities, because if you become a show's regular "expert" on a given topic, you will have devised a P.R. annuity that keeps paying dividends for a long time.

MEDIA FACTS

• 93.1 million U.S. households have at least one television (that's 98 percent of us).

• 91.3 million of them have color TV.

• 56 million American households currently receive cable.

• VCR sales in 1990 totaled 10 million units.

• There are 1,527 TV stations in the United States: 691 VHF and 836 UHF. Of those, 314 are public stations and 1,186 are commercial.

• The typical household tunes in to TV 48.5 hours a week.

• The average cost of a prime-time 30-second TV commercial is $122,000.

• The top cable networks are: (1) ESPN (55.9 million subscribers); (2) CNN (54.4 million); (3) TBS Superstation (54 million); (4) USA Network (51.5 million); (5) Nickelodeon (50 million); (6) MTV (50.4

million); (7) Nashville Network (50 million); (8) C-Span (49.7 million); (9) Discover Channel (49.7 million); and (10) Family Channel (49.1 million).

MAKING RADIO WAVES

All this talk about TV skirted one obvious issue: with television, you almost always have to go to them. The national morning shows can send a crew to interview you if need be, but if you want to hit the major U.S. cities with a TV blitz, you're going to have to buy a fistful of airline tickets to hit each town, a nice way to blow your entire Guerrilla P.R. budget. However, this isn't so with radio.

From the comfort of your own bedroom, you can do forty radio interviews across the country in a couple of days, covering as much if not more ground than with television. Radio is clearly the easiest and least expensive method for reaching a maximum number of people. Unlike TV, there are practically no boundaries on radio in terms of taste and subject matter (not that TV talk shows are all that tasteful). I once heard a morning talk-radio segment devoted to the issue of Asian immigrants capturing and eating neighborhood dogs. The show was known as "The Breakfast Edition."

Radio, especially the Guerrilla P.R.–rich target of talk radio, is ever on the lookout for controversy, for something different. If it ties in with the news of the day, great. It was talk radio that a few years ago launched a nationwide campaign to mail in teabags to congress-men contemplating a hefty pay raise for themselves. People *are* listening out there.

Most cities have at least one talk-radio show. Some are nationally broadcast, like Tom Snyder and Rush Limbough, who are heard by astronomical numbers of people (up to half a million at any given quarter hour). Getting on radio is easier than getting on TV, although it's never a cakewalk. Many of the same rules apply, i.e., know the show you're pitching, send written material first, find out the name of the producer. But you do have more latitude because you're free of the visual component.

One effective way of reaching talk-radio producers is to submit your name and project to *Newsmaker Interviews*, a publication sub-scribed to by dozens of radio stations across the country. In its simple format, potential guests and their topics are described in detail, with a contact name and number listed at the bottom.

I urge you to send your information to *Newsmaker Interviews* (see details in Appendix). Otherwise, you'll need to track down the myriad talk-radio shows across the country. Some published listings do exist. Try *Radio & Records*, a respected industry trade newspaper based in Los Angeles. They have a comprehensive talk-radio section and editor, as well as published specials on the format. I list R&R in the appendix as well.

Whether you're shooting for a local, regional, or national talk-radio campaign, once you've nailed down your contacts, keep these pointers in mind:

• Most producers get their ideas from the other media like newspapers and TV, and *not* from publicists or direct appeals. It's wise to link your idea with some other current item in the news.

• Like other media producers, talk-radio producers are extremely overworked. Because they don't really cover breaking news like TV and newspaper journalists, they may not be as accessible. Be persistent. Eventually you'll hear back from them.

• Talk-radio producers and hosts really like controversy. Maybe you have a new theory of nutrition that says fat and cholesterol are healthy in the diet. That'll get you on the air very quickly. Talk radio is America's contemporary version of the soapbox in the town square, and anyone can climb on top of it.

• Demonstrate you know the show by mentioning something you heard on the air recently, and perhaps tie that in with your pitch.

As a Guerrilla, you want maximum exposure, so I recommend linking as many radio shows as possible in a given amount of time. Set a goal of, say, five shows, five cities, within two weeks. It will not only help your P.R. effort, but will vastly improve your skills as an interview subject.

Once you're asked to go on the air, you may do the interview in the studio or by phone at home. If the station is in your area, try to go down there. That way you meet the staff face to face, and grease the wheels for possible future appearances. Otherwise, doing the interview by phone is just fine.

Usually, the producer will call you and hook you into a special extension. You'll hear the show over the line, and within a few minutes you'll be introduced. *You don't have to be nervous.* It's just like talking to a friend. Obviously you want to keep your language clean and diction clear. This is an audio medium, so modulate your speaking tone to give your voice a little more color, and keep answers concise.

Take your cues from the host/interviewer. He or she calls the shots. Never interrupt the host or step on his or her words. Apply what you've learned about steering the conversation, but keep that deference to the host in mind. Unlike TV, they can cut you off in a second. One nice thing about radio: because you're "invisible" you can jot down notes to yourself while on the air to remind yourself of other points you want to make.

Media consultant Peggy Klaus urges her clients to "make a fan" of the microphone. "I tell them to imagine someone they love and who loves them is sitting there just dying to get the information," she says. "This helps elevate the enthusiasm in the voice."

As with print, you should collect your radio "clips," i.e., record your appearances, and assemble a little cassette of your best sound bites. You can use this as part of an "audio press kit" to help line up future radio appearances.

Even if your talk-radio show efforts fizzle this time, don't give up on radio. You can always call in to the talk-radio show as a regular citizen. You can cloak your call around some current event, but there's no reason why you can't slip in commentary related to your project.

All radio stations have community affairs programming, and even pop-music DJs announce upcoming events. Check with local stations to see how and when to submit press releases for announcement. Speaking of DJs, many stations have loony morning and afternoon announcers who throw into their shows every crass and crazy concept they can dream up. If you have the right personality, you just might fit in with your local shock jock.

Every station has a news department, and though they're microscopic compared to TV, don't neglect them. Sending a press release only costs a stamp. A single mention on the air may not have a dramatic impact, but taken cumulatively, radio is a superb outlet. You reach more people in one shot than you do with the average newspaper, and it's easier to obtain than a TV appearance. Radio is America's clearinghouse of ideas, so step up to the mike!

FROM THE GUERRILLA P.R. FILE

In 1990, California celebrated the twentieth anniversary of the personalized license plate. One car-car company sponsored its own star search for the best vanity plate in the nation. The winners included "04A4RE," found on a Pennsylvania Honda; OUT50GZ seen on the back of a Mercedes-Benz; and the grand prize winner adorning the rear bumper of a frenzied movie executive "IM2BZ2P."

COMPUTERIZE YOURSELF

If this book were being written ten years ago, this section would not have been included, but that's how fast personal computers have changed the landscape. Although not free, another novel way of gaining publicity is to have your project mentioned on a computer bulletin board system, or BBS. Thousands of people subscribe to services like Prodigy, CompuServe, and The Source, and you might find them a very useful resource.

These BBS's post an amazing array of information, from simple announcements to controversial opinions. It's like a high-tech CB radio on which any subscriber can air his or her feelings or news. Although there are many hundreds of BBS's, if you're serious about this, sign up with one of the commercial on-line companies, such as the ones mentioned above. They offer such features as electronic mail, databases, even on-line conferencing.

Even though it costs to join the service, posting bulletins is free to members. Someday most Americans will be linked up with one service or another, but you might not want to wait for someday.

GUERRILLA P.R. COMMANDOS: LUKE DOMMER

"Having had more guns pointed at me than I can count, I knew I was fighting a cultural value system," recalled the late Luke Dommer, founder of CASH (Committee to Abolish Sport Hunting) and crusader on behalf of American wildlife. By passionately taking on a cherished institution, Luke embarked on a long-term struggle that took him face-to-face with angry hunters, a well-organized gun lobby, and the ire of America's macho faction, all the while fighting a losing battle with the cancer that recently took his life.

A burly ex-Marine and ace marksman, Dommer made a good living as a graphic artist before recognizing the devastating impact society wreaked on the environment. He chose to devote his life to preserving life on the planet, relying on old training for guidance. "I looked at this from a military point of view," said Dommer. "First, you reconnoiter the enemy and find the weakest point in his line. I determined hunting was the weakest link in the chain of animal and ecological abuses."

Working on his own, Luke established CASH and filed a series of lawsuits to stop hunting in New York state parks. His actions drew the fury of hunters, whom he credited with his first P.R. successes. "They're the ones that promoted me," said Luke. "I was routinely written about in hunting magazines, and when the lawsuits began, I was naturally the one the media contacted for comment."

Luke also had himself listed in the "Directory of Experts, Authorities, and Spokespersons," a bible for talk-show producers. Soon he was appearing on radio and TV, first regionally, and later nationally. He wrote articles for op-ed pages and magazines, printed in such publications as *USA Today*, the *New York Times*, the *Philadelphia Inquirer*, and animal rights tracts. He was written up in *Omni* magazine and newspapers in communities where hunting was an issue.

Because he sold himself as a genuine expert, Luke cornered the market in his field. He debated more hunters than anyone else, and appeared on at least 400 radio and TV programs since 1976. One lesson he learned: let a belligerent opponent ride roughshod over you. "I had one guy interrupt me, be rude to me on a talk show," Luke recalled in his interview with me in 1991. "He got lots of complaining letters, even from hunters."

Years of experience taught Luke much about the nature of

media. "I had to reach beyond the animal rights movement and give the mass media a logical reason to look at sport hunting," he noted. Luke didn't believe Guerrillas should look for too much too soon. "I believe in starting at the first rung of the ladder," he told me. "You gain experience gradually on your way to the top. For example, don't go on a show you can't handle. Eventually, like me you make it to the top of the ladder."

Luke enjoyed doing his own media campaign. "I reach more people than anyone else in the movement," he said. "It doesn't cost the animals a dime. My opponents spend millions each year on propaganda, but the media I've done came because they called me."

Luke continued his struggle, knowing full well he might not see his dream of the abolition of hunting in his lifetime. "Scientists predict we may lose another million species of plant and animal life in the next ten years," he noted somberly. "There's a continuum of death going on. But whatever I do, when I weigh it against the universe, I know I'm just a speck. But seeing this become a national issue after fourteen years of sacrifice has been my greatest reward."

The world will miss Luke Dommer, one of the best Guerrilla P.R. masters I have ever encountered.

7

RESERVE AMMO: PRESS CONFERENCES, PARTIES, AND MORE

If people around you will not hear you, fall down before them and beg their forgiveness, for in truth you are to blame.

—FYODOR DOSTOYEVSKY

THE PRESS CONFERENCE

It's a publicist's dream come true: assembled under one roof, the cream of the national media—TV, print, radio, wire services—gathered together to hear a special announcement from you. That night, every station in town runs a piece, and the next morning, every newspaper carries a story and photo taken at the conference. It's the ultimate high.

In reality, few press conferences (or "news conferences" as they're sometimes called) are ever as well attended as hoped. But we keep staging them because they remain one of the most efficient ways to disseminate information to media. When they go well, you experience a powerful feeling of accomplishment.

Although they're a staple of the professional publicist, Guerrillas should not devote an inordinate amount of energy to press conferences. For one thing, they are often boring and are way too respectable. Guerrillas stir things up, and unless you plan an audacious event, a p.c. may be too tame a tactic.

For another thing, media people resent turning out for any event that imparts information that could just as easily have been mailed in press release form. But, despite the risks, the press conference can be an important weapon in your arsenal. So here's what you need to know.

The central function of a p.c. is to announce and exhibit something specific: Marla Maples is named No Excuses Jeans' butt-of-the-month; Michael Jackson heads out on tour; General Motors phases out gasoline-powered cars in favor of non-polluting electric engines (I can dream, can't I?). P.c.'s are often cut and dry, and though the media ask questions, the inquiries are usually limited to the subject at hand.

You don't do a press conference to announce how happy you are to be in business, or tell the world your product is simply maaahvelous, or that you're in favor of more money for AIDS research. A p.c. has to scream a headline; otherwise, skip it. If you have something clear-cut and enticing to present to the media en masse, terrific! Consider a press conference, but brace yourself. Most likely, media people won't give a darn. Making them care enough to attend is your main task.

Start by sending out a special press release/invitation. Tease them by holding one or two details back while alluding to a surprise. Be dramatic. A touch of theater doesn't hurt, since a p.c. is by definition theatrical. You have a stage, performers, and an active audience. So make your invitations inviting. Here's a sample:

PRESS CONFERENCE   April 17, 1993
PRESS CONFERENCE
PRESS CONFERENCE

LANCEL CORPORATION TO ANNOUNCE NEW POLLUTION-FREE
AUTOMOBILE ENGINE

The goal of creating affordable non-polluting transportation will take a giant leap forward when Lancel Corporation unveils its new Paracel A-1 automobile engine *at a press conference to be held May 5 at the Lancel Manufacturing Plant in Norwood*. With manufacturing orders from the Big 3 automakers already in hand, Lancel predicts the solar-powered Paracel A-1 will revolutionize the automobile industry.

Speaking at the press conference will be Lancel president Mitchell Barlow and chief designer Evita Cheslow, who will demonstrate the engine's capabilities and answer questions.

WHAT: Press conference announcing Paracel A-1 solar automobile engine.

WHEN: May 5, 1993 at 9:00 A.M.

WHERE: Lancel Corporation, 4567 Geary Ave., Norwood

PHOTO OPPORTUNITY: Design staff, executive staff, prototypes of engine will be available

CONTACT: John Jones
213-999-1111

Mail your invitations no later than two weeks beforehand. It's one thing to send a press release and follow up with a call. That's no skin off anyone's back. But to ask a news organization to dispatch a reporter or crew to a p.c. is asking a great deal more, so you have to give them time. Make follow-up calls a few days after you send the invite and see if you get any nibbles.

In these conversations, build on the excitement. Will there be any special guests? Will there be any kind of unexpected stunt? Will you bring on dancing girls or barking seals? Whatever it may be, make an effort to tease the media, to spark their curiosity. Then, call again two days before the event and one more time early on the day of the event for final confirmations of attendance.

Timing is important. Did you notice I scheduled the conference for early in the morning? That's important, so journalists can attend and still meet any of their regular deadlines. Location and setting are also important. It should be held somewhere easy to reach for the media in your area. Indoors at a hotel conference room. Your company parking lot. Your front lawn. If you're demonstrating some kind of cause, say an anti-drug message, how about holding the p.c. in front of a school with a known drug problem? If it's for an upcoming homelessness charity, go to skid row to dramatize the problem. Think in terms of visuals that may heighten the dramatic effect.

Make sure you also provide food and adult drinks. It may sound petty, but the media expect to be fed, so pop for refreshments. Other amenities to consider are easy and free parking, availability of telephones, restrooms, and seating. See that there are electrical outlets for TV lights if your p.c. is held indoors, and place the cameras in the back of the room. And make sure, for photographic purposes, the background behind the lectern or dais is plain and simple—a curtain or unadorned wall will do fine.

Once assembled, hand the media any additional materials necessary to put together a full and accurate story, such as an updated press release, press kit, etc. Begin on time, and don't drag it out. You may feel nervous performing before so many people, but if you're prepared you have nothing to worry about (sound familiar?).

Your opening remarks should be concise and to the point, recapping the information in your press release. Visual aids are a plus (à la General Schwartzkopf in his masterful post–Gulf War press conference). These add color and reinforce your message. If other people are due to speak, move them right along. Everyone should make his or her presentation, and then open up the floor to questions.

As in so many aspects of this business, the best-laid plans often get turned on their head. If you can stay loose with it, though, you may come out all right. I recall one incident in which my client Dr. Joyce Brothers was in town to attend a press conference. The night before, she had left her shoes in the hotel hallway to be picked up for shining. The hotel lost her shoes and, because of time constraints, she was forced to attend the p.c. in her stocking feet. Turned out she got more coverage because of that than for anything else that day.

The key to answering questions is preparation. Before a presidential news conference the chief executive runs through a series of mock questions so that he can be ready for any inquiry. You should do the same.

In one-on-one interviews elsewhere, you may turn off the tape and say something off the record, but not at a gathering like a p.c. Everything done and said at a press conference is on the record. So be careful not to mention anything you don't want discussed or reported.

In fact be careful about what you say, period. You know the expression about the camera never blinking. Microphones are equally vigilant. The way you express yourself can determine whether you have a positive, neutral, or negative impact on the media and the public. Even the president of the United States has to watch what he says. In the 1992 election race, George Bush was overheard making some rather incomprehensible remarks to voters in New Hampshire while the cameras rolled. I quote them verbatim:

Somebody said we prayed for you over there. That was not just because I threw up on the prime minister of Japan either. Where was he when I needed him? But I said, Let me tell you something. And I say this. I don't know whether any ministers from the Episcopal Church are here. I hope so. But I said to him this. You're on to something here. You cannot be president of the United States if you don't have faith. Remember Lincoln, going to his knees in times of trial in the Civil War and all that stuff? You can't be. And we're blessed.

I include this not out of disrespect for George Bush, but to show how easy it is, when we speak off the cuff, to fail to convey what we mean. When you're "on" during the p.c., you are on, and everything you say can and will be scrutinized.

Once the conference is over, stick around for any informal follow-up questions the press may have. It's a good idea for you to tape the event to check for media accuracy, as well as study your own performance. If it goes well, ideally this first press conference won't be your last.

FROM THE GUERRILLA P.R. FILE

To make its own kind of statement about fighting the recession (and, not coincidentally, to gain some favorable P.R.) the *Boston Globe*, the Hub city's major daily paper, began offering in March of 1992 free situation-wanted ads submitted during a limited time by unemployed individuals. More than 500 submissions a day flooded the paper, with the *Globe* promising to keep the campaign up until every single ad has run.

LET'S PARTY

People think we Hollywood types spend our days doing lunch and our nights attending parties. Well, they're right. Only we don't have any fun doing it. Actually, parties are one of the best ways to spread goodwill, good cheer, and good P.R. At most parties, few people overtly discuss business, yet a lot seems to get done. That's because in America, everybody wants to feel like he or she has tapped into the Good Life, and a party invitation is the quintessential membership card.

Why throw a party? Perhaps you're celebrating the expansion of a business, the release of a new product, the arrival of an honored guest, or the beginning of a new campaign. Parties get things off to a festive start, and media people, if not the media themselves, love them. Unless there are celebrities in attendance, parties don't often get direct media coverage, but I believe in their efficacy as wheel-greasers.

As a Guerrilla, you don't want to spend a lot of money. The good news is it's definitely possible to mount a successful party on the cheap. All you need are the bare necessities: food, drink, music, and people. Start by making your invitation alluring. Make people want to come. Whom to invite? Your network, business associates, some friends, any media people you've become acquainted with, and even some you may not know.

Though you don't want anything like a kiddie party, consider attaching a theme to your affair. Whether a color scheme, or a consistency in the decor, dress, music, or food, make your party an event by giving it thematic structure. How about a sixties party, with blacklight posters and Jimi Hendrix music? How about something Oriental, where the guests must first remove their shoes before hitting the sushi table?

Pamper your guests. Washington diplomatist hostess Perle Mesta used to say the secret to a successful party is in the greetings and good-byes. When each of her guests arrived she would say, "At last you're here," and when they departed, "I'm sorry you have to leave so soon." Keep food lines short, supply ample, and make sure guests know where the restrooms are.

As for you, you're a Guerrilla, so mix it up. Work the room, visiting as many people as you can. Concentrate on the individual you're talking to, listen carefully, and don't let your eyes wander from the other person's. Feel free to move on when the conversation has run its course. Go into it with a burst of energy and leave when the energy fades. Try lines like "Excuse me, but I see someone I haven't seen in ages," or "I think I'll try one of these hors d'oeuvres." They sure have worked for me.

If you see people you don't recognize, introduce yourself with a smile. A friendly face will break the ice, and, as I've said, a handshake can be as important to your public relations as a packed press conference.

Above all, remember a party is not the place to conduct serious business. Take numbers, exchange cards, make promises, but keep the conversation—and the party—on a spirited note. If feasible, grab a microphone, make a toast, thank people for attending. Mention your project in brief, but don't distract your guests from their pleasure. If your project was the reason they came, they'll remember the next day, and the next.

TIPS & TRAPS

* Don't overdo the tables and chairs. People tend to cluster at parties and not spread out. With less places to sit, more partygoers will mingle. It can be risky, but sometimes you end up with a fantastic party that way.

* Have enough help on hand to handle things. Whether you hire people or have friends and family helping out, make sure they dress appropriately, know what they're doing, and keep things running smoothly and unobtrusively. You don't want guests to feel burdened or neglected.

* Plan surprises. Midway through the proceedings, stage some kind of novel event involving the project. Don't let it go on too long, but definitely make this a key part of the evening.

* Timing for a party is tricky. If you plan it for mid-week, many working people (including media) are too tired to come out. If it's on a weekend, oftentimes people prefer to do other things. Consider carefully.

* If you can't remember the name of the person you're greeting, extend your hand and say your name. The other will likely do the exact same thing.

* Lighten up! Once the party begins it takes on a life of its own. Just go with it and have a good time.

MONKEY-WRENCHING

This section is not for everyone. It's not even for me. But being Guerrillas, some of you may have projects that require bold action. If your project involves a political or social cause you believe in strongly, there may be times when you need to go a step beyond the mainstream to bolster your P.R. profile. Sometimes those steps involve walking a line dangerously close to law breaking, something I do not *in any way* advocate. But I'm not against the concept of tantalizing the media with the potential for controversy or confrontation.

I cherish our right to protest, even when I don't agree with the protesters. Though most Americans give lip service to that right, some get uptight over the sight of angry demonstrators and picket signs. That's understandable. As the L.A. riots in 1992 showed, sometimes the line is crossed from legitimate protest to civil insurrection. Most of us prefer to go about our lives without having other people's concerns thrust in our faces, especially if we don't agree. But America is a great country precisely because we have the right to protest. As a Guerrilla, you may wish to take advantage of that right to engage the media, thus furthering your cause.

Don't be torn because you think you're just "using" the media to draw attention. The media are as jaded as can be, but they know a good story when they smell it. If you mount a demonstration over some scurrilous local abuses, and you get a significant volume of people to join you, let the media know.

A few guidelines: Don't give too much advance warning. Unlike other events, a protest has to seem spontaneous, a convulsive expression of the will of the people. If the media smell friction, they'll be there, you can be sure. I'd say forty-eight hours' notice should suffice.

When you call, let the assignment editor know you're in charge. When the crew arrives at your protest site, introduce yourself, hand the reporter or producer your literature, offer yourself as an interview subject, and help them get situated. Make your protest noisy and passionate. Have colorful signs with cogent slogans carried by your comrades. Most such protests are completely peaceful and tolerant. Occasionally not so, especially if you draw counter-protesters. A shouting match between opposing sides of an issue always makes great copy, or great video for the evening news.

If, unfortunately, law enforcement is involved, only you can decide how far you want to take things. As we saw with the anti-abortion protests in Wichita during the summer of 1991, sometimes things get out of hand. For true believers, the threat of arrest is no obstacle. That's a decision you have to make on your own. But I don't recommend it. Jail food stinks and it's tough getting fingerprint ink off your hands.

You also run the risk of being branded a publicity seeker. Personally, I have nothing against that. After all, that's what I do, but you know how people think. Anybody in the public eye, championing a cause, is subject to derision, and usually he or she is blamed for cunning in gaining the media spotlight. There's a price to pay no matter what you do in life; in my opinion, you're better off opting for wider media exposure. That way, your message will get out to the people. Otherwise, you can sit at home with your scruples and shout your slogans at the TV screen.

PSA'S AND EDITORIAL REPLIES

Part of your Guerrilla P.R. campaign is the effort to establish yourself as an expert in your field. One way to do that is to take advantage of public service announcements (PSA's) and editorial replies. All television stations that broadcast editorials (and most do) are required to provide airtime to opposing points of view. They are also required to devote a certain portion of their programming to PSA's, which are, in effect, free commercials on matters of public interest.

If you see an editorial that in some way relates to your project, consider contacting the station to respond. Editorial replies provide an opportunity to have your face and name broadcast across the city and further solidify your expert standing. To make this happen, contact the news department at the station and ask for the editorial director. Tell him or her you represent citizens with an opposing view and you'd like to reply. Send information on yourself and your project, such as your press kit.

If they give you the green light, you'll be informed of the parameters. You'll probably have sixty seconds to make your point.

When writing your reply, think in bursts of quick three-sentence paragraphs, with your opening comments being the most potent. Begin by summarizing the station's view and stating why they're dead wrong. Detail a handful of reasons, again expressed in short easy-to-understand phrases. Close by urging a different direction, chiding the station for taking its position. That's it! You're a politician now!

As for PSA's, both TV and radio stations make available air time with a ten- or thirty-second "commercial" for your project if it's a bona fide charity or message of cultural, medical, or safety interest to the community. Contact your local stations' community affairs department, explain your mission, and inquire whether you can make a PSA.

Because you have such an extreme time limitation, you must make your points quickly and effectively. Approach the writing of your PSA as if it were a TV commercial, that is, you must leave a strong impression on the viewers or listeners.

TIPS & TRAPS

* *Start out with a bang.* You must grab your audience from the outset, and the best way to do that is with a punchy and arresting lead sentence or two. Watch and listen for other PSA's and you'll see what I mean.

* *Stay focused.* With only thirty or sixty seconds, you have time to make only one main point with a couple of illustrations. Don't lose sight of your main point.

* For TV, *provide interesting visuals for use as backdrop.*

* Most PSA's are read by on-air announcers, whether TV or radio. That being the case, *you must have a well-crafted script.* Write it with very narrow margins, and be sure to time it before you send it in. Obviously, you must include your name, address, and phone number, just as with a regular press release.

TRADE SHOWS AND CONVENTIONS

It's a common sight. Bikini-clad co-eds reclining on car rooftops or demonstrating some new Japanese techno-toy; famous athletes signing autographs for the mobs crowding the floors of large convention halls; spectacular sets with all kinds of electronic bells and whistles on display. The trade show is a modern-day carnival of commerce, and there's not an industry in America that doesn't stage one of its own. When the next convention comes to town, the wise Guerrilla should seriously consider a preemptive strike.

Trade shows, such as the annual Consumer Electronics Show in Las Vegas, and conventions, like the National Association of Theatre Owners, a movie business conclave, bring together under one enormous roof virtually everyone who's anyone in a given industry. It's the perfect setting for gladhanding, politicking, protesting, viewing what's new in the industry's products, making a scene, making a friend, or just plain learning.

My friends Sandy and Howard Benjamin, when launching their independent celebrity radio interview business, descended upon the National Association of Broadcasters annual get-together, and plastered the place with flyers, and remained, as they put it, "in their faces" for the entire three days. It got their fledgling company off to a good start.

If you have the wherewithal to travel to a convention in your line of work, do so. It's worth the registration fee to mingle with your own and to test whether your Guerrilla P.R. plan has merit. Use a touch of showmanship, salesmanship, and marksmanship to score your points. These events are people, not media, oriented. They provide you with a perfect opportunity to practice your personal P.R. skills.

When get-togethers are held in hotels, many corporate participants open up their suites to all visitors. Work these rooms. Make friends, expand your network, make an impression. This is P.R. on the micro-scale, rather than the macro-scale, but it is no less important. Any one of those conventioneers could be the person to turn your business around, open a new door, or offer an unexpected opportunity. There's something about the convivial atmosphere that lends itself to solidifying relationships with colleagues. Take advantage.

Sometimes you can strike gold in other settings. Jerry Porter, president of Metrospace Corporation, a large commercial real estate consulting firm, makes a point of landing new clients by attending shareholders' meetings. If he isn't a stockholder, he simply buys a few shares of stock, entitling him entry to the annual shareholders' shouting-match (sometimes). Says Jerry, "While the company puts on its dog-and-pony show and the executives are shmoozing with the people, I'm out there greeting them, shaking hands, and scheduling follow-up meetings." Now, that's clever.

GOOD WORKS

I don't care if it sounds crass to you, but being a Good Samaritan is good for business. Those individuals and companies that do charity work go a long way in cementing a positive image within their surrounding community. I believe it's important for you too to weigh your options in this area.

Sometimes this can indeed become crass. I recall the cynical manager of a famous pop musician who called me in a desperate search of a charity outlet for her artist, because he'd recently been mentioned in unfavorable press accounts linking him with drugs and alcohol. She thought a picture of her wigged-out guitar player giving a teddy bear to a terminally ill child would solve her artist's problems.

I'm not talking about that kind of thing.

I'm talking about top sports agent Leigh Steinberg who, before he negotiates the contract of an NFL or major league rookie, has the athlete set down on paper the extent of his charitable works. If the athlete doesn't commit to extensive charity appearances and donations, Steinberg won't represent him.

I'm talking about the corporate blood drives, where a factory parking lot is turned into a temporary sea of gurneys, with employees rolling up their sleeves to give a unit of blood. I'm talking about sponsoring a fundraiser for Jerry's Kids, or organizing a litter pick-up. I'm talking about the San Diego donut shop that regularly gives away thousands of day-old donuts to mission rescues and halfway houses.

I believe business is inextricably linked with the well-being of the community, and as a matter of simple justice, it is incumbent upon us to help make this a better world, whether we receive much publicity for our efforts or not. At the same time, I have no problem with making sure the rest of the world knows about it.

If you were to sponsor a similar charitable effort—say a 10K run for cancer research, or a turkey dinner for the homeless—it's beneficial to all for the media to be informed and to cover the event. You gain better employee and citizen involvement, you spread the word that such activities are worthwhile, and you gain that all-important positive public perception of you and your company or project, even if the P.R. you get from it is relatively narrow-focused.

How about a holiday tie-in? Andy Lipkis of TreePeople sponsored an urban beautification tree planting on Martin Luther King Jr. Day in Los Angeles. Do you have out-of-date computer equipment in your office? Why sell it when you can reap much greater P.R. benefits by giving it away to your neighborhood elementary school? Is it feasible to have schools visit and tour your operations? Can you provide employment or intern opportunities to area youth? Did you ever consider sponsoring the preservation of a nearby historical landmark?

These kinds of projects are so easy to do. If you're not sure how to proceed, try hooking up with established charities like the Red Cross or the American Cancer Society. With their vast experience, they can help you organize and publicize your event (unless, being the Guerrilla publicist that you are, you opt to do that yourself). The main thing is, you're helping to repair the world just a little bit. And like I said, that's good for business.

SPEECHMAKING

It was one of the highlights of my life. Standing before an assembly of graduate students at the Harvard Business School, I delivered a lecture, stating my observations about the current business climate. As I spoke I thought to myself, "Imagine, me, who never finished college, addressing America's best and brightest."

I concluded my remarks that day with a wonderful quote from author H. G. Wells: "Some ideas are so stupid, only intellectuals believe them." Several hundred future captains of industry leaped to their feet, cheering my words. Clearly, I had struck a nerve.

Giving speeches ties in with our oldest and greatest human legacy, that of oral communication. All P.R., indeed all of human communications, technological and otherwise, is simply an extension of it.

In this day and age, too many people have unfortunately mangled the meaning of the word "rhetoric." Politicians and pundits use the term to mean insincere blather, deliberate obfuscation, or, in plain English, ka-ka. Yet "rhetoric" actually means the fine use of spoken language. It is a lost art; indeed the very word to describe it is lost. But I don't want it to get lost on you. Hitting the speakers' trail can be one of the very best adjuncts to your Guerrilla P.R. campaign strategy.

Even though your reach per audience is much smaller with speechmaking than it is with media, you shouldn't underestimate the impact. There are drawbacks to conventional press exposure. Someone leafing through a newspaper might spot an article about you and your project, give it a passing glance, or perhaps even read the entire piece, and then, with the turn of a page, move on to the next article. In a flash, you're yesterday's news.

Not so with public speaking. In such a setting you have the full undivided attention of an audience ostensibly there to hear you speak. If you deliver a strong speech, the effect can linger far longer than in many other forms of P.R.

Do you have anything to say? The answer is "yes." If you are the owner of a business, you can address business gatherings on the subject of your specific industry, or on general business topics. If you are in a specialized field, such as medicine, education, law, entertainment, or sports, you can set yourself up as a perceptive insider. What you think matters; you'd be surprised just how expert in your field you probably are already.

Getting a forum for your public speaking career isn't as hard as you may think. Schools, churches and synagogues, health care facilities, business clubs like Rotary, Kiwanis, and Chamber of Commerce, seminars, conventions, political clubs, and many others all use and are in constant need of speakers. Speakers' bureaus abound. Find them and offer yourself. You do not need extensive prior experience to sign up with a speakers' bureau—only a willingness to present your ideas.

If your only public speaking experience is limited to your bar mitzvah or the fifth grade Thanksgiving pageant, fear not. It's not as terrifying as you remember. I don't want to take too much space in this book to teach the art of speechmaking, but a few choice tips are in order.

TIPS AND TRAPS

* Before you make that speech, you need to know a few things about the venue and your audience. James Robinson, in his terrific volume, *Winning Them Over*, suggests you find out how much time you've been given to speak; when you're expected to arrive; how the evening's program is to be structured; will a lectern and a p.a. system be in place; who will introduce you; and will there be a Q&A period after the speech. Knowing just what to expect will help you to relax.

* Write out your speech completely. Even if you prefer to work without a script and appear spontaneous, you should put down on paper the gist of your remarks. It will help orient you. If you choose to work with a script, transfer the speech to 3 × 5 cards in large type. Cards are easy to work with and fit easily into your pocket.

* If given a choice of short speech or long, opt for the short. Unless you're a mesmerizing orator, going on too long is the kiss of death. As a rule-of-thumb, I'd say twenty minutes maximum.

* Use simple, plain English, full of action and rhythm. Keep the ten-cent words for your college theses. At the same time, don't be afraid to draw on your natural eloquence. You may not be Martin Luther King, Jr., but it's all right to take advantage of our beautiful language.

* This is one bit of advice you probably already know: lace your speech with humor. Levity loosens up a room and makes you instantly more likeable. Humor sourcebooks for speechmakers and toastmasters abound in the library.

* Making a speech can be nerve-wracking, and often the voice tends to rise. Be aware, and try to keep your voice in the mid-range.

* Join Toastmasters, an organization devoted to making you adept at public speaking. It's a great investment of your time.

GUERRILLA P.R. COMMANDOS: DICK RUTAN

December 23, 1986—the day Dick Rutan and Jeanna Yeager landed their storm-battered *Voyager* aircraft after nine days of non-stop flight around the globe—was not only a glorious day in aviation history. It also marked a signal achievement in the annals of Guerrilla P.R. For the *Voyager* would never have gotten off the ground if not for the nationwide support for the project generated by Rutan's skillful handling of the press. Clearly, he piloted the media as well as his plane.

Flying since the age of sixteen, Rutan is a decorated Air Force lieutenant colonel who, after retiring from the service, settled into a family-owned aircraft company. He developed a sterling international reputation as an ace test pilot; but Dick's dreams encompassed greater achievements. In 1981 he launched the idea of the *Voyager*, a lightweight aircraft that could fly around the world without stopping for refueling.

Though Dick was well-known within the aviation press, he and Jeanna would need massive financial and moral support from the public to make this dream come true. From his Mojave Desert base east of Los Angeles, Dick carefully courted the media to spread the word about *Voyager*. "We had a couple of philosophies that worked well for us," says Dick. "We always maintained a sense of openness and sincerity. Sometimes people try to use the press for some hidden agenda, but when they came here they found genuine people who would take the time to talk with them."

In preparing his and Jeanna's encounter with the media, Dick studied the history books. "I went back to Charles Lindbergh," he notes. "He served as a model for how not to handle the press. If someone wrote a story on him that wasn't 100 percent accurate, he would rant and rave at the reporter. Because he grew more reclusive, writers had little information to write about him. It all snowballed, and the more recalcitrant he became, the more the press hated him."

Dick took this lesson to heart. When articles appeared that were at least 50 percent accurate, he took the time to thank the writer. However, he always insisted all interviews be taped, which led to 90 percent accuracy in most stories. "We never alienated anybody," says Dick. "They usually stayed on the right subjects: adventure, human spirit, volunteerism." Dick also had another trick up his sleeve. "I'd give the reporters about 90 percent of what they wanted, but I'd always hold something back so they'd return again."

His openness with the press even included the tabloids. When the *National Enquirer* requested an interview, Dick was a little hesitant because of the paper's trashy reputation. But he invited the reporter up, treated him with the customary graciousness, and, believe it or not, ended up with a highly favorable and accurate story in America's favorite scandal sheet.

Working with media, Dick quickly learned the ground rules. "They may talk with you for thirty minutes," notes Dick, "but all they'll end up using is four or five sentences, and you have to be sure to give them those. Make them dramatic and personal."

Today Dick Rutan is one of the most requested speakers on the circuit, inspiring audiences across the country with his message of opportunity and vision.* As for advising others on any dealings with the media, Dick cautions against Lindbergh-style criticism. "You have to be open and friendly with the media," he notes. "Goodwill is very infectious, and you can build strong personal relationships. You should also understand the constraints the press is under, and work with them, not against them."

Dick often closes his speeches with these words, which also express the heart of the Guerrilla P.R. credo: "What you can accomplish is limited only by what you can dream." Amen.

---

*As of this writing, Dick Rutan is a declared candidate for the U.S. Congress.

8

MAY DAY, MAY DAY

When I make a mistake, it's a beaut!

—FORMER NEW YORK MAYOR FIORELLO LA GUARDIA

WHEN THINGS GO WRONG

The man who coined the phrase "When life deals you a lemon, make lemonade" has my sympathy. On more than one occasion, I've found his book—with that title—mired in the cooking section of my neighborhood bookstore.

Early on I said P.R. is an art. For that reason, Guerrilla P.R. doesn't take a by-the-numbers approach. You can't go by the book because there is no book. So even the best-laid plans of Guerrillas and pros sometimes go awry, just as half-baked schemes occasionally succeed.

My aim has been to reorient your thinking, to alter your habits of imagination, so you devise a strategy that works *for you*. Despite my tips, Guerrilla P.R. is entirely instinctive and self-directed, and thus subject to no immutable laws. So, having implemented your campaign, you may find things haven't exactly gone according to plan. Either you aren't getting the publicity you hoped for, or you're getting the kind you don't need: the *negative* kind. But relax, there are ways to circumvent such problems.

When fighter pilots lose power in an engine, they don't consult the manual. They respond instinctively. The information in this chapter will help you react in much the same way when things go wrong.

Because how you handle bad news reflects greatly on how your good news will be accepted by the media in the future.

MAJOR DISASTER NO. 1: NO PRESS

It's a sad sight I've grown accustomed to in every city I visit. Mini-malls, America's immortal contribution to late twentieth century architecture, stand on nearly every corner, offering shoppers a startling array of choices in nail boutiques, tanning salons, donut shops, and one-hour photo labs. The mini-malls stand as mute testament to the power of the American dream of entrepreneurship and captaining one's destiny.

They also stand as very eloquent testament to the failure of that elusive dream.

Strip-mall business bankruptcies and space vacancies have skyrocketed in the last few years, surely due in large part to the persistent recession, but also, I believe, to the lack of P.R. initiative on the part of new business owners. Every single one of these malls and their stores seems identical. Each needs to stand out from the pack. Each needs some good press. Yet few ever seem to go for it.

Mini-mall businesses comprise the perfect example of those who need press and usually never get it. But what about you? Whether you own a business or are involved in some other kind of project, perhaps the most devastating response you can get from the media, should you seek their attention, is to get no attention at all.

You've got an impressive mailing list, selected targets, assembled a press kit, mailed press releases, called papers, TV, and radio. You're pumped, primed, ready to take on the world. But you find your tracking sheets are blank. Nobody gives a damn. What now?

First, let's do a reality check. Reexamine your written materials. Bring trusted friends and family back into the discussion. Look for signs of poor presentation or unimaginative pitches. You should have noted these long ago when you sensed the media were yawning as you pitched them. But these kinds of problems should be remedied now.

If you feel your fundamentals were sound, look to your outlets. Could you have chosen the wrong ones? Reconsider your target audience and media. Perhaps you should expand in another direction? If you were going for financial press, maybe *Business Week* was a little too out-of-reach at this time. How about a smaller business journal in your neck of the woods? Take another long look at your list. Comb through the names you have. Perhaps you should move up to regional and national media? Or, ratchet down to local and smaller press? This kind of retooling can often make a miraculous difference.

Although you may think you've exhausted the possibilities, go back to the library, newsstand, or bookstore. Seek out different media guides with expanded listings, and add new names to your master list. Every week, fledgling publications make their debut, and perhaps you can get in on the ground floor with some of them. The key here is to reignite your initial enthusiasm and keep up the search.

Recontact the journalists you've contacted before. Being careful to keep the focus on newsworthiness, inquire again whether they can run something—anything—on your project. If your presentation has been professional, courteous, and energetic, you should rouse a certain degree of sympathy on the part of the reporter or editor. But never ever say anything like, "We really need some publicity." Reporters were not put on this earth to give you publicity, and they will invariably take great offense at such a statement.

And don't forget, you have at your disposal a variety of Guerrilla techniques: magnet events, press conferences, protests, parties, mailings. Stir new ingredients into your P.R. stew. Maybe now you should conduct that survey, poll, or trend prediction, and thus generate a new slate of releases? Could this be the time to throw a gala party? Have you called local TV stations to see about an appearance on a public affairs program? Maybe this would be a good time to send that picture to the paper, or write a letter to the editor? Just like a big-league hurler, you want to mix up your pitches to become as effective as possible.

What if you don't have time to waste? What if your charity event is just around the corner? You'll have to work quickly. Select the two or three most important outlets and concentrate efforts there. Do as much of the journalistic legwork as you can, re-present it to the outlets and this time stress the urgency of the matter. If you still get no response, at least make sure all local calendar listings are reserviced, make your follow-up calls, and get a mention that way.

The main point is, if you're being ignored, you have to shift your focus to something un-ignorable. Synthesize the key elements of your project and create something controversial, newsworthy, challenging, funny, or unprecedented. Even if it's tangential to the heart of your project, it will get you coverage, and that's what you want. Don't beat yourself up if you have to make changes. George Bernard Shaw said, "Progress is impossible without change, and those who cannot change their minds cannot change anything."

MOI?

What if you've followed all these steps and still find the media turning their back? Publicist, heal thyself. Maybe there's something about you that needs a little work.

Don't be hurt or offended by this. I'm talking about a little fine-tuning to make that personality engine of yours hum. Start by taking stock of the basics. Examine your dress, grooming, and interpersonal performance. If these check out, move on.

If you did or said something you shouldn't have (after all, you *are* new at this), keep your composure. The more relaxed you are, the less you will appear to have screwed up. Only a creep would write you off for one gaffe. If you accidentally misled a reporter, offer a sincere apology, make amends, and pick up the pieces. Don't resolutely avoid mention of your mistake; it makes you look sneaky. People appreciate openness and honesty.

Above all, forgive yourself. You don't have to be perfect. That's one of society's most pernicious lies: that we can do it all, have it all, and be it all. You're a human being. You have your own mission on this earth, but that's between you and God, not between you and the daily paper. Carry on with that mission. Return to your Guerrilla P.R. posture. What's the worst that can happen? What's the best?

MAJOR DISASTER NO. 2: BAD PRESS

There it was on "ABC World News Tonight." An exposé revealed that a new series of history textbooks for high schoolers, published by the top educational publishers in the nation, were riddled with inaccuracies, over 5,000 in fact. Among the mistakes, the books claimed we dropped "the bomb" on Korea, and both Martin Luther King, Jr. and Robert Kennedy were killed during the Nixon administration (it was, of course, during the Johnson years).

A senior executive of one of the publishers courageously faced the cameras to explain the disaster. He blamed human error and admitted there was no justification, then, helping to trash his own case, he added, "History is more than dates." I had to avert my eyes.

I don't know which is worse, too little good publicity or too much bad publicity. The former is no doubt frustrating, but the latter can be devastating. It can ruin a business, it can ruin lives. I hope you would do everything possible to avoid negative press in the first place, but should you get sideswiped by it, don't freak out. Here's what to do.

If faced with a crisis, e.g., the media are all over your tail for some alleged misconduct, impropriety, or misstatement, your first duty is to respond *immediately.* Do not delay in dealing with the problem. Remember how the Soviets covered up Chernobyl? They couldn't have looked worse. In fact, the fallout from their secrecy and cover-up was arguably more damaging than the reactor explosion itself.

How you handle the bad news will play a large role in how your good news will be met by the media in the future. But to meet a crisis head-on, you have to prepare in advance. While designing your Guerrilla P.R. campaign up-front, ponder also a few worst-case scenarios. Make a list of potential problems, then opposite them list all your explanations and courses of action. That way, you'll be ready when a hostile press knocks on your door.

And I do mean hostile. It's a chilling experience staring into glaring TV lights, having a steel bouquet of microphones thrust in your face, and being battered by terse questions from people you don't know. If you're confronted with this, center yourself as best you can, and remain calm. Answer positively, offer facts, and show an up-beat attitude. If you don't know the answer to something, say so.

If worse comes to worst, you can always say "no comment," but those two words have a dreadful ring to them. It's better to say something like, "I'd really prefer not to comment about that at this time." But a "no comment" can't be attacked. It keeps you in balance while the crisis blows over. You don't want the heat of the moment to cause you to say something you'll regret. Remember, today's headline is tomorrow's fish-wrapping.

One of the worst drubbings I ever saw anyone take from the press was Rob Lowe, following the embarrassing release of his home-made pornographic video in which he engaged in sex with an underage Georgia girl. Some of my friends and colleagues still say his career never recovered, but I think he played it smart. He refused comment for a while, then came back with what I felt was a sincere apology. Later, he was able to joke about his circumstances with an appearance on "Saturday Night Live," in which he made fun of himself. This diffused the discomfort people felt and allowed him to return to the mainstream, tossing off the incident as "youthful indiscretion." Today his film career is back on track.

But I'd say the textbook illustration of skillfully handling bad press came with the Tylenol tampering tragedy a few years back. As you probably recall, some lunatic laced several bottles of the pain medication with lethal doses of cyanide, and before anyone could do anything about it, seven people were dead.

The manufacturer met the crisis head-on. Without delay, all Tylenol products were withdrawn from the shelves. An all-out effort to find the culprits was launched; immediately, new tamper-proof measures were introduced that changed the industry, and, most importantly, the company took the time to let a jittery nation heal. The company was prepared, acted coolly and responsibly, did not duck the tough questions, and in the end, retained their dominance in the market. They used the media to show their genuine concern and their determination to take the lead in resolving the crisis. It was a message of courage and leadership via public relations.

One of the single most important points to keep in mind when facing a negative situation of your own is to follow the old dictum: the best defense is a good offense. You must never go on the defensive. By anticipating negative questions you can stand ready to counter with positives.

For example, let's say you're a developer who bought a large apartment complex occupied by senior citizens, and you plan to turn it into a luxury hotel. The old folks are due to be turned out. That's the kind of juicy Simon Legree story the media love. But if reporters demand to know why you're putting seniors on the street, don't say, "We're not putting seniors on the street." That's like Nixon saying "I am not a crook." It merely confirms what you're denying.

Instead, you should say something like this: "I'm glad you asked me that because now I have a chance to explain to the public what we *are* doing. Not only does every resident have six months rent-free to search for alternative housing, but we'll give them a six-month extension if need be. In addition, we're actively helping the residents find new housing, and we'll pay their moving costs. If anyone in this neighborhood is willing to do more, I'd like to meet him."

Here's another hypothetical scenario: you're launching a new manufacturing center in a small neighborhood worried about increased traffic, air pollution, and noise. Instead of denying, or getting defensive, tell the media (and, thus, the public) that you're offering staggered work shifts, increasing the local tax base, increasing property values, that you're donating a certain percentage of your profits to a local charity. In other words, you take away from the hostile press the very weapons they plan to wield against you.

If I were to boil it down to one word, it would be this: courage. That's what it takes to weather such a storm.

I know these guidelines seem hard, but you *must* follow them or you'll come across as just another low-life caught by the vigilant free press. *It's how you come across that matters.* So act your heart out. Be a De Niro or a Streep. Pretend to feel differently than you do. It takes an emotional toll, but in the end it will be worth it.

FROM THE GUERRILLA P.R. FILE

Though we've all experienced a bad meal every once in a while, nothing can compare to the queasy stomachs the directors of a major book publisher (not this one) experienced in February, 1992, when it was discovered that one of the ingredients in a recipe in a recently published cookbook presented a potential health hazard. The cookbook featured a recipe recommending lilies-of-the-valley as an edible flower for cake decoration. Turns out this is a poisonous plant, to eat (though not to grow and handle). The publisher immediately sent out a press release, recalled all copies of the book from wholesalers and retailers, and offered a toll-free number for all customers who desired a full refund. A good example of a responsible company acting promptly and correctly.

MAJOR DISASTER NO. 3: INACCURATE PRESS

Actually, I don't think of this as such a disaster, but it could create problems. As I've said, P.R. is a gamble because you don't have authoritative control over what appears in print or on the evening news. Sometimes your message is truncated, misinterpreted, or juxtaposed with issues or symbols that defeat your purpose. Sometimes, they just plain get it wrong.

For example, a couple I know, Richard Epcar and Ellyn Stern, both actors, did a segment for a national TV magazine show. The setup showed them performing a scene for a noted Hollywood casting director. The scene went well and the casting director raved about the couple's acting. The magazine show's producer asked the casting director, "Isn't there anything you can say that's not quite so positive, just to give it some balance?" The casting director replied, "Well, I suppose the scene did go on a little bit too long."

Wouldn't you know it—the only sound byte that wound up on the show was the director's single negative line. Not one word about what wonderful actors Richard and Ellyn were.

Sad to say, there's not much you can do about this sort of thing. The media are often in a hurry, and frequently get facts wrong or cut a piece to fit given space or time limitations. If a newspaper gets something wrong, you can request a retraction or a correction (though the publications don't always comply). The same is sometimes true of TV news. You should make your request firmly, but without rancor. If a retraction does run, then you've gotten two mentions for the price of one.

But by and large, you'll have to let this sort of thing go. You just have to take your lumps and look on the bright side. After all, you did get some media coverage, and that means your message got through on some level. Generally, I feel it's better to get skewed press than none at all. If you keep your cool, you can always come back to them later. Handling it psychologically is no mean trick. Just don't take personally anything negative or incorrect the papers write about you. The longer you play this game, the thicker your skin will become, believe me.

MONEY TROUBLES

Guerrilla P.R. is grounded in low-cost techniques. But what if they're not low enough? I speak often of appearance, perception, quality, and these things can't be plucked out of thin air. They require an unavoidable minimum outlay of money. So in this section, I offer a few tips that help you save some dough.

Your biggest costs will likely be printing, mailing, and telephone. As for the first, obviously you should shop around for the least expensive copy store. Many now have computer terminals which offer desktop publishing. I don't recommend handwriting envelopes, so if you don't own a typewriter, head for your local library, college, neighbor, or print shop that offers typewriters (better yet, buy one). Photocopying costs are low, usually no more than a nickel a copy, so that shouldn't bust your budget.

Perhaps you can ask local printing firms if they'd be willing to tack your materials on to the end of a big job at a reduced cost. They may be more inclined to do this if your project is of a charitable nature. It's a good way for them to use up excess paper that might otherwise go unused or tossed.

Photo duplication is another matter. If you want photos reproduced in bulk, it can be very expensive. One way to minimize costs is to get the photo right the first time. Professional photographers, however, charge an arm and a leg, so you may be better off taking your own. If you do, be sure to use a quality 35mm camera with a single lens reflex. Have a photo lab produce a proof sheet, rather than prints of everything on the roll. That way you select the one or two pictures you want and make copies only of them. Of course, bulk copies bring the unit price down, but that can still be expensive. Work with smaller quantities at first until you need or can afford more photos.

Press kit covers can run you quite a bill too. Instead of having them printed, run off a quantity of attractive 3- × 5-inch labels with your logo on them. These you can place on blank press kit covers, which you can buy at any stationery store. Again, be conservative in your initial quantity. The unit price is high, but it will still be far less than if you were to buy bulk. You simply may not need large amounts in the early going, especially if your P.R. focus is primarily local.

As for mailing, a stamp is a stamp. You will probably never generate the quantity of mail that may entitle you to a Postal Service discount. But you can still keep your expenses down with a degree of vigilance. Hand-deliver materials if the addressees are close by. Make sure your list doesn't have any duplicate names or titles. For example, both the assignment editor and planning desk coordinator at Channel 12 may not need to be on your list.

You should also avoid heavy packaging material like thickly padded jiffy bags or cardboard inserts to protect photos. Usually, mail is delivered in tip-top shape. These items only serve to drive up your costs (not to mention creating needless waste).

Saving on phone costs is easy. For long distance, call before 7:00 A.M., especially if you live in the western U.S.A. and you're calling east. One trick you may try is to deliberately leave a message, making the other party call you back and pick up the tab, though you risk making the other party very sore unless *they* want *you*. But most long distance and local phone companies offer myriad savings plans, like Reach Out America, and some can prove economical to you. Call your phone company for details, but beware, some plans don't amount to much.

If you get a G.P.R. campaign going full steam, people are going to want to talk with you and meet with you. That may mean travel to other cities to meet the media. Although some, especially the national shows, will pay your transportation, most do not. You're on your own. However, you have to weigh the cost of a plane ticket against the potential gain. In the end, the extraordinary exposure you receive on a national TV appearance could more than pay for itself.

Overall, like anything in society, to do a P.R. campaign right involves expenditures. But unlike marketing or advertising, P.R. is dramatically inexpensive and the return potentially tremendous. You get most of the benefits of a well-planned ad campaign without the burdensome costs. So even though Guerrilla P.R. isn't free, it's darn close.

THE ART OF TROUBLESHOOTING

Don't you just hate those Pollyanna types who always look on the bright side? Who whistle while they work, with a song in their heart? Who always think the sun'll come up tomorrow? Well, sorry, but I'm one of those types. I am a natural-born optimist, which partly explains my obsession with opportunity. The problems we all face day to day are no less fraught with opportunity than the good things that come our way. It's possible to make something positive out of the tough situations I described above.

Look at losing political candidates. After investing so much of their money, prestige, time, energy, and personal life, they so often walk away with nothing but a massive campaign debt. Yet, so often I see them carrying on and smiling all the way. Sure, they hurt inside, but I suspect by and large they adopt an attitude of, "Well, I gave it everything I have, and there's nothing to hang my head about."

I'm not saying you have to enjoy the hard times, but you can develop a new perspective on life's challenges. In terms of Guerrilla P.R., it means seeing your efforts framed by a wider view. Your business, your project, your life and well-being do not revolve around a guest shot on "Geraldo." P.R. is something you want, not necessarily something without which you die.

It's one of life's great ironies: sometimes, the less you "care" to have something, the more you're likely to achieve it. Go for everything you want with all your heart, but keep something in reserve just for you. If you win, great. If you lose, hey, it's only a game.

GUERRILLA P.R. COMMANDOS: WAYNE PERRYMAN

Wayne Perryman, a former gang member, is an author, labor relations executive, and one of his city's most active community leaders. But his favorite endeavor is helping the disadvantaged African-American youth in his native Seattle. Among his notable achievements: the nationally lauded Role Models Unlimited, a program designed to provide positive adult male role models for kids; and the Harold Reynolds Children's Foundation, run in tandem with the Mariners' great second baseman.

In fact, Wayne has so many projects going simultaneously it's a wonder he has any time to breathe, let alone direct his own publicity campaigns. But from the very start of his community service work, Wayne has run his own P.R. show, learning as he went along exactly how to entice the media.

"The media want something newsworthy," he says. "Selling newspapers meant they had to have something unique in terms of public interest. No matter what I was doing, I tried to give it a new twist to make sure, from a journalistic standpoint, there would be some excitement in covering it."

That's precisely what he did by publishing the nation's first anti-drug storybook for young children, "What Mary Found," as part of the Harold Reynolds Children's Foundation. Wayne knew Reynolds wanted to do something for kids, but warned him against doing anything that had been done a hundred times before. "All it takes is thinking your project through," says Perryman, "and presenting it in such a unique way, it touches the emotions."

That's the key to any Perryman pitch: emotion. "When your project is devoid of emotional appeal, the chances of selling it are almost nil," he notes. "If you reach the heart, you generally will get the response you want."

To get there, however, requires a solid foundation, as Perryman well knows. "Anyone doing their own P.R. should take a community college course in creative writing and/or public speaking," says Wayne. "Monitor news anchors and journalists. Watch 'Good Morning, America.' Guests on these have only seconds to make their points. The question is, when the lights hit you, can you tell your story? You have only one chance, and you'd better be prepared."

Given Wayne Perryman's sterling reputation in the Northwest, he considers his good name a priceless possession. "You use P.R. to build on your credibility," he says. "The collective press you receive over time helps you sell your projects. Even if you sometimes end up with bad press, they can't damage you if you have a good reputation preceding you."

Though his Role Models project has received network attention, Wayne continues to focus his energies on a local basis. That's just fine with him; making a difference in Seattle has always been Wayne Perryman's main mission, and fortunately for him, it's a "mission accomplished."

9

INTELLIGENCE GATHERING: PLANNING YOUR NEXT STEP

One man that has a mind and knows it can beat ten men who haven't and don't.

—GEORGE BERNARD SHAW

HOW'M I DOING?

Assessing the success of your Guerrilla P.R. campaign can be simple. If your project is a church carnival and, come event day, it's packed to the rafters, then you did your job well. But if your project involves longer-range goals that aren't so easy to measure, like increasing community awareness of a public policy issue, or getting a new storefront business off to a good start, then you have to read different tea leaves to know how well you're doing.

One of the truisms of a well-mounted professional public relations campaign is its pervasiveness. When a big star has a new summer movie coming out, or a top author hits the talk-show circuit to push a new book, the cumulative publicity effect hits like a hurricane. You'll see that person's face everywhere you look, on magazine covers and round-the-clock TV interviews, even if the movie's a turkey or the book's a loser.

The well-connected P.R. pros wield enormous clout, and many face a good deal of criticism, some justifiable, with naysayers decrying the outsized demands of a select group of top Hollywood publicists. That certainly isn't the case with Guerrilla P.R. While the pros may brew hurricanes, you're looking to create a stiff breeze. You'll still make the trees bend, but not snap.

To calculate the effectiveness of your Guerrilla P.R. campaign, take stock of the following:

- Are sales up?

- Is attendance increasing?

- Are the phones ringing more?

- Have people commented on seeing your project mentioned in the media?

- Do you notice an increase in donations?

- Are calls being returned more than before?

- Are people treating you differently? (You know how awestruck folks get when encountering anyone deified by media celebrity.)

These sorts of things can be explained by forces other than a P.R. campaign, e.g., ancillary marketing efforts, word-of-mouth, seasonal timing, etc. So to pinpoint the impact of your Guerrilla P.R. campaign, you have to conduct some kind of survey. Either by verbal inquiry or written form, poll your customers and find out what drew them to your project. If they read about it in the paper, get specific. Which articles did they read? What impressed them about it? Some small business owners I know regularly hand out to their customers little cards with specific questions about how they first heard of the store, and other similar points of inquiry. I would urge you to do the same.

The best and simplest way to honestly assess your progress and performance is to play schoolteacher. I mean you should literally give yourself letter grades in various categories. The categories should include specific P.R. objectives (i.e., the local daily paper; the morning talk-radio show, etc.), success in reaching target audience, ability to define your own message (as opposed to having the media inaccurately shape the definition), and diversity of media (i.e., did you get no TV or radio? Were you only featured in trade press, when you were also going for consumer press?).

Here's what each grade should mean:

A. All your objectives were met. The coverage you received was extensive, the spin given your project was positive, and response from your target audience met or exceeded expectations. Pat yourself on the back, but only for a moment, because success is a short-term affair unless you keep on top of it.

B. You got most of what you wanted. Response was generally favorable, but perhaps one or two important goals were not met. Perhaps you felt your own performance was not as dynamic as you would have liked. Reexamine your plan, take note of what went right, and emphasize those aspects in the next leg of the campaign.

C. There was some press coverage on your project, though not enough of it was positive or prominent. Perhaps you achieved some of target media coverage, but it turned out to be the wrong choice, and goals for your project were unmet because of judgment error. You need to begin the formulation process again, exploring new angles, new pitches, new avenues for publicity.

D. Nothing went right. Despite your best efforts, you received little or no press, or bad press, or nobody showed up or cared. It's time to start from scratch, developing your interpersonal skills and rethinking your strategy for media. All is not lost, but you have your work cut out for you.

E. Forget about it. You have to either change careers, hire someone like me, or join a Tibetan religious order.

Take a look at your grades, and see where you flourished, and where you floundered. This will give you an instant picture on where you need to improve and where your strengths lie. Also look beyond the grades themselves, and analyze your data in terms of the quantity and quality of coverage. We professionals do this all the time in refining our techniques for the next campaign. Presuming you too will want to take your P.R. efforts to the next level, assessing your P.R. data is crucial.

As carefully as we may try to select our targets, often we take shots in the dark. P.R. reminds me of the old "linguini on the wall" routine. "How do you know if the linguini is done? Throw it on the wall. If it sticks, it's done." You may try many different Guerrilla P.R. techniques to publicize your project, but whatever sticks is what works, and vice versa. If your data show more people responded to your appearance on a local radio call-in show than to a guest shot on the local morning show on channel 6, then that tells you where some of your personal strengths lie, as well as which media respond best to your project.

Once you isolate your successful media efforts, retrace your steps. Go over your tracking from the campaign, examining your pitch style, responses, and reactions. Do this not only with your successes but also with your failures, to determine why some aspects of your campaign didn't work. I see nothing wrong with recontacting media people with whom you had success and "debriefing them" on what it was about you and your campaign that worked for them. You can use this information for future appeals.

Next go-around, you may return to the well, appealing again to publications and broadcasts that covered you previously. Or you may wish to retackle those outlets that said "no" early on. Both strategies have merit, but be aware: many media will not touch a story a second time, especially if it's within a year of the first article or segment. But this is not the eleventh commandment, and if you can continually come up with fresh new project hooks, there's no reason why you cannot sustain an ongoing media presence.

In addition, thanks to your successes, when you return to the naysayers to pitch again, you will now have evidence to show just how media-worthy you are. You will have gained new-found credibility that keeps building as you go. That's the beauty of publicity. You're the same worthwhile and deserving person you always were, but now the media have knighted you thus, which makes it *really* true.

TIME TO TRADE UP

So, you've surveyed your customers, collected data, pinpointed the media sources of your P.R. success, reexamined your success with those outlets, and sketched a second-tier plan. Most likely you can proceed upward on your own, following essentially the same path you took before. You should be better at writing, phoning, and interviewing than you were the first time; your increased confidence should mushroom into bigger and better results.

Managing an ongoing campaign is different from launching one. You may not always have a splashy announcement or a magnet event to draw attention. But you should maintain regular contact with media to keep your profile high. Once you have your links at the outlets, regularly send them releases. I don't mean every day, and I don't mean to announce your Doberman had his tonsils out. But if you hire a new employee, begin distributing an interesting product, or move to a new building, then let the media know about it. You may not get coverage, but the constancy of regular mailings keeps you in their faces, and they'll definitely remember you.

If you were lucky enough to cultivate friendships with any media people during your initial campaign, now is the time to cement them. Do lunch, do dinner, take time to fraternize. It doesn't guarantee a story next time you need one, but it does guarantee a fair hearing, which is not something everyone gets from the media.

This is the time to solidify a perception of yourself as an expert in your field. If you own a downtown fishmarket, you must be the one the local newspaper calls when it's doing a story on fish. How do you do this? Careful cultivation of your prior media success. This is where reprints of clips can be most valuable. You should be sending out mailings to your list, even if you have no immediate news angle. If you keep the editors informed of your standing as an "expert," I promise you they will eventually come to believe it too.

Also, make sure you're listed in the *Yearbook of Experts, Authorities, & Spokespersons*, the bible of talent bookers on radio and TV (see Appendix Two). It may cost a couple of hundred bucks to run your ad, but it will be seen by influential media personnel. And see to it the media are part of any consumer marketing effort you undertake, that is, keep them fully informed. Again, even if they do no reporting this time, they will remember who you are the next time you need them.

What if your reach exceeds your grasp? What if you set your sights on loftier P.R. goals? Can you pull it off on your own, or is it time to trade up? If you're willing to relinquish a measure of control to establish a long-term high publicity profile, if you find your ability to make contacts has hit a ceiling, and if you've got the bucks, you may wish to consider hiring a pro.

Don't think a professional will solve all your problems. Pros strike out as often as they get base hits, and home runs are never a sure thing. They will still likely utilize you as the spokesperson, and you may end up expending nearly as much time and energy on their

P.R. campaign for you as you would on your own.

Obviously, having written this book, I believe anyone can successfully mount his or her own Guerrilla P.R. campaign. But deciding on going the professional route rests on the following criteria:

• You have the financial resources to afford the $1,000 to $5,000 monthly retainer.

• You are simply too busy reaping the rewards of your first G.P.R. campaign to devote more time to future publicity efforts.

• Your new targets include cream-of-the-crop outlets like *Life* magazine, the *Wall Street Journal*, or the "CBS Evening News," and you have been unable to make any headway with them.

• You need to maintain an ongoing long-term very high-level national P.R. presence that would best be maintained by an independent professional.

Only a fool would do his own dental work. Similarly, someone who wants to become the next Madonna will need help on the P.R. front. Madonna was too busy doing her thing to spend time calling attention to it. Although she is a P.R. genius, she is not the one picking up the phone dialing *Rolling Stone* or faxing press releases to UPI. Her coterie of publicists do that for her.

But let me put in a plug for hanging in there on your own. As you have gleaned from the G.P.R. Commandos info, this is indeed something you can do yourself. Relying on her own initiative, Candy Lightner made it to the network news, as did Angelyne and Dick Rutan. Before they started, none knew much about how media functioned, but they learned as they went along. Their instincts were sharp, but no sharper than yours.

Moreover, you keep control when you do it yourself. Sometimes, pros alter a client's persona to entice the media. That doesn't mean we lie; we just emphasize certain media-genic qualities over others. But that can backfire. You know yourself better than anyone, and you can't help but develop a more honest profile if you handle the P.R. chores yourself.

Besides, it's very rewarding to pull it off yourself. I'm in the P.R. game for a living, in no small part because I enjoy the rush of success. You will experience that with your own successes too, and the longer you hang in, the greater will be your achievements.

HAVE I GOT A CAREER FOR YOU

Who knows? You may be so good at this, you might want to make a career out of it. Don't laugh. If you have a knack for persuading media to do your bidding, then you possess an extremely marketable skill. Perhaps you can hook up with a local P.R. firm on a part-time basis, or find a mentor who can teach you further techniques or steer clients your way. Maybe you can do *pro bono* P.R. work, for charities or causes you believe in, or work as an intern for an established firm. *New Choices* magazine listed P.R. as one of the twelve hot careers for the 1990s, with mid-level salaries ranging from $45,000 to $90,000. There's always room for talented newcomers.

In fact, I have an offer you may just want to take me up on. Remember that feature article I wrote on the subject of interning? I was deadly serious about it. If you feel you can benefit from a tour of duty as an intern, I'll take you on at my firm in Los Angeles.

Really. No kidding.

Write to me at the address given in the Postscript of this book; tell me about yourself and why you'd like to intern at my company. Of course it's not a paid position, but you will get priceless hands-on experience at a top P.R. firm, learning from the professionals on my staff. There is no real education without experience. This is a golden opportunity to gain that experience. Drop me a line. I do have openings, and I would love to hear from you.

Also, if you like doing P.R. or learning more about it, I suggest you subscribe to the various professional journals (see Appendix Two), enroll in workshops, join professional associations, or take a college course. These kinds of activities can't help but improve your mind as well as your business.

Can you make it as a pro? First, ask yourself if you're merely interested in the field, or whether you have a burning maniacal rage. There's a big difference. Without the burning maniacal rage to succeed, you'll have trouble making it. For the first five years of my P.R. career, I worked two shifts, first from 9:00 A.M. to 6:00 P.M., then, after a quick trip home for a shower, I'd return to the office, and work from 7:00 P.M. to midnight. People would ask me how long I'd been a publicist, and I'd say "ten years" because of those two shifts.

It's not for everyone. Even today, about twice a week I hand in my resignation to myself. But whether you pursue a career in P.R. or not, you can continue to move up in your own ongoing G.P.R.

campaign. You'll find maintenance easier than starting up, because you will have a growing list of media contacts on whom you can rely time and again. In your second- and third-tier campaigns, you can take greater risks, and attempt to reach higher targets. Before you know it, the media will be calling you. That doesn't mean you drop the ball. You'll always need to keep yourself visible; but the sledding gets easier when the media want you before you want them.

STRUT YOUR STUFF

I told my staff the other day that you *don't* have to have goals. You only need them if you want to succeed. This is true in all areas of life, including P.R. Someone once said, "Scratch a publicist and you get a milkman." That is, we milk our ideas for all they're worth. You too must expand your vision in order to do Guerrilla P.R.

As with the simple exercises in the first chapters of this book, you should continue to build a portfolio of ideas. Henceforth, spend fifteen minutes a day jotting down ideas. I mean all kinds of ideas: from new brainstorms to clever witticisms to incorporate in your next press release.

Do it on a notepad, or talk into a dictaphone. It doesn't matter how, only that you do it. Your ideas may stink at first, but watch how quickly you refine your mind. Soon your manilla folder marked "IDEAS" will begin to bulge. Because ideas can come anytime, keep pads everywhere, at home, in the car, at work, by the bed. Ideas are like slippery fish. If you don't spear them with a pencil right away, they'll be gone. But remember, the good Lord did not issue you a limited supply of creative energy. Once you get one idea, there's plenty more where that came from.

Besides, you will want to begin thinking long-term. Most Guerrilla P.R. efforts are geared to short-term, isolated event publicity. But you may wish to cultivate a longer-range game plan as well. No matter who you are or what you do, whether you're project oriented or personality oriented, well-managed ongoing media relations is no longer a luxury in business: it is a stone-cold necessity.

By sustaining your contacts with the media, you reserve for yourself a twenty-four-hour hotline to the people. You not only create interest in specific events, but you *establish a permanent presence in the consciousness of your target audience and the public at large.* That's the difference between short-term and long-term P.R. goals. One is event-oriented, the other consciousness-oriented. When people think of hope for the gang problem, they'll think of the Mid-Valley Youth Center. When they think of whatever it is your project entails, they'll think of you.

The operative phrase here is "ongoing." You should maintain a steady stream of press releases or other P.R. efforts to keep the media aware of you and your project. You can't believe how quickly they forget: media people are hard-wired for the present. The old adage, "Live for today," is the blood credo of the media, so if you're not on their minds today, they'll have forgotten about you by tomorrow.

I'll give you one classic example, although it's more of a marketing and advertising story than a P.R. story. Remember when Nissan used to be called Datsun? The company in Japan knew changing their name would be a long and difficult adjustment for Americans. But over a ten-year period of gradual but *constant* reminders in their ads, in their showrooms, and in the media, they managed to remove one name from our consciousness and replace it with another. Now, the term "Datsun" sounds funny; Nissan sounds natural. That happened to you and me because the company understood the importance of uninterrupted media manipulation.

As for you, perhaps your project isn't as complicated as an international automobile company, but given your own scale, you will want to keep up an equally compelling long-range media profile. Remember, it hardly costs a thing, and the payback is beyond measure.

GUERRILLA P.R. COMMANDOS: ANDY AND KATIE LIPKIS

TreePeople is known around the world not only for its extraordinary efforts to plant trees, but also for planting a love of trees in the hearts and minds of children and adults everywhere. Founded in the early seventies by Andy Lipkis when he was only fifteen, TreePeople exemplifies the kind of originality of purpose that not only gets good things done, but also brings out the best kind of Guerrilla P.R. Today, with his wife Katie, Andy Lipkis and TreePeople remain the premier organization of its kind.

Considering the fact that TreePeople always worked at a grassroots level, it's not surprising that Andy and Katie took a guerrilla approach to P.R. From their L.A. headquarters atop Coldwater Canyon, they have directed large-scale urban tree planting projects, visited schools to give away seedlings and educate young people on the ecological importance of trees, undertaken massive ad campaigns, written a best-selling book *(The Simple Act of Planting a Tree)*, and maintained a sprawling tree nursery to fuel their dreams of international reforestation.

To pull this off, Andy knew he had to sell himself as hard as his ideas. As he wrote in his book, "People who cared about the environment were portrayed on television as outcasts, and people who expressed concern over this issue were do-gooders." Andy changed that image to one of lively enthusiasm, backed by a spirit of fun and genuine concern. With Katie's writing skills, the two made a formidable team.

To illustrate just how effective they were at organizing and publicizing, let's take a quick look at their successful three-year campaign in the early eighties which they called "The Million Trees Story." The goal was to plant one million trees in southern California before the 1984 Los Angeles Olympics. First, TreePeople enlisted the aid of a top ad agency, which donated all its services. The campaign rallied around the slogans, "Turn Over a New Leaf, L.A.—Help Plant the Urban Forest" and "Urban Releaf."

The nobility of the campaign goals led to a PSA starring actor Gregory Peck. Radio's help was enlisted too, with thirty-second and sixty-second taped PSA's and scripts for on-air announcers sent to every station in town. Fresh scripts were sent regularly during the two-year campaign, with each good-for-use (timely) for around a month. A billboard company donated ad space. The local ABC news affiliate signed on with a five-part series on the campaign. In the end, by securing high-visibility media and *pro bono* services, and enlisting corporate sponsorship for its cause, TreePeople succeeded in its ambitious Million Trees campaign.

Though there were pitfalls, basically the organization emerged all the more savvy. "We've never had a public relations budget," writes Andy. "In every case, the national media attention we've received has been unsolicited. Why is this? We believe it has something to do with our genuine respect for most of the media folk we've worked with. They're a priceless resource. Don't overuse or try to trick them."

10

THEME AND VARIATIONS

Innovation has never come through bureaucracy and hierarchy. It's always come from individuals.

—JOHN SCULLY, CHAIRMAN, APPLE COMPUTERS

Throughout this book, I have offered my concept of how a Guerrilla P.R. campaign can be mounted. Many of the illustrations came from my own personal experience, and others were drawn from my knowledge of other people's efforts. The Guerrilla P.R. Commandos spotlighted between chapters are, in my mind, the cream of the crop, but they certainly aren't the only ones who exemplify the approach I urge.

There are many people in all fields who recognize the critical importance of P.R., and who wage and win publicity battles every day. Most of them had little or no money to invest in a P.R. campaign. Few or none had any formal training in this area. Yet all had the moxie and the instincts to use the media and their interpersonal P.R. skills to achieve their goals. I'd like to now share with you several examples of real-life people I've known who showed me just how tenacious and inventive the Guerrilla P.R. practitioner can be.

THE ACTORS

Los Angeles is a town where every waiter is a struggling actor, and every shop clerk has a script he's trying to sell. The competition among wanna-bes and almost-theres in the film, theater, and TV communities is unimaginably fierce, with the average member of SAG (Screen Actors Guild) earning only an annual pittance from his/her acting ability.

The only way for actors and actresses to make it—aside from the talent and dumb luck factors—is to work as hard on marketing themselves as they do on remembering their lines. Two young actors who personify that kind of perseverance are Richard Epcar and Ellyn Stern, a married couple who have managed to maintain successful careers in entertainment by relying on their own ingenuity to reach their target audience.

Richard had a big role in the 1992 Chevy Chase film, *Memoirs of an Invisible Man*, appeared in many TV shows such as "Cheers" and "Beverly Hills 90210," and has written and directed scores of children's films and English-language adaptions of foreign film hits like *Cinema Paradiso* and *Women on the Verge of a Nervous Breakdown*. Ellyn has worked in many motion pictures, including *The Man Who Loved Women*, such TV shows as "St. Elsewhere" and "General Hospital," provided scripts and voices for Saturday morning cartoons and foreign films like *Babette's Feast*, and has written several children's books of her own. The two of them are constantly working, while many of their peers wait for the phone to ring. And there's a good explanation.

"Without P.R., we don't work," says Richard, "and we've been doing this for fifteen years." What they've been doing is simply applying P.R. techniques to keep their names and faces constantly in front of their target audience: casting directors and producers. They send out a steady barrage of postcards with their pictures on one side and a personalized note on the back. They take advantage of the "Breakdown" service, which furnishes casting directors and production companies with casting information, by having their materials included on daily deliveries.

"It's like a mail service, but not many actors know about it," says Ellyn, who notes that names and addresses of casting directors are easily obtained from listings kept by the Casting Society of America. The two also scored a major P.R. coup a few years back when they created their own one-on-one showcase for casting directors. "We and other actors pitched in to rent a small theater. Then we would pay the casting people a small honorarium to get them down," recalls

Richard. "We would each do a short five-minute scene, and that way get to know personally these important people."

Later on, the actors' and producers' unions battled over the ethics of paying casting directors to watch actors work. It was a mini-controversy in Hollywood, yet even in this case, Ellyn's comments about the issue were constantly quoted in *Variety*. The two never failed to make their presence felt in the trades.

Every time either landed a job, they'd send an announcement to the telecastings and filmcastings columns in *Variety* and the *Hollywood Reporter*. By reading the trades and learning their formats, Richard was easily able to write usable copy for those particular columns.

Richard has booked himself on cable TV talk shows, and both made sure they were photographed at the Hollywood parties they occasionally attend. "You have to use all your connections," notes Richard, "and you can't be shy about it." Adds Ellyn, "You also have to have a positive attitude. That's what propels you."

So, by combining initiative to do the P.R. legwork, and never dropping the offensive, Richard Epcar and Ellyn Stern have managed to sustain their careers in the ultimate dog-eat-dog business.

Lessons from Richard Epcar and Ellyn Stern: Persistence and relentless efforts are vital if one seeks to impress decision-makers who don't remember what they had for breakfast. Find P.R. resources nobody else has thought of yet, and seize the opportunity.

THE REALTOR

Realtors are the most optimistic people in the world. The market's never bad, sales have never been better, and any house they show is the most perfect dwelling ever constructed. It's enough to make you sick sometimes. But other times, you meet people in the real estate business who sincerely try to do the best possible job for their clients, and make sure they find the right house for the right price.

One realtor who exemplifies this first-rate service attitude is Dale Fay, owner of the Century 21 Oak Tree franchise in California's San Fernando Valley. Dale has been a realtor for thirty years, working her way through the ranks to become one of the Valley's top salespersons. She bought her franchise at a time when the real estate market in southern California was in a true tailspin. Friends called her crazy, but Dale knew what she was doing.

"People in the community need to know you," she says. "I figured it would take two years before anybody would get to know us, and opening then would establish us to be there at the right time when the market picked up."

To ensure that once and future clients will remember her, Dale relies on several strategies. Since referral is the most important source of business, she makes sure her present clients are happy. She's always ready to go the extra mile, clean up the house she's showing if the owners aren't home, make herself available by phone literally twenty-four hours a day, and she carries a few bottles of champagne in the trunk of her car in case she closes a deal on the spot. Her attitude is "Once a client, always a client." Dale mails out forty pieces of literature and information to clients up to five years *after* the sale of a property. "It keeps our name in front of them."

But she also has to court potential customers. To do that, Dale regularly offers free seminars to likely first-home buyers; sends out cards and mailers offering free home market analysis; and for good community relations, sponsors food drives and Easter Seals benefits.

"Our P.R. message is, 'We're different because we know more and we serve you better," says Dale. To impart that message, Dale has simply lived up to it. As for the media, she maintains cordial relationships with the real estate reporters for L.A.'s two daily papers. "I bombard them with press releases, knowing full well they can't run them all. But if I send them ten, I know they'll run at least two."

Dale's principal G.P.R. tactic: "If you show interest in others, they will like you," she says. "I have six kids, so I'm prepared to deal with people in all kinds of situations, and that's all this business is."

Lessons from Dale Fay: Pinpointing a target audience and finding new ways to reach and keep this public attentive is essential to long-range growth in P.R. and business.

THE USED CAR DEALER

"I'm pretty lazy," says Dave Schwartz, founder of the Rent-A-Wreck chain of auto rental and sales outlets that deals with slightly unsightly but perfectly functional automobiles. "I found making mistakes takes extra time, so by avoiding mistakes, I save a lot of time and aggravation." That kind of self-effacing approach has taken Dave far, from the unassuming owner of a small L.A. used car lot when he was a teenager, to the multi-million-dollar franchise of Rent-A-Wreck's across the nation.

His original company, Bundy Very Used Cars, drew attention not only for its amusing name, but also for its first-rate service. Once he changed the name to Rent-A-Wreck in 1973, he was hardly prepared for the torrent of attention he received.

"The same day I changed the name, CBS was here filming a story," recalls Dave of the power the new name held. Soon—totally unsolicited—Dave was written up in *People*, the *New York Times*, the *Wall Street Journal*, and appeared on the "Donahue" and "Tom Snyder" shows. The name drew attention, the attention drew overwhelming business, the business drew more attention. "Our name was our biggest asset," he says. "We just used reverse psychology."

Despite his phenomenal success, Dave still works at his original used car lot every day, greeting customers and perpetuating the good service that made Rent-A-Wreck such a hit. "We never have an argument at the counter," he notes. "If a guy's a few hours late, or the gas tank isn't topped off, we don't worry about it. For us, service is everything. Again, it's because I'm lazy. I don't want anybody uptight because that takes extra work to sort out."

Because he doesn't in any way fit the tycoon mold, Dave has had fun with his media encounters. He was given a standing ovation at a national used car convention, well covered by the media. For his profile on "Lifestyles of the Rich and Famous," Dave drove around in one of his old clunkers. But his interpersonal P.R. tools are, for him, the most important. "You have to bring someone down to the comfort zone immediately," he says. "The reason U.S. business is down is because Americans don't take that extra step. A guy who just works for the money is in a bottomless pit."

So, with Dave, starting out with a fantastic business name got his foot in the door. But it took a potent dose of personal P.R. power to sustain his business over twenty years.

Lessons from Dave Schwartz: Coming up with an irresistible name for his business, Dave generated not only overwhelming press coverage, but launched an empire. In one tongue-in-cheek phrase he defined his company and captured the essence of his easy going attitude. Yet he never forgot that service is the key to commercial longevity. His business flourished because he cared about his customers' needs. That, combined with his company's name, attracted media attention.

THE HOAXSTER

It's likely you never heard the name Alan Abel, but I'll bet my last dollar that you're familiar with his "work," if that's what it can be called. Alan is much more than a Guerrilla P.R. genius. He's a pure Guerrilla, a true saboteur, a troublemaker of the highest order. The only people he makes trouble for, however, are members of the news media. The rest of us can't help but snicker with glee at his antics.

Alan is the guy that stages monumental media hoaxes. Like the time he faked Ugandan dictator Idi Amin's wedding to a New England debutante; like the time he arranged a photo-op for the Ku Klux Klan symphony, sitting at their music stands, robes and all; like the time he had his own lengthy obituary very prematurely printed in the *New York Times*.

He says he does it to educate and amuse the public, while at the same time catching lazy reporters off guard. Time and time again journalists have run with his phony stories, only to turn around red-faced shortly thereafter. Some pundits praise his wit and skill; others condemn him as a two-bit scoundrel doing harm to the public. I say he's a P.R. genius who has an unmatched eye for what the press goes for.

Other examples of his handiwork include Omar's School for Panhandlers, the International Sex Bowl Olympics, and Princess Di's chocolate pumps, which she supposedly wore and later ate at a royal function. None were true, but the press dutifully reported them all, proving the veracity of those immortal words from the late New York newspaper publisher James G. Bennett, "Many a good story has been ruined by oververification."

Lessons from Alan Abel: The press will jump overboard for a good hook. After all, the media consists of nothing more than curious individuals. Combine Abel's knack for ideas with your own "true" stories, and you cannot fail to attain coverage.

THE COMIC

"Life is an improvisation," says funny lady Claire Berger. "You don't have a script." Maybe not, but when it came to piloting her own stand-up career through the competitive waters of the comedy business, Claire must have done something right. Especially when it came to guiding her own publicity, it seems she was blessed with as much P.R. talent as comedic gifts.

Today, happily married for fifteen years, and mother of two young children, Claire is something of an anomaly as a comedienne. She doesn't go out on the road for fifty weeks a year, but rather found a place for herself as a warm-up comedienne for top network sitcoms like "Seinfeld," "Murphy Brown," and "Night Court." A warm-up keeps the studio audience entertained before filming and in between set changes. But when she migrated to L.A. from Chicago eight years ago, she didn't know a soul.

"I hate people that say, 'It's who you know.' I say, 'It's who you get to know.'" That attitude made her many friends in Chicago, no two-bit town itself. While working for the city library, she hosted her own radio talk show, worked stand-up, and was a member of the ensemble cast of *Second City*. She was always successful, in part because she comprehended the power of media.

In Chicago, the entertainment columnists for the two daily papers are especially powerful. A mention in their columns can mean a major career boost. Claire hounded them until both caught her show, helping to establish her in her hometown. Her last booking in Chicago came when she was seven months pregnant. She dubbed it "The Raging Hormones Tour," which caught the eye of the media, and all shows were sell-outs.

Once she moved to L.A., she found her niche as a warm-up. When the *New York Times* came out to do a story on the subject of warm-ups, Claire made sure she was interviewed. The piece ended up more like a glowing profile of Claire than anything else, and this she used to get herself more work. Her clip file was so thick with first-rate press that she was actually turned away by a professional publicist, who told her, "What do you need me for?"

Claire was also clever in going after jobs. When the TV series "Chicken Soup" was looking for a warm-up comedian, Claire sent the *New York Times* article wrapped around a pint of chicken soup. Of course she got the job.

Lessons from Claire Berger: Creativity in pitch will pay off. Finding a unique niche and becoming the best in it helps pave the way to success. Especially in the entertainment field, columnists wield great power. Even a one-line mention in a column can have long-ranging after-effects. Use every option at your disposal.

THE RESTAURATEUR

Sometimes it's impossible to trace the origins of a movement. Innovations in art, language, and pop culture often seem to emerge out of the collective unconscious. But it's not at all difficult to identify the start of the surge in popularity of Thai food in this country. Tommy Tang, a Thai refugee who personifies the classic rags-to-riches tale, is the master chef who introduced Thai food to the trendy L.A. and New York restaurant scene. Today, with his two Tommy Tang's restaurants and a complete line of retail food products, a video, and best-selling cookbook *Modern Thai Cuisine*, he remains the undisputed king of the Thai food movement.

Much of his success is due to his wife, Sandy, a marketing analyst by training who helped launch Tommy's career through clever use of Guerrilla P.R. and self-directed marketing. "The first couple of years of the restaurant, I did all the P.R. myself," recalls Sandy. "I'm a firm believer in P.R. Once a restaurateur starts thinking he/she doesn't need it, that's the beginning of the end."

For starters, back in 1982 Sandy and Tommy threw an opening night party at the restaurant, inviting all their loyal patrons from the previous restaurant where Tommy worked. Press came, celebrities came, and the resulting mystique catapulted the restaurant to immediate notoriety. Sandy made a point of personally greeting and mingling with customers every night, and she maintained constant contact with the local food press. "There's an element among the population very interested in what's going on," says Sandy. "They read restaurant reviews, and want to know the hot places to go."

Sandy also made sure Tommy Tang's was involved with charities, such as S.O.S. (Save Our Strength), a hunger-fighting organization, and AIDS research. The restaurant also caters the famed Comic Relief benefits that combat homelessness.

Other catchy and provocative innovations devised by Sandy included staging yearly parties on the restaurant's anniversary; the introduction of a preferred diner's card; and stocking a full line of retail products, such as Thai seasonings and sauces, cookbooks, and a home video.

Sandy's key advice is, to make sure the media are given sufficient information. "If you don't, you won't spark their interest, and then you can't blame them if you don't get the press you want." Though their operation is now too big for Guerilla P.R., Sandy never takes it for granted. "Every day," notes Sandy, "I wake up and think, 'What if this was all taken away?' That keeps me on my toes."

Lessons from Sandy Tang: Keep in close personal contact with your customers. They are the ones who ultimately ensure your success. Even though the critics are unable to review a restaurant over and over, the press need to be in your corner, so keeping them up-to-date regularly is a good investment of your time and energy. And don't sit on your laurels. As quickly as success appears, it can be taken away. Like the Tangs' strategy, it's a wise course to be ever innovative, looking for new ways to expand.

THE ENTREPRENEUR

They say nothing is as powerful as an idea whose time has come, and that was certainly true for Jeffrey Ullman, the man who pioneered the concept of video dating. His company, Great Expectations, founded in 1976, spawned an entire industry, born out of our modern-day explosion of alienated singles. A self-described video guerrilla prior to forming his company, Jeffrey had a good sense of the *zeitgeist* (German for "spirit of the times"), and his idea of pairing singles who meet each other via extended videotaped interviews took off quickly.

But that doesn't happen without tremendous effort. As a journalism major, Jeff had a keen awareness of the central role the media might play in his company's success, and he wasted no time in securing publicity for his fledgling dating service. "When we started," recalls Jeff, "I called up the local papers and asked for their Singles Reporter. They didn't know what I was talking about, so I asked to talk to a reporter who was single."

Trusting the validity of his own entrepreneurial idea, Jeff persuaded reporters to actually experience a video date. "It was a crap shoot," he says, "because they might not have had a good experience, but it turned out they did." After a story would run, and sometimes even before it ran, he'd call up the wire services, ask for an unmarried reporter, and inquire whether he'd seen the article in the paper. Inevitably, he got them curious, and an entirely new wire story would be generated.

At the time, the "Merv Griffin Show" was an important TV outlet. "I booked myself," says Jeff, recalling one of his most audacious moves. "I called up and asked for the executive producer. When the secretary answered, I said, 'Did Jean (the talent coordinator) call you?' When the secretary got flustered, she put her boss on the line, and I pitched him. He liked the idea of booking me, and said he'd check with Jean. I then called Jean and asked, 'Did Murray call you?' It was the presumptive close all the way." Jeff ended up making four appearances on the show over the years. He also was featured on CBS' "48 Hours" twice, *Newsweek*, and other important media outlets.

Having fended off the competition for so long, Jeff has drawn some valuable conclusions about media and P.R. "Print is more powerful in generating ideas," he notes. "When people are exposed to a new concept, such as video singles introduction, they need to mull it over, sort of intellectually kick the tires. That isn't possible with TV. With reading, your mind has to be active."

Jeff's advice to fledgling Guerrilla publicists: "Know what it is you're selling," he says. "Reduce it to as simple a statement or phrase as possible. Imbue it with both facts and emotion so that others will feel about it as you do. And above all, always tell the truth to the media, or else they will bite you back very badly."

Lessons from Jeff Ullman: Don't be afraid to be a little outrageous. Jeff was aggressive with the media and it paid off for him. Because he was so sure of the validity of his idea, he easily mustered the confidence to assertively pursue press.

THE MUSIC MAN

Although he has always personally detested the term "New Age," there's no doubt that Windham Hill Records founder Will Ackerman almost single-handedly launched that genre of music in the late seventies, and guided his own fledgling company, operated out of his garage, into a multi-million-dollar enterprise. Windham Hill Records, known for its pristine audio quality, elegant graphics, and tranquil acoustic instrumental music, took the lead in a musical format that has by now swept the world. It's hard to imagine that it all began in 1976 when Will, a house builder at the time, had to borrow $300 to record his debut album of guitar music, *In Search of the Turtle's Navel.*

"I'm flattered by the articles that see me as some marketing genius who saw a niche in the U.S. music scene and understood demographics," he says, "but nothing could be further from the truth." Will only knew he wanted the best, so he tracked down the finest pressing plant in America to make the records, insisted on top-quality album artwork, and, of course, signed only those musicians who moved him. Though he had no money in the beginning, his enthusiasm and naiveté worked for him. "I was utterly genuine," says Will. "That's why everyone went for it. There was no pretense, no hype. This was something done with a great deal of love and quality."

In the sphere of publicity, Will started out as a novice, but soon mastered it as well. "My ambitions were modest at first, but once I taste blood I go after something," he notes. "I went for publications like the *Boston Weekly, Village Voice,* making cold calls." The unusual quality of the music attracted attention, while Will's articulate manner and passion for his product helped establish him as a forceful spokesman, not only for Windham Hill, but also for the genre of New Age music, though he never enjoyed that label. "It wasn't flattering to me. The press has a desperate need to codify."

Windham Hill grew so large that, by the early eighties, he had signed a distribution deal with A&M Records, which shifted the company from a handmade cottage industry to a major player in the international record business. Until that time, however, all marketing functions, including P.R., were performed in-house. The label was featured in articles in virtually every news and music publication in America.

Ackerman attributes the company's success not only to the quality of its music, but to the intense pioneering spirit exemplified by him and his staff. "The world is thirsty for anything genuine," says Will. "I believe the audience responds with extraordinary loyalty when they find something they can believe in."

Today, he's also embarking on an exciting new project, the G7 label, which features spoken-word recordings by contemporary essayists and humorists. It's a daring gamble, but that's certainly in keeping with Ackerman's track record. As he says, "I was once asked,

'Will, when will you compromise?' I replied, 'Where is it indicated in my past that compromise has ever been advantageous to me? I've gotten where I am because I didn't compromise. The lesson I've learned is quite the contrary. The more adamant I am about doing something different from the trends of society, the more likely I am to distinguish myself in what I'm doing, and to find a loyal following.' "

Lessons from Will Ackerman: This brilliant man speaks for himself. That last quote of his says everything one needs to know about initiative, courage, imagination, and the Guerrilla P.R. attitude. Will Ackerman is a model, not just for P.R., but for life.

The people profiled in this brief chapter embody the Guerrilla P.R. spirit I've tried to describe in this book. No two are alike, as no two should be alike. Each found distinct prescriptions for pursuing his or her distinct P.R. challenges. You cannot precisely copy what they did, because their circumstances were unique, but you certainly can pattern your demeanor and your outlook after these winners.

It's my great hope that someday, in future editions of this book, I will add your name to this list of champions.

11

CONCLUDING THOUGHTS:
A CALL TO BATTLE

There is only one success—to be able to spend your life in your own way.

—CHRISTOPHER MORLEY

ETHICS

Maybe you've heard the old joke, "What do you call 500 lawyers at the bottom of the ocean?" Answer: "A start." A little macabre, perhaps, but funny because, fairly or not, we tend to perceive lawyers as unethical. Americans don't take kindly to cheaters, even though a large number of good citizens play fast and loose with society's rules. How many of us are 100 percent honest on our taxes? Who among us has never rolled through a stop sign, swiped a pen from the supply cabinet, or called in sick when we really weren't?

Most people look on the P.R. profession as one populated by liars, cheats, and tellers of tall tales. It would be untrue to say we don't have our share of miscreants, but most publicists are honest and principled. That doesn't mean we don't bend the truth when it suits our purposes. We do. Likewise, in your own Guerrilla P.R. efforts, you too may find yourself at times facing moments of choice: do I stretch the truth or do I blow an opportunity?

Here's what the *Dartnell Public Relations Handbook* has to say on the subject: "There is no branch of public relations that can stand up under misleading or tricky tactics without hurting the practitioner."

It's vital that we take some time to explore issues of ethics. They apply in every field, from medicine to law to simple commerce. Ethics constitute the unwritten and unenforceable laws that allow us to get along with each other. Without ethics—as we saw in the tragic L.A. riots of 1992—we have a complete breakdown in the moral order of society. The riots were an example of that on a grand scale. You represent only yourself, but within that self-contained universe, you must uphold the highest sense of ethics.

At the outset, I say to you *never deliberately lie*. By that I mean the following:

- Do not make a promise you know you cannot keep.

- Do not fabricate anything about your project that you cannot in some way substantiate.

- Do not mislead the media as to any of the central merits and attributes of your project.

Do any of these, and, as they say in the movies, you'll never work in this town again.

Media are, however, accustomed to embellishment, aggrandizement, and hype. For example, here's my reconstruction of an actual phone call I overheard from a publicist to a newspaper reporter regarding one of her clients:

I'm telling you, (the client) is to die. Her talent is so . . . well, let's just say I never heard a singer as gifted, ever. I'm not kidding. She makes Whitney Houston sound like my father does in the shower. Have I sent you a tape? What??? I haven't?? I'm getting one over to you by messenger right this very second. I'm packing it up as we speak. You must hear her. I guarantee you're going to mention her in your column next week. Not because I said so, but because you're gonna want to. I'm telling you, she's to die.

There is absolutely nothing wrong with this. It is merely thrusting an emotional component into your pitch. If you want to give the media an enthusiastic spiel, they may not buy it, but they would certainly not accuse you of lying. Nevertheless, this is a far cry from intentional fabrication.

Ethics is more than a simple matter of right and wrong. You will truly hurt yourself if you behave unethically. For one, you can't get away with falsehoods, with backstabbing, with intentional and malicious manipulation of people and media outlets. The folks out there are far too smart to be taken in. The only result will be the complete discrediting of you and your project. So if you're one of those people who has no moral problem with unethical behavior, think of such a stance simply as bad for business. You can take the morality right out of the equation. But I would hope you could see it as more than just a business decision.

Ethical behavior is important in all aspects of life. I cringe when I see decent people justifying abhorrent business practices simply because "that's the way it's done." There's no excuse for that. Maybe powerful people—including powerful publicists—can get away with it. But you, as a Guerrilla, cannot. So walk the straight and narrow. Do what you can to aggressively pursue your P.R. objectives, but don't cross the ethical line. You'll sleep better at night.

EXCELLENCE

Former Secretary of State Henry Kissinger tells the story of a young assistant whom he asked to prepare a lengthy policy analysis. After several days of slaving away, the aide submitted his work to the boss. Kissinger returned it with a note, demanding it be redone. The assistant stayed up all night revising it, but the second draft was returned again. After three drafts, the exasperated aide asked to see Kissinger, telling him, "I've done the best I can do."

Kissinger replied, "In that case, I'll read it now."

What is easy is seldom excellent. Some people believe excellence can be achieved through cunning; that being tricky is a valid substitute for hard work. That's bull, plain and simple. Guerrilla P.R. is like any other effective business strategy in one respect: it only works if you put the proper effort into it. There is no shortcut through the firewalk.

I have presented to you in this book a path and a direction. It is up to you to find your way. To have given nothing but ultra-specific ideas and formulas would have been to dishonor your native gifts of invention, improvisation, and ingenuity. Implicit between the lines is the conviction that each person knows what is best for himself or herself. Only you know how far you can push things; only you know when you haven't pushed hard enough.

With all my emphasis on perception, in truth perception only goes so far. You can't pretend to lead. If you want to be perceived as a leader, start leading. If you haven't yet become the leader you want to be, then be what you are becoming. That's not psychobabble, but sound advice. I've applied it many times in my career. When faced with unfamiliar situations, I try to imagine how I want to perform. Then I work backward and figure out how to do it. It's easier than you think. It just takes a little self-confidence.

That, in fact, is one of the fringe benefits of Guerrilla P.R. Anyone with enough money can buy an ad in a newspaper or rent a plane to scrawl a message in smoke in the skies. But to bring about a real article in a newspaper or a segment on the evening news, something that will impact millions of people, and to do it using only one tool—your brain—well, not everybody can do that. I believe you can. As was once said to me, "The only real voyage of discovery consists not in seeking new landscapes, but in having new eyes."

While putting together this book, I remembered an incident from a noisy Hollywood bash I attended a few years back. Among all the pretty people mingling, drinking, and attempting to impress one another, I noticed a world-famous director standing by the bar unnoticed, talking quietly with someone.

A woman standing next to me poked my arm and said, "Look who's over there." I acknowledged the great man. The woman said to me, "He certainly made his mark on history, didn't he?" My reply to her: "We can all leave our mark on history."

Go, and make yours.

APPENDIX ONE:
TWO INTERVIEWS

Not everyone with a Guerrilla P.R. outlook is a Guerrilla publicist. Some are involved in other fields, yet have developed a keen understanding of the Guerrilla view of things. Two such people, both good friends of mine, are Bart Andrews and Alan Caruba. One is a noted author and literary agent, the other a professional publicist, albeit an unconventional one.

In researching and preparing this book, I spoke with dozens of people, both Guerrilla P.R. practitioners and media representatives, and all were universally helpful to me. However, Bart and Alan were exceptionally wise in their insights and experience. The interviews I conducted with them proved to be extraordinarily astute, and in reviewing these, I felt they should be reproduced here.

As you read them, try to get a feel for both Bart's and Alan's dynamic view of the P.R. process. Neither views P.R. in a strictly linear fashion, that is, Task A precedes Task B which precedes Task C. Rather, they see it as an ongoing multi-linear process, interconnected, geodesic in shape. Read on, and glean as much as you can from them.

BART ANDREWS

A former TV comedy writer, Bart began researching the life and career of Lucille Ball in 1975 for a book which has now become a best-selling classic, *The "I Love Lucy" Book*. Bart went on to write many other books, including a companion volume to his first Lucy book, *Loving Lucy*. Bart is at the same time a highly successful literary agent, having represented such authors as Vanna White, Sally Jesse Raphael, Smokey Robinson, and many others.

Although his specialty is book publishing, his comments can be applied to any P.R. endeavor:

MICHAEL LEVINE: Bart, do you think authors generally need to hire outside publicists, or should they do their own P.R.?

BART ANDREWS: I discourage hiring out because, (A) it's very expensive, and (B) it's a big gamble for an author to expect to recoup that money based on royalties. It's simply not money well spent. The question is, do you want your face out there for reasons of ego, or are you doing it for the book?

ML: Does P.R. serve a narrower function in publishing than in other fields?

BA: P.R. success is much more difficult to gauge in realms other than publishing. For an individual to really know if you're getting anything out of personal P.R. is nearly impossible. You can't monitor it the way you can with a book. If you appear on "Good Morning, America," your sales will substantially increase overnight. You can punch up the numbers on a computer. All you can do with an individual or, say, an idea, is head for the nearest street corner and ask someone, "Hey, did you hear about so-and-so?" If they say, "I just read about him in the paper," then you know.

ML: What are some of your general observations about P.R. and media?

BA: There are certain things you do to publicize anything. In my area they usually involve radio, TV, and print. Those are generic. I happen to have a knack for keeping my eyes open when opportunities present themselves. I met Sally Jesse Raphael in 1976 when she was doing a radio talk show in New York. I appeared on her show for the Lucy book, and we became great friends. I never forgot about her after that first interview, and kept in touch with her. Today, I'm able to pick up the phone and book myself or one of the authors I represent on the show.

ML: What do you need to know going in, before you contact the media?

BA: You've got to know whether your pitch fulfills some requirement of the show's audience. If you're selling a cookbook, don't pitch Geraldo. It amazes me how people still do things like that. You've got to watch or listen to the shows, or read the paper or magazine. True, TV and talk radio are hungry for subjects. I hear constantly how viewers send in ideas for Oprah and Sally segments. They're not ivory towers. But you have to give them ideas that will fill up an hour. Once you're on with something people want to hear about, you become a Good Guest. They'll call you from then on. But you have to sustain the relationship. Keep sending them your material.

ML: What is more important, marketing or publicity?

BA: Between the two, I'd take publicity. For each dollar spent you get more out of P.R. I sent a copy of a book by one of my authors to USA Today. Total cost was $8 for the book and $3 for postage. The book's theme caught someone's fancy and the paper ran an entire page on it. How much do you figure a full-page ad in USA Today would cost?

ML: I often stress communication skills. What about you?

BA: People in the media are too used to professional quality to put up with crap. I get stuff submitted to me hand-written, with typos. Even if they have the kernel of a good idea, if the presentation is poor, I file-and-forget in the wastebasket.

ML: What advice would you give to people contemplating their own, self-directed P.R. campaign?

BA: If you really want to make the effort to get publicity, you can do it. It takes perseverance. People always want the end product, but too often they don't want to do the work to get the end product or they don't have the ingenuity to figure out how to get it. You've got to be really cold about yourself, and decide if you've got the right stuff. But it's definitely possible.

ALAN CARUBA

Although he's one of the most in-demand public relations counselors, and counts major associations, corporations, and celebrities among his clients, Alan Caruba of Maplewood, New Jersey, possesses the soul of a Guerrilla P.R. master. His resourcefulness, creativity, and almost superhuman energy have allowed him to benefit not only his clients, but himself as well.

In 1984, for example, he launched The Boring Institute as a lark, and now he sends out his eagerly awaited annual list of the year's "Most Boring Celebrities" to the international media. His National Anxiety Center has become a resource for insightful commentary on the national stress caused by daily scare headlines. Both these ventures reflect not only his own imagination, but his skills in securing media exposure.

In a recent conversation with Alan, we talked about many aspects of P.R. On some things we agreed; on many others we did not, but I reproduce for you the text of our interview, to give you a fresh alternative perspective.

MICHAEL LEVINE: How do you define P.R.?

ALAN CARUBA: P.R. is a craft. It doesn't lend itself to committee approach. It's an information gathering, packaging, and dissemination process.

ML: I suspect many people view P.R. people as hypesters and liars.

AC: That is a mistaken viewpoint, often encouraged by the media, who are almost entirely dependent on P.R. to perform their work. I would say 80 percent of any newspaper or news broadcast is utterly dependent on news stories and ideas from P.R. professionals. Today's journalists are often less newsgatherers than "news processors." Most journalists sit at the desk working the phones and complaining bitterly they're getting too much mail, too many news releases going to too many editors. Media people sometimes sound to me like crybabies.

ML: You're not really so bitter about reporters, are you?

AC: On the contrary, I have many friends who work in the media and, having been a former fulltime journalist, I feel a real kinship. I have always viewed everything I do in terms of journalistic standards. When I write a news release I am writing a news story. That's the way every news release should be written, as if it could go in a newspaper or magazine, or be read on TV verbatim. The first question any P.R. person should ask himself is: *Is this newsworthy?* Does this product or service lend itself to what is happening in the news these days? Is this a product or service which will help people lead better lives?

ML: What kinds of obstacles do publicists run into?

AC: Commonly, it's the expectation of a client that he will be on page one of the *Wall Street Journal* or the cover of *Business Week* within a matter of days. Most clients have no idea what P.R. is, or they believe it requires no significant skills or background. It's important that they understand that developing and maintaining a level of recognition and credibility for the product or service, or the company and principals, doesn't happen overnight. In terms of street-smart P.R., you have to figure on three to four months start-up before there's any real response to what you're doing, because it takes the media that long to get familiar with what you're sending them.

ML: What are your thoughts about American journalism?

AC: For the past decade we've had some of the worst journalism imaginable. They ignored the S&L debacle, totally missed the looting of HUD, and were caught totally off-guard by the break-up of the Soviet Union. We've had major problems sneak up on America without a single journalist noticing. We had to have the *Challenger* blow up in front of our eyes before anybody asked whether NASA was doing anything wrong. The media, which love to complain about publicists, should remember that many of us have tried to bring to light significant national problems, trends, and even scandals. I think P.R. people represent the best definition of the First Amendment, because we *do* believe in free speech and freedom of the press. It's essential to our own function of advocacy.

ML: How do you feel about the increase in media outlets in the last ten years?

AC: We've gotten nothing but more of the same. Though we have more cable stations, the news remains largely homogenized both at the national and local levels. There isn't a single local news show that doesn't begin with five minutes of murder, mayhem, and fires. It's a major misrepresentation of the real issues affecting the people watching. Viewers are lucky to get a nine-second sound byte of the governor saying something really important. The rest of the time, what passes for local news is mostly drivel. We have more coverage, but we're often not getting news of much value.

ML: What about your personal responsibilities as a public relations counselor to be attuned to the media?

AC: I read the *New York Times*, the *Wall Street Journal, USA Today,* and my local daily every day, and easily fifty publications from various industries and political points of view every month. Anybody in P.R. has to be a bit of a renaissance person in that you cannot function from a narrow perspective. You always have to understand *the larger context* in which people make their decisions, including the economy, current political issues, social and cultural factors. One does have to read rather widely among the more serious publications like the *New Republic, U.S. News and World Report,* to understand what's happening. Moreover one must also read trade publications like *Magazine Week* and *Advertising Age.*

ML: What does a P.R. professional need to know about media in order to succeed?

AC: First, a handful of newswire services determine what we read and hear today. Many people don't understand—if your story is picked up by AP, UPI, Reuters, or Gannett, to name a few, you reach out instantly with enormous impact. If your story is in the *New York Times*, I don't care if it's only two paragraphs, the impact is a smash. There is a relatively small group of print media that determine to a great extent the national news agenda.

ML: What about TV?

AC: The networks have been steadily losing audience share, and one network may be close to abandoning the news function almost entirely, which would be a tragedy. You see news playing a lesser role on the networks, because they've taken a beating from one of the most extraordinary enterprises to come along in years, Cable News Network. We're seeing the news function reformulated on the networks in shows like "20/20," "Prime Time," and, of course, the old standby "60 Minutes." We also get a lot of news from the talk shows, which desperately try to fill an hour every day. Much of what starts out as chatter on talk shows ends up as major news stories and vice versa.

ML: Have you observed serious blunders on the part of neophyte public relations practitioners?

AC: Many people don't understand that you have to *think in advance*. Whom among the media will I approach? What kind of package of information should I give them? Most media professionals don't have a lot of time. A one-page fact sheet may be more effective than a fat press kit. Most media people don't enjoy being called directly. In fact, the thing they hate the most is the call asking, "Did you get my news release?" You circumvent that by making sure the news release you *do* send is so well-constructed in terms of headline and presentation that it is *absolutely irresistible.* I see the most god-awful P.R. press releases every day.

ML: What makes them awful?

AC: They're dull, they're boring. The headline, if one exists, does not interest me in the contents in the slightest bit. The first paragraph doesn't say anything about why I should bother reading any further. P.R. is a craft. It requires a lot of know-how to understand the mindset on the receiving end of your news release or story. In a typical media organization, you have a limited staff of people working very hard to meet deadlines. These people are under tremendous pressure. That's why I say don't waste their time, don't insult their intelligence, and be sure you're giving them something they can use.

ML: What kinds of materials are useful in a P.R. campaign?

AC: While it may be applicable in some cases, the big heavy-duty press kit is more a burden than a help. It's useful usually if you represent a client with a major research study, and you have to provide a lot of documentation. In most cases, you don't need anything more than a one-page news release. There isn't that much media space available to begin with, and if you deliver your story in the first two paragraphs, you're well ahead of the game. A good press kit has three elements: a fact sheet on the company and/or product, a bio of the key individual involved, and a ready-to-use canned feature story. These are essential starting points for any client. They set up the story.

ML: What about follow-up?

AC: There's no point to follow-up if you've done it right. The follow-up will come *from* the media *to* you. It's a fallacy that you must follow-up. Ninety percent of the time you're going to piss someone off, anyway. Get the package right the first time.

ML: What's your conclusion about the nature of mass media and its effect on the public?

AC: Most people don't understand that news moves like wildfire. You have to get on the back of the tiger very quickly. You've got to ride it until the tiger gets tired and wants somebody else for dinner. Most stories have a shelf life of less than two weeks. We go from kidnapped children to some new environmental hazard to the latest skin rash in a month's time. The attention span of the public is very brief, so it's better to *create news* and be the trend-setter than try to catch up.

ML: What about the people who comprise the media?

AC: People have higher expectations of media professionals than they should. They're working stiffs like you and me, and must live with the internal politics of wherever they work. I've known thousands of them, and most are damn nice people who should be approached with the best possible story; then you should get out of their way in terms of whether they go for it or not.

ML: What do you mean?

AC: People don't understand that in the P.R. process much of the time the answer is "no." It's like prayer. To some degree, P.R.—even in the best professional's hands—is a crapshoot. The story you've worked on for weeks can go right down the toilet because there's been a plane crash, a volcano has erupted, or the president fell on his tush playing golf. Any number of things can wash your story away, whether you've invested $2 in it or whether you've got $200,000 on the line. The job can be done beautifully, but get nothing and nowhere because the world is turning and events overtake it.

APPENDIX TWO:
LADIES AND GENTLEMEN . . . START
YOUR ROLODEX

Developing a master mailing list is a big job. To help save you time and effort, I've included here a comprehensive mailing list direct from my own files. This is the most current information available, checked and rechecked up to the moment of publication. You can be confident the listings are as accurate as possible.

I've divided the list into three broad categories: Print Media, Electronic Media, and Resources. I further subdivided these into newspapers, magazines, wires and syndicates, TV, and radio. As you compile your own listings, it's vital to include not only names, addresses, and phone numbers but key information about the outlet as well: air times, whether it's a weekly column or daily feature, the name of the producer, etc. It's up to you to fill out your file card as extensively as you feel it must be.

Keep in mind, this is essentially a national list. (You will likely want a more localized list, which only you can put together to suit your needs.) Because these are major publications, you shouldn't expect to get the editors on the phone right away. But persistence will pay off. You will be directed to the right person, and in time you will make headway.

Newspapers of National Significance

CHRISTIAN SCIENCE MONITOR
One Norway St.
Boston, MA 02115
617-450-2000

JOURNAL OF COMMERCE
2 World Trade Center
New York, NY 10048
212-425-1616

THE LOS ANGELES TIMES
Times-Mirror Square
Los Angeles, CA 90053
213-237-5000

THE NEW YORK TIMES
229 W. 43rd Street
New York, NY 10036
212-556-1234

USA TODAY
1000 Wilson Blvd.
Arlington, VA 22229
703-276-3400

THE WALL STREET JOURNAL
200 Liberty Street
New York, NY 10281
212-416-2000

THE WASHINGTON POST
1150 15th Street
Washington, DC 20071
202-334-6000

Newspapers in Major Markets

Some papers have two names marked by a slash. These are papers under identical ownership. One is the morning paper, the other the afternoon paper. They share an address but are usually competitive.

AKRON BEACON JOURNAL
44 E. Exchange St.
Akron, OH 44309
216-375-8111

ALBANY TIMES-UNION
645 Albany-Shaker Rd.
Albany, NY
518-454-5694

ALBUQUERQUE JOURNAL
7777 Jefferson NE
Albuquerque, NM 97103
505-823-3800

ARIZONA DAILY STAR
4850 S. Park Ave.
Tucson, AZ 85726
602-573-4233

ARIZONA REPUBLIC
120 E. Van Buren
Phoenix, AZ 85004
602-271-8000

ARKANSAS GAZETTE
112 W. 3rd St.
Little Rock, AR 72203
501-371-3723

ASBURY PARK PRESS
3601 Rte. 66
Neptune, NJ 07754
908-922-6000

ATLANTA JOURNAL/CONSTITUTION
72 Marietta Street NW
Atlanta, GA 30302
404-526-5151

AUSTIN AMERICAN-STATESMAN
166 E. Riverside
Austin, TX 78767
512-455-3500

BALTIMORE SUN
501 N. Calvert St.
Baltimore, MD 21278
301-332-6000

BATON ROUGE ADVOCATE
525 Lafayette St.
Baton Rouge, LA 70821
504-383-1111

BIRMINGHAM NEWS
2200 4th Ave., N.
Birmingham, AL 35202
205-325-2222

BOSTON GLOBE
P.O. Box 2378
Boston, MA 02107
617-929-2000

BOSTON HERALD
1 Herald Square
Boston, MA 02106
617-426-3000

BUFFALO EVENING NEWS
1 News Plaza
Buffalo, NY 14240
716-849-3434

CAMDEN COURIER-POST
301 Cuthbert Blvd.
Cherry Hill, NJ 08034
609-663-6000

CHARLESTON GAZETTE/DAILY MAIL
1001 Virginia St., S.E.
Charleston, WV 25301
304-348-5140

CHARLOTTE OBSERVER
600 Tryon St.
Charlotte, NC 28232
704-379-6300

CHICAGO SUN-TIMES
401 N. Wabash Avenue
Chicago, IL 60611
312-321-3000

CHICAGO TRIBUNE
435 N. Michigan Ave.
Chicago, IL 60611
312-222-3232

CINCINNATI ENQUIRER
617 Vine St.
Cincinnati, OH 45201
513-721-2700

CINCINNATI POST
125 E. Court Street
Cincinnati, OH 45202
513-352-2000

CLEVELAND PLAIN DEALER
1801 Superior Avenue NE
Cleveland, OH 44114
216-344-4500

COLUMBIA STATE
1401 Shop Rd.
Columbia, SC 29202
803-771-8374

COLUMBUS DISPATCH
34 S. 3rd St.
Columbus, OH 43216
614-461-5000

DALLAS MORNING NEWS
508 Young Street
Dallas, TX 75202
214-977-8222

DAYTON DAILY NEWS
45 S. Ludlow Street
Dayton, OH 45401
513-225-2000

DENVER POST
1560 Broadway
Denver, CO 80202
303-820-1010

DES MOINES REGISTER
715 Locust St.
Des Moines, IA 50304
515-284-8000

DETROIT FREE PRESS
321 W. Lafayette
Detroit, MI 48226
313-222-6400

DETROIT NEWS
615 W. Lafayette Blvd.
Detroit, MI 48226
313-222-2300

EVANSVILLE COURIER/PRESS
300 E. Walnut
Evansville, IN 47702
812-464-7711

FLINT JOURNAL
200 E. First St.
Flint, MI 48502
313-766-6100

FLORIDA TIMES-UNION
1 Riverside Ave.
Jacksonville, FL 32231
904-359-4111

FORT LAUDERDALE NEWS
200 E. Las Olas Blvd.
Ft Lauderdale, FL 33301
305-761-4000

FORT WAYNE JOURNAL-GAZETTE
600 W. Main Street
Fort Wayne, IN 46801
219-461-8333

FORT WORTH STAR-TELEGRAM
400 W. 7th St.
Ft. Worth, TX 76102
817-390-7400

FRESNO BEE
1626 E Street
Fresno, CA 93786
209-441-6111

GRAND RAPIDS PRESS
155 Michigan St. NW
Grand Rapids, MI 49503
616-459-1400

GREENSBORO NEWS & RECORD
200 E. Market St.
Greensboro, NC 27420
919-373-7000

GREENVILLE NEWS/PIEDMONT
305 S. Main St.
Greenville, SC 29602
803-298-4100

HARRISBURG PATRIOT-NEWS
812 Market St.
Harrisburg, PA 17105
717-255-8100

HARTFORD COURANT
285 Broad Street
Hartford, CT 06115
203-241-6200

HONOLULU STAR-BULLETIN
605 Kapiolani Blvd.
Honolulu, HI 96802
808-535-8660

HOUSTON CHRONICLE
801 Texas Ave.
Houston, TX 77002
713-220-7171

HOUSTON POST
4747 S.W. Freeway
Houston, TX 77210
713-840-5600

INDIANAPOLIS STAR/NEWS
307 N. Pennsylvania Ave.
Indianapolis, IN 46206
317-633-1240

JACKSON CLARION-LEDGER
311 E. Pearl St.
Jackson, MS 39205
601-961-7000

KANSAN
901 N. 8th St.
Kansas City, KS 66101
913-371-4300

KANSAS CITY STAR
1729 Grand Ave.
Kansas City, MO 64108
816-234-4300

KNOXVILLE NEWS SENTINEL
208 W. Church Ave.
Knoxville, TN 37950
615-523-3131

LANCASTER NEW ERA
8 W. King St.
Lancaster, PA 17603
717-291-8734

LOS ANGELES DAILY NEWS
21221 Oxnard St.
Woodland Hills, CA 91367
818-713-3636

LOUISVILLE COURIER-JOURNAL
525 W. Broadway
Louisville, KY 40202
502-582-4011

MEMPHIS COMMERCIAL APPEAL
495 Union Ave.
Memphis, TN 38101
901-529-2211

MIAMI HERALD
1 Herald Plaza
Miami, FL 33132
305-350-2111

MILWAUKEE JOURNAL
333 W. State St.
Milwaukee, WI 53201
414-224-2000

MILWAUKEE SENTINEL
918 N. 4th Street
Milwaukee, WI 53201
414-224-2198

MINNEAPOLIS STAR & TRIBUNE
425 Portland Ave. S.
Minneapolis, MN 55488
612-372-4141

NASHVILLE TENNESSEAN
1100 Broadway
Nashville, TN 37202
615-259-8000

NEWARK STAR-LEDGER
Star-Ledger Plaza
Newark, NJ 07101
201-877-4141

NEW HAVEN REGISTER
40 Sargent Drive
New Haven, CT 06511
203-789-5200

NEWSDAY (Long Island, NY)
235 Pinelawn Road
Melville, NY 11747
516-454-2020

THE NEW YORK DAILY NEWS
220 E. 42nd Street
New York, NY 10017
212-210-2100

NEW YORK POST
210 South Street
New York, NY 10002
212-815-8000

NORFOLK LEDGER-STAR
150 W. Brambleton Ave.
Norfolk, VA 23501
804-446-2000

NORFOLK VIRGINIAN-PILOT
150 W. Brambleton Ave.
Norfolk, VA 23501
804-446-2000

OAKLAND TRIBUNE
409 13th Street
Oakland, CA 94623
415-645-2000

OKLAHOMAN
9000 Broadway
Oklahoma City, OK 73125
405-232-3311

OMAHA WORLD-HERALD
1334 Dodge Street
Omaha, NE 68102
402-444-1000

ORANGE COUNTY REGISTER
625 N. Grand Ave.
Santa Ana, CA 92711
714-835-1234

ORLANDO SENTINEL
633 N. Orange Ave.
Orlando, FL 32801
305-420-5000

PALM BEACH POST
2751 S. Dixie W.
Palm Beach, FL 33416
407-837-4100

PEORIA JOURNAL STAR
1 News Plaza
Peoria, IL 61643
309-686-3100

PHILADELPHIA INQUIRER/DAILY NEWS
400 N. Broad Street
Philadelphia, PA 19101
215-854-2000

PITTSBURGH POST-GAZETTE
50 Blvd. of the Allies
Pittsburgh, PA 15230
412-854-2000

PITTSBURGH PRESS
34 Blvd. of the Allies
Pittsburgh, PA 15230
412-854-2000

PORTLAND OREGONIAN
1320 S.W. Broadway
Portland, OR 97201
503-221-8327

PROVIDENCE JOURNAL-BULLETIN
75 Fountain Street
Providence, RI 02902
401-277-7000

RALEIGH NEWS & OBSERVER RECORD
215 S. McDowell St.
Raleigh, NC 27601
919-829-4500

RICHMOND NEWS
LEADER/TIMES-DISPATCH
333 E. Grace Street
Richmond, VA 23293
804-649-6000

ROANOKE TIMES & WORLD NEWS
201-09 W. Campbell Ave.
Roanoke, VA 24010
703-981-3100

ROCHESTER DEMOCRAT &
CHRONICLE/TIMES-UNION
55 Exchange Blvd.
Rochester, NY 14614
716-232-7100

ROCKY MOUNTAIN NEWS
400 W. Colfax Ave.
Denver, CO 80204
303-892-5000

SACRAMENTO BEE
2100 Q St.
Sacramento, CA 95852
916-321-1000

SACRAMENTO UNION
301 Capitol Mall
Sacramento, CA 95812
916-442-7811

ST. PAUL PIONEER PRESS-DISPATCH
345 Cedar St.
St. Paul, MN 55101
612-222-5011

ST. PETERSBURG TIMES
490 First Ave.
St. Petersburg, FL 33731
813-893-8111

SALT LAKE CITY TRIBUNE
143 S. Main St.
Salt Lake City, UT 84111
801-237-2045

SAN ANTONIO EXPRESS-NEWS
Ave. E & Third Street
San Antonio, TX 78297
512-225-7411

SAN ANTONIO LIGHT
420 Broadway
San Antonio, TX 78291
512-271-2700

SAN DIEGO UNION/TRIBUNE
350 Camino de la Reina
San Diego, CA 92112
619-299-3131

SAN FRANCISCO CHRONICLE
901 Mission
San Francisco, CA 94103
415-777-1111

SAN FRANCISCO EXAMINER
110 5th Street
San Francisco, CA 94103
415-7772424

SAN JOSE MERCURY
750 Ridder Park Dr.
San Jose, CA 95190
408-920-5000

SEATTLE POST-INTELLIGENCER
101 Elliot Ave. West
Seattle, WA 98111
206-448-8000

SEATTLE TIMES
1120 John Street
Seattle, WA 98109
206-464-2111

SHREVEPORT TIMES
222 Lake St.
Shreveport, LA 71130
318-459-3200

SOUTH BEND TRIBUNE
223 W. Colfax
South Bend, IN 46626
219-233-6161

SPOKANE SPOKESMAN-REVIEW
W. 999 Riverside Dr.
Spokane, WA 99210
509-459-5485

SPRINGFIELD UNION
1860 Main St.
Springfield, MA 01102
413-788-1332

ST. LOUIS POST-DISPATCH
900 N. Tucker Blvd.
St. Louis, MO 63101
314-622-7000

SYRACUSE HERALD-JOURNAL
Clinton Square
Syracuse, NY 13221
315-470-2265

TACOMA NEWS TRIBUNE
1950 S. State Street
Tacoma, WA 98411
206-597-8675

TAMPA TRIBUNE
202 S. Parker St.
Tampa, FL 33601
813-272-7650

TIMES PICAYUNE/STATES ITEM
3800 Howard Ave.
New Orleans, LA 70140
504-826-3279

TOLEDO BLADE
541 Superior St.
Toledo, OH 43660
419-245-6000

TULSA DAILY WORLD
318 S. Main Mall
Tulsa, OK 74102
918-581-8300

WICHITA EAGLE & EAGLE BEACON
825 E. Douglas
Wichita, KS 67201
316-268-6000

WISCONSIN STATE JOURNAL
1901 Fish Hatchery Rd.
Madison, WI 53708
608-252-6200

WORCESTER TELEGRAM
20 Franklin St.
Worcester, MA 01615
508-793-9100

YOUNGSTOWN VINDICATOR
107 Vindicator Sq.
Youngstown, OH 44501
216-747-1471

Alternative Publications

Most major cities have a weekly or monthly alternative publication that features in-depth local political, arts, and entertainment coverage, with extensive calendar listings. These kinds of outlets, often distributed free, can be among your best bets in print. The following is a list of some of the most important of these publications.

Austin Chronicle
600 W. 28th St.
Austin, TX 78705
512-473-8995

Baltimore City Paper
800 N. Charles St.
Baltimore, MD 21201
301-539-5200

Boston Phoenix
100 Massachusetts Ave.
Boston, MA 02115
617-536-5390

Chicago Reader
11 E. Illinois St.
Chicago, IL 60611
312-828-0564

City Pages
P.O. Box 59138
Minneapolis, MN 55459
612-375-1015

Cleveland Edition
401 Euclid Ave.
Cleveland, OH 44114
216-579-6071

Creative Loafing
750 Willoughby Way
Atlanta, GA 30312
404-688-5623

Dallas Observer
P.O. Box 190289
Dallas, TX 75219
214-637-2072

East Bay Express
3234 Adeline St.
Berkeley, CA 94703
415-652-4610

Gambit
921 Canal St.
New Orleans, LA 70112
504-525-5900

In Pittsburgh
P.O. Box 4286
Pittsburgh, PA 15203
412-488-1212

Isthmus
14 W. Mifflin St.
Madison, WI 53703
608-251-5627

L.A. Weekly
2140 Hyperion Ave.
Los Angeles, CA 90027

Los Angeles Reader
5550 Wilshire Blvd.
Los Angeles, CA 90036
213-933-0161

Maine Times
41 Main St.
Topsham, ME 04086
207-729-0126

Metro Times
800 David Whitney Building
Detroit, MI 48226
313-961-4060

New Times
P.O. Box 2510
Phoenix, AZ 85002
602-271-0040

Oklahoma Gazette
P.O. Box 2178
Oklahoma City, OK 73101
405-235-0798

Philadelphia City Paper
603 Fitzwater Street
Philadelphia, PA 19147
215-735-8444

Phoenix's New Paper
131 Washington St.
Providence, RI 02903
401-273-6397

Riverfront Times
1221 Locust St.
St. Louis, MO 63103
314-231-6666

San Antonio Current
8838 Tradeway
San Antonio, TX 78217
512-828-7660

San Diego Reader
635 State St.
San Diego, CA 92101
619-235-3000

San Francisco Bay Guardian
2700 19th St.
San Francisco, CA 94110
415-255-3100

Santa Barbara Independent
607 State St.
Santa Barbara, CA 93101
805-965-5205

Seattle Weekly
1931 Second Ave.
Seattle, WA 98101
206-441-6240

Shepherd Express
804 E. Wright St.
Milwaukee, WI 53212
414-374-0648

Tucson Weekly
P.O. Box 2429
Tucson, AZ 85702
602-792-3630

Washington City Paper
724 Ninth St. NW
Washington, DC 20001
202-628-6528

Westword
1621 18th St.
Denver, CO 80202
303-296-7744

Willamette Week
2 NW Second Ave.
Portland, OR 97209
503-243-2122

Worcester Magazine
44 Front St.
Worcester, MA 01614
508-799-0511

Magazines

The following are, in descending order, the nation's top twenty magazines, starting at over 20 million in circulation down to 2.5 million. Lead times are generally very long, so make sure you give them plenty of time.

MODERN MATURITY
3200 E. Carson Street
Lakewood, CA 90712
213-496-2277
Editor: Henry Fenwick

READER'S DIGEST
Reader's Digest Road
Pleasantville, NY 10570
914-238-1000
Managing Editor: John Panitza

TV GUIDE
4 Radnor Corporate Center
Radnor, PA 19088
215-293-8500
Editor: Roger Youman

NATIONAL GEOGRAPHIC
1145 17th St. NW
Washington, DC 20036
202-857-7000
Editor: William Graves

BETTER HOMES AND GARDENS
1716 Locust Street
Des Moines, IA 50336
515-284-3000
Editor: David Jordan
Features Editor: Margie Daly

FAMILY CIRCLE
110 5th Ave.
New York, NY 10011
212-463-1000
Editor: Jackie Leo

GOOD HOUSEKEEPING
959 Eighth Ave.
New York, NY 10019
212-649-2200
Articles Editor: Joan Thursh

McCALL'S
110 5th Ave.
New York, NY 10011
212-463-1000
Editor: Kate White

LADIES' HOME JOURNAL
100 Park Ave.
New York, NY 10017
212-953-7070
Managing Editor: Mary Mohler

WOMAN'S DAY
1633 Broadway
New York, NY 10019
212-767-6000
Editor: Jane Chesnutt

TIME
1271 Avenue of the Americas
New York, NY 10020
212-586-1212
Managing Editor: Henry Muller

REDBOOK
224 W. 57th Street
New York, NY 10019
212-649-3450
Features Editor: Diane Salvatore

PLAYBOY
680 N. Lake Shore Dr.
Chicago, IL 60611
312-751-8000
Editor: Jonathan Black

SPORTS ILLUSTRATED
1271 Avenue of the Americas
New York, NY 10020
212-522-2445
Features Editor: Chris Hunt

NEWSWEEK
444 Madison Ave.
New York, NY 10022
212-350-4000
Editor: Maynard Parker

PEOPLE
1271 Avenue of the Americas
New York, NY 10020
212-522-1212
Managing Editor: Landon Jones

PREVENTION
33 E. Minor St.
Emmaus, PA 18098
215-967-5171
Managing Editor: Louis Vaughn

AMERICAN LEGION
700 N. Pennsylvania Street
Indianapolis, IN 46206
317-635-8411
Managing Editor: Miles Epstein

COSMOPOLITAN
224 W. 57th Street
New York, NY 10019
212-649-3570
Editor: Helen Gurley Brown

SOUTHERN LIVING
2100 Lakeshore Drive
Birmingham, AL 35209
205-877-6000
Features Editor: Bill McDougould

The following are various other important trade, business, and general consumer periodicals you should have on your media list:

ADVERTISING AGE
6255 Barfield Rd.
Atlanta, GA 30328
404-256-9800

ADWEEK
49 E. 21st St.
New York, NY 10017
212-995-7323

AMERICAN BABY
475 Park Avenue South
New York, NY 10016
212-689-3600

ARCHITECTURE
370 L'Enfant Promenade SW
Washington, DC 20004
202-646-7476

ATLANTIC
745 Boylston St.
Boston, MA 02116
617-536-9500

AUTOMOTIVE NEWS/AUTO WEEK
1400 Woodbridge Ave.
Detroit, MI 48207
313-446-6000

BARRON'S
200 Liberty Street
New York, NY 10281
212-416-2700

BILLBOARD
1515 Broadway
New York, NY 10036
212-764-7300

BON APPETIT
5900 Wilshire Blvd.
Los Angeles, CA 90036
213-965-3600

BROADCASTING
1705 DeSales St. NW
Washington, DC 20036
202-659-2340

BUSINESS MARKETING
740 Rush St.
Chicago, IL 60611
312-649-5200

BUSINESS WEEK
1221 Avenue of the Americas
New York, NY 10020
212-512-2000

CAR AND DRIVER
2002 Hogback Road
Ann Arbor, MI 48105
313-971-3600

COMMUNICATIONS NEWS
12936 Falling Water
Strongsville, OH 44136
216-243-8100

COUNTRY LIVING
224 W. 57th St.
New York, NY 10019
212-649-3570

DIRECT MARKETING
224 7th St.
Garden City, NY 11530
516-746-6700

DISCOUNT STORE NEWS
425 Park Ave.
New York, NY 10022
212-371-9400

EBONY
820 S. Michigan Ave.
Chicago, IL 60605
312-322-9250

ELECTRONIC NEWS
825 7th Ave.
New York, NY 10019
212-887-8318

ELLE
1633 Broadway
New York, NY 10019
212-767-5800

ENTERTAINMENT WEEKLY
1675 Broadway
New York, NY 10019
212-522-5681

ENTREPRENEUR
2392 Morse Ave.
Irvine, CA 92714
714-261-2325

ESQUIRE
1790 Broadway
New York, NY 10019
212-459-7500

ESSENCE
1500 Broadway
New York, NY 10036
212-642-0600

FINANCIAL WORLD
1328 Broadway
New York, NY 10001
212-594-5030

FORBES
60 5th Ave.
New York, NY 10011
212-620-2200

FORTUNE
1271 Avenue of the Americas
New York, NY 10020
212-522-1212

GENTLEMEN'S QUARTERLY
350 Madison Ave.
New York, NY 10017
212-880-7901

GLOBE
5401 NW Broken Sound Blvd.
Boca Raton, FL 33487
407-997-7733

GOURMET
560 Lexington Ave.
New York, NY 10022
212-371-1330

HARPER'S BAZAAR
1700 Broadway
New York, NY 10019
212 903 5000

HOUSE BEAUTIFUL
1700 Broadway
New York, NY 10019
212-903-5084

IN HEALTH
475 Gate Five Road
Sausalito, CA 94965
415-332-5866

INC.
38 Commercial Wharf
Boston, MA 02110
617-248-8000

INFORMATION WEEK
600 Community Dr.
Manhasset, NY 11030
516-562-5000

LEAR'S
655 Madison Ave.
New York, NY 10021
212-888-0007

LIFE
1271 Avenue of the Americas
New York, NY 10020
212-586-1212

MADEMOISELLE
350 Madison Ave.
New York, NY 10017
212-880-8800

MEDIA WEEK
49 E. 21st Street
New York, NY 10010
212-529-5500

MEDICAL WORLD NEWS
600 Harrison
San Francisco, CA 94107
415-905-2200

MODERN BRIDE
475 Park Ave. South
New York, NY 10016
212-779-1999

MODERN HEALTH CARE
740 N. Rush Street
Chicago, IL 60611
312-649-5342

MODERN OFFICE TECHNOLOGY
1100 Superior Ave.
Cleveland, OH 44114
216-696-7000

MONEY
1271 Avenue of the Americas
New York, NY 10020
212-522-1212

MOTHER JONES
1663 Mission Street
San Francisco, CA 94103
415-558-8881

MS.
230 Park Ave.
New York, NY 10169
212-551-9500

NATIONAL ENQUIRER
600 South East Coast Ave.
Lantana, FL 33462
407-586-1111

NEW YORK
755 2nd Ave.
New York, NY 10017
212 880 0700

NEW YORKER
25 W. 43rd Street
New York, NY 10036
212-840-3800

OPPORTUNITY
73 Spring St.
New York, NY 10012
212-925-3180

OUTDOOR LIFE
2 Park Ave.
New York, NY 10016
212-779-5243

PARADE
750 3rd Ave.
New York, NY 10017
212-573-7000

PARENT'S MAGAZINE
685 3rd Ave.
New York, NY 10017
212-878-8700

POPULAR MECHANICS
224 W. 57th St.
New York, NY 10019
212-649-2000

POPULAR SCIENCE
2 Park Ave.
New York, NY 10016
212-779-5000

PREMIERE
2 Park Ave.
New York, NY 10016
212-725-3437

PUBLISHING NEWS
911 Hope St.
Stamford, CT 06907
203-358-9900

ROAD AND TRACK
1499 Monrovia Ave.
Newport Beach, CA 92663
714-720-5300

ROLLING STONE
1290 Avenue of the Americas
New York, NY 10104
212-484-1616

SALES AND MARKETING
MANAGEMENT
870 Belleville Dr.
Valley Cottage, NY 10989
914-268-5120

SATURDAY EVENING POST
1100 Waterway Blvd.
Indianapolis, IN 46202
317-636-8881

SCIENCE
1333 H St. NW
Washington, DC 20005
202-326-6400

SCIENTIFIC AMERICAN
415 Madison Ave.
New York, NY 10017
212-754-0550

SELF
350 Madison Ave.
New York, NY 10017
212-880-8850

SEVENTEEN
850 3rd Ave.
New York, NY 10022
212-759-8100

SOFTWARE MAGAZINE
1900 West Park Dr.
Westborough, MA 01581
508-366-2031

SPIN
6 W. 18th Street
New York, NY 10011
212-633-8200

SPORTS ILLUSTRATED
1271 Avenue of the Americas
New York, NY 10020
212-522-2445

SPY
5 Union Square West
New York, NY 10003
212-633-6550

STAR
660 White Plains Rd.
Tarrytown, NY 10591
914-332-5000

SUNSET
80 Willow Road
Menlo Park, CA 94025
415-321-3600

TEEN
8490 Sunset Blvd.
Los Angeles, CA 90069
310-854-2222

TELECOMMUNICATIONS REPORTS
1333 H Street NW
Washington, DC 20005
202-842-3006

TELEVISION DIGEST
2115 Ward Ct. NW
Washington, DC 20037
202-872-9200

TOWN & COUNTRY
1700 Broadway
New York, NY 10019
212-903-5000

TRAVEL & LEISURE
1120 Avenue of the Americas
New York, NY 10036
212-382-5600

TRAVEL WEEKLY
500 Plaza Dr.
Secaucus, NJ 07096
201-902-1500

USA WEEKEND
2400 N St. NW
Washington, DC 20037
202-955-2000

U.S. NEWS & WORLD REPORT
599 Lexington Ave.
New York, NY 10020
212-326-5300

US
1290 Avenue of the Americas
New York, NY 10104
212-484-1616

VANITY FAIR
350 Madison Ave.
New York, NY 10017
212-880-8800

VARIETY
475 Park Ave. South
New York, NY 10016
212-779-1100

VIDEO MAGAZINE
460 W. 34th St.
New York, NY 10001
212-947-6500

VOGUE
350 Madison Ave.
New York, NY 10017
212-880-8800

WASHINGTON JOURNALISM REVIEW
4716 Pontiac St.
College Park, MD 20740
301-513-0001

WOMAN'S WORLD
270 Sylvan Avenue
Englewood Cliffs, NJ 07632
201-569-6699

WOMEN'S WEAR DAILY
7 W. 34th St.
New York, NY 10001
212-630-4000

WORKING MOTHER
230 Park Ave.
New York, NY 10169
212-551-9412

WORKING WOMAN
230 Park Ave.
New York, NY 10169
212-551-9500

Wire Services and Syndicates

Most major wire services have bureaus in many cities around the world, including yours. It's best to deal with your local bureau, but your list should include national info as well. For the biggest, I've included a few of their major bureaus as well.

ASSOCIATED PRESS
50 Rockefeller Plaza
New York, NY 10020
212-621-1500

221 S. Figueroa St.
Los Angeles, CA 90012
213-746-1200

2021 K Street NW
Washington, DC 20006
202-828-6400

230 N. Michigan Ave.
Chicago, IL 60601
312-781-0500

CANADIAN PRESS
1825 K Street NW
Washington, DC 20006
202-828-9669

COLLEGE PRESS SERVICE
64 E. Concord St.
Orlando, FL 32801
800-322-3068

COLUMBIA FEATURES
36 W. 44th Street
New York, NY 10036
212-840-1812

COPLEY NEWS SERVICE
123 Camino de la Reina
San Diego, CA 92112
800-445-4555

GANNETT NEWS SERVICE
1000 Wilson Blvd.
Arlington, VA 22229
703-276-5800

KING FEATURES SYNDICATE
235 E. 45th Street
New York, NY 10017
212-455-4000

KNIGHT-RIDDER
790 National Press Building
Washington, DC 20045
202-383-6085

NEW YORK TIMES NEWS SERVICE
229 W. 43rd St.
New York, NY 10036
212-556-1927

NORTH AMERICA SYNDICATE
235 E. 45th Street
New York, NY 10017
212-867-9000

REUTERS
1700 Broadway
New York, NY 10019
212-603-3300

311 S. Wacker Dr.
Chicago, IL 60606
312-408-8700

1333 H St. NW
Washington, DC 20005
202-898-8300

445 S. Figueroa St.
Los Angeles, CA 90071
213-680-4800

SCRIPPS-HOWARD NEWS SERVICE
1090 Vermont Ave. NW
Washington, DC 20005
202-408-1484

THOMPSON NEWSPAPERS
1331 Pennsylvania Ave. NW
Washington, DC 20004
202-628-2157

TRIBUNE MEDIA
64 E. Concord Street
Orlando, FL 32801
407-839-5600

UNITED MEDIA ENTERPRISES
200 Park Ave.
New York, NY 10166
212-692-3700

UNITED PRESS INTERNATIONAL
461 8th Ave.
New York, NY 10001
212-560-1100

316 W. Second Street
Los Angeles, CA 90012
213-620-1230

1400 Eye St. NW
Washington, DC 20005
202-898-8000

203 N. Wabash
Chicago, IL 60601
312-781-1600

ELECTRONIC MEDIA

National Television News and Talk Shows

CBS THIS MORNING
524 W. 57th Street
New York, NY 10019
212-975-2824
Producer: Pat Shelvin

TODAY
30 Rockefeller Plaza
New York, NY 10112
212-664-4238
Producer: Robert Wheelock

GOOD MORNING, AMERICA
1965 Broadway
New York, NY 10023
212-496-4803
Producer: Jack Reily

The addresses listed above are the same for the CBS Evening News, NBC Nightly News, and ABC World News Tonight, respectively, as well as for New York's three network-owned and -operated affiliates, WCBS, WNBC, and WABC. The phone numbers for those are:

CBS EVENING NEWS: 212-975-3691
(for WCBS: 212-975-2161)

NBC NIGHTLY NEWS:
212-664-4444

ABC WORLD NEWS TONIGHT:
212-456-7777

CNN
One CNN Center
100 International Blvd.
Atlanta, GA 30348
404-827-1500

PUBLIC BROADCASTING SERVICE
1320 Braddock Place
Alexandria, VA 22314
703-739-5000

FOX BROADCASTING COMPANY
10201 W. Pico Blvd.
Los Angeles, CA 90035
310-203-3442

USA NETWORK
1230 Avenue of the Americas
New York, NY 10020
212-408-9100

LARRY KING LIVE
820 First Street NE
Washington, DC 20002
202-898-7983
Producer: Tamara Haddad

NIGHTLINE
47 W. 66th St.
New York, NY 10023
212-887-4995
Producer: Tom Bettag

DONAHUE
30 Rockefeller Plaza
New York, NY 10112
212-664-6501
Producer: Lorri Benson

THE OPRAH WINFREY SHOW
110 N. Carpenter
Chicago, IL 60607
312-633-0808
Producer: Debbie DiMaio

GERALDO
524 W. 57th Street
New York, NY 10019
212-265-8520
Producer: Dan Weaver

SALLY JESSY RAPHAEL
510 W. 57th Street
New York, NY 10019
212-582-1722
Producer: Burt DuBrow

ENTERTAINMENT TONIGHT
5555 Melrose Avenue
Los Angeles, CA 90038
213-956-4900
Managing Editor: Rob Yarin

LIVE WITH REGIS AND KATHY LEE
7 Lincoln Square
New York, NY 10023
212-887-3054
Producer: Michael Gelman

THE TONIGHT SHOW
3000 W. Alameda Ave.
Burbank, CA 91523
818-840-2222
Producer: Helen Gorman Kushnick

LATE NIGHT WITH DAVID LETTERMAN
30 Rockefeller Plaza
New York, NY 10112
212-664-5908
Talent Booker: Betsy Steyer

THE JOAN RIVERS SHOW
555 W. 57th Street
New York, NY 10019
212-975-5522
Producer: Marlene Selip

Local TV Network Affiliates in Major Markets

Atlanta
WSB (ABC)
1601 W. Peachtree NE
Atlanta, GA 30324
404-827-8900

WAGA (CBS)
P.O. Box 4207
Atlanta, GA 30302
404-875-1611

WXIA (NBC)
1611 W. Peachtree NE
Atlanta, GA 30309
404-892-1611

Chicago
WBBM (CBS)
630 N. McClurg Ct.
Chicago, IL 60611
312-944-6000

WLS (ABC)
190 N. State Street
Chicago, IL 60601
312-750-7777

WMAQ (NBC)
454 N. Columbia Dr.
Chicago, IL 60611
312-836-5555

Cleveland
WKYC (NBC)
1403 E. 6th Street
Cleveland, OH 44114
216-344-3300

WEWS (ABC)
3001 Euclid Ave.
Cleveland, OH 44115
216-431-5555

WJKW (CBS)
5800 S. Marginal Rd.
Cleveland, OH 44103
216-431-8888

Dallas/Ft. Worth
KDFW (CBS)
400 N. Griffin Street
Dallas, TX 75202
214-720-4444

KXAS (NBC)
3900 Barnett Street
Ft. Worth, TX 76103
817-429-5555

WFAA (ABC)
606 Young Street
Dallas, TX 75202
214-748-9631

Denver

KCNC (NBC)
1044 Lincoln
Denver, CO 80203
303-861-4444

KUSA (ABC)
1089 Bannock
Denver, CO 80204
303-871-9999

Houston

KTRK (ABC)
3310 Bissonnet St.
Houston, TX 77005
713-666-0713

KPRC (NBC)
P.O. Box 2222
Houston, TX 77252
713-771-4631

KHOU (CBS)
Box 11
Houston, TX 77001
713-526-1111

Los Angeles

KABC (ABC)
4151 Prospect Ave.
Los Angeles, CA 90027
213-557-7777

KNBC (NBC)
3000 W. Alameda Ave.
Burbank, CA 91523
818-840-4444

KCBS (CBS)
6121 Sunset Blvd.
Los Angeles, CA 90028
213-460-3000

KTTV (FOX)
5746 Sunset Blvd.
Los Angeles, CA 90028
213-856-1000

Miami

WCIX (CBS)
8900 Northwest 18th Terrace
Miami, FL 33172
305-593-0606

WTVJ (NBC)
316 N. Miami Ave.
Miami, FL 33128
305-379-4444

Milwaukee

WTMJ (NBC)
720 East Capitol Drive
Milwaukee, WI 53201
414-332-9611

WITI (CBS)
5445 N. 27th St.
Milwaukee, WI 53209
414-462-6666

WISN (ABC)
759 N. 19th St.
Milwaukee, WI 53233
414-342-8812

Nashville

WKRN (ABC)
441 Murfreesboro Road
Nashville, TN 37210
615-248-7222

WTVF (CBS)
474 James Robertson Parkway
Nashville, TN 37219
615-244-5000

WSMV (NBC)
P.O. Box 4
Nashville, TN 37202
615-353-4444

New Orleans

WDSU (NBC)
520 Royal Street
New Orleans, LA 70130
504-588-9378

WVUE (ABC)
1025 S. Jefferson Davis Parkway
New Orleans, LA 70185
504-486-6161

WWL (CBS)
1024 N. Rampart St.
New Orleans, LA 70116
504-529-4444

Philadelphia

KYW (NBC)
Independence Mall East
Philadelphia, PA 19106
215-238-4700

WCAU (CBS)
301 City Ave.
Philadelphia, PA 19131
215-668-5752

WPVI (ABC)
4100 City Line Ave.
Philadelphia, PA 19106
215-878-9700

Phoenix

KTVK (ABC)
P.O. Box 5068
Phoenix, AZ 85010
602-263-3333

KTSP (CBS)
511 W. Adams Street
Phoenix, AZ 85003
602-257-1234

KPNX (NBC)
P.O. Box 711
Phoenix, AZ 85001
602-257-1212

Pittsburgh

KDKA (CBS)
1 Gateway Ctr.
Pittsburgh, PA 15230
412-392-2200

WPXI (NBC)
11 Television Hill
Pittsburgh, PA 15214
412-237-1100

WTAE (NBC)
400 Ardmore Blvd.
Pittsburgh, PA 15221
412-242-4300

St. Louis

KTVI (ABC)
5915 Berthold Ave.
St. Louis, MO 63110
314-647-2222

KMOV (CBS)
1 Memorial Dr.
St. Louis, MO 63102
314-621-4444

KSDK (NBC)
1000 Market St.
St. Louis, MO 63101
314-421-5055

San Diego

KGTV (ABC)
Hwy. 94 & 47th
San Diego, CA 92102
619-237-1010

KFMB (CBS)
7677 Engineer Rd.
San Diego, CA 92111
619-571-8888

KCST (NBC)
8330 Engineer Rd.
San Diego, CA 92111
619-279-3939

San Francisco/Oakland

KRON (NBC)
1001 Van Ness
San Francisco, CA 94119
415-441-4444

KPIX (CBS)
855 Battery
San Francisco, CA 94111
415-362-5550

KGO (ABC)
900 Front St.
San Francisco, CA 94111
415-954-7777

Seattle

KOMO (ABC)
100 4th Ave. North
Seattle, WA 98109
206-443-4000

KIRO (CBS)
2807 Third Ave.
Seattle, WA 98121
206-728-7777

KING (NBC)
333 Dexter Ave. North
Seattle, WA 98109
206-448-5555

WUSA (CBS)
4100 Wisconsin Ave. NW
Washington, DC 20016
202-364-3900

WRC (NBC)
4001 Nebraska Ave. NW
Washington, DC 20016
202-885-4000

Washington, D.C.
WJLA (ABC)
3007 Tilden St. NW
Washington, DC 20008
202-364-7777

Radio

The following is a sampling of important radio networks as well as key talk-radio hosts around the country with powerful influence in their communities. You will most likely be aware of high-impact shows in your area. A word to the wise: with talk-radio outlets, write, don't call.

AP RADIO
1825 K St. NW
Washington, DC 20006
202-955-7250

BLACK RADIO NETWORK
166 Madison Ave.
New York, NY 10016
212-686-6850

GROUP W NEWSFEED
400 N. Capitol St.
Washington, DC 20001
202-508-4400

MUTUAL BROADCASTING SYSTEM
1755 S. Jefferson Davis Hwy.
Arlington, VA 22202
703-685-2000

NATIONAL PUBLIC RADIO
801 2nd Ave.
New York, NY 10017
212-490-2444

UPI RADIO NETWORK
5 Penn Plaza
New York, NY 10001
212-560-1190

RUSH LIMBOUGH
2 Penn Plaza
New York, NY 10121
Producer: Kit Carson

MICHAEL JACKSON
KABC
3321 S. La Cienega Blvd.
Los Angeles, CA 90016
Producer: Ted Lekas

RON OWENS
KGO
900 Front Street
San Francisco, CA 94111
Producer: Mikel Cleland

ROGER HEDGECOCK
KSDO
5050 Murphy Canyon Road
San Diego, CA 92123
Producer: Gayle Falkenthal

BOB GRANT
WABC
2 Pennsylvania Plaza
New York, NY 10121
Producer: Roy Fredriks

GENE BURNS
WRKO
3 Fenway Plaza
Boston, MA 02215
Producer: Sheryl Gipstein

PRESTON WESTMORELAND
KTAR
301 W. Osborn Rd.
Phoenix, AZ 85013

RADIO & RECORDS MAGAZINE
1930 Century Park West
Los Angeles, CA 90067
213-553-4330
Talk Radio Editor: Randall Bloomquist

RESOURCES

Directories

POWER MEDIA SELECTS
2233 Wisconsin Ave.
Washington, DC 20007
202-333-4904

The best directory on the market, available in
three-ring volume or on floppy disk. If you
get only one directory, this is the one.

EDITOR & PUBLISHER
11 W. 19th Street
New York, NY 10011
212-675-4380

Superb listing, especially of daily newspapers
across North America. Also contains weeklies,
college papers, African-American newspapers,
syndicates, and much more. Updated
annually.

BACON'S PUBLICITY CHECKER
332 S. Michigan Ave.
Chicago, IL 60604
800-621-0561

Similar to E&P. Bacon's has several volumes
covering print and electronic media. Superb
directory.

BPI MEDIA SERVICES
1695 Oak Street
Lakewood, NJ 08701
800-753-6675

BPI offers several directories: radio, TV, cable,
syndicated columnists, TV news, and news
bureaus. Comprehensive and easy to read, but
expensive.

GEBBIE PRESS
Box 1000
New Paltz, NY 12561
914-255-7560

Over 21,000 listings. All American daily
papers, weeklies, TV and radio, consumer
magazines, business press, ethnic press, you
name it. And it's less expensive than many
other directories. Comes in 500-page
spiral-bound volume or floppy disk.

WRITER'S MARKET
1507 Dana Ave.
Cincinnati, OH 45207

Over 4,000 listings to help you sell what you
write. Valuable information about scores of
specialized publications.

DIRECTORY OF EXPERTS, AUTHORITIES,
AND SPOKESPERSONS
2233 Wisconsin Avenue NW #540
Washington, DC 20007
202-333-4904

This is a directory you want to be in. Write
or call for information on how you can be
included. It will cost you a few hundred
dollars to run your advertisement. This could
be your ticket to bookings on TV and radio
talk shows.

NEWSMAKER INTERVIEWS
8217 Beverly Blvd.
Los Angeles, CA 90048

This newsletter will include you in its
monthly listing as a potential talk show
guest. A powerful resource.

Professional Organizations

PUBLIC RELATIONS SOCIETY OF
AMERICA
33 Irving Place
New York, NY 10003

NATIONAL SCHOOL PUBLIC RELATIONS
ASSOCIATION
1501 Lee Highway
Arlington, VA 22209

INTERNATIONAL ASSOCIATION OF
BUSINESS COMMUNICATORS
870 Market Street
San Francisco, CA 94102

WOMEN IN COMMUNICATIONS, INC.
3724 Executive Center Drive
Austin, TX 78731

Professional P.R. Trades and Newsletters

BULLDOG REPORTER
25115 4th St.
Berkeley, CA 94710
415-227-4568

COMMUNICATIONS BRIEFING
700 Black Horse Pike, Suite 110
Blackwood, NJ 08012

MDS PUBLICITY STRATEGIST
307 W. 36th Street
New York, NY 10018

O'DWYER'S NEWSLETTER
271 Madison Ave.
New York, NY 10016

PUBLIC RELATIONS JOURNAL
33 Irving Place
New York, NY 10003
212-995-2230

PR NEWS
127 E. 80th Street
New York, NY 10021

PUBLIC RELATIONS QUARTERLY
P.O. Box 311
Rhinebeck, NY 12572

PR REPORTER
14 Front St.
Exeter, NH 03833
603-778-0514

PUBLIC RELATIONS REVIEW
10606 Mantz Road
Silver Springs, MD 20903

RAGAN REPORT
407 S. Dearborn St.
Chicago, IL 60605
312-922-8245

POSTSCRIPT

I'm vitally interested to know if this book was a help to you in your P.R. efforts. In future editions, I hope to include real-life success stories from readers like you. Please share with me your triumphs, questions, and comments by writing to me at:

Michael Levine
c/o GUERRILLA P.R.
8730 Sunset Blvd., 6th floor
Los Angeles, CA 90069